Incorrectly P

Incorrectly Political

Augustine and Thomas More

PETER IVER KAUFMAN

University of Notre Dame Press

Notre Dame, Indiana

Library of Congress Cataloging in-Publication Data

Kaufman, Peter Iver.
Incorrectly political : Augustine and Thomas More / Peter Iver Kaufman.
p.   cm.
Includes bibliographical references and index.
ISBN-13: 978-0-268-03314-9 (pbk. : alk. paper)
ISBN-10: 0-268-03314-5 (pbk. : alk. paper)
1. Augustine, Saint, Bishop of Hippo. 2. More, Thomas, Sir, Saint, 1478–1535.
3. Christianity and politics—History of doctrines. 4. Political science. I. Title.
BR65.A9K38   2007
261.709—dc22
2006034392

Contents

Acknowledgments

Incorrectly Political is better because of the careful reading and wise counsel of generous friends and tremendously insightful colleagues, notably, Robert Dodaro, John Headley, David Hunter, Ralph Keen, Clarice Neumann, Al Rabil, and Carolyn Wood. I am grateful also for the kindness of strangers, John von Heyking and especially Eugene TeSelle, who gave the manuscript a good scrubbing. Marcia Colish is my beacon and became this book's feisty critic and outstanding benefactress. Where it and I appear to run aground, though, blame my stubbornness and not Marcia's—or any of those others'—good sense and great goodwill. And I am lucky also to have found those special yet rare qualities, discernment and decency, at the University of Notre Dame Press. Barbara Hanrahan, Rebecca De Boer, Jack Kirshbaum, and Margaret Gloster are invaluable collaborators.

———

More than thirty years ago, Bernard McGinn arrived to examine my doctoral dissertation at the University of Chicago, carrying editions of my primary sources with countless Post-its, showing that he had patrolled those pages as carefully as I had. I do recall being worried by those yellow notes that seemed to stick out like fixed bayonets. But Bernie was unfailingly kind and helpful, then and thereafter. Although *Incorrectly Political* comes somewhat late, missing his recent retirement, it is for him—with thanks.

Introduction

When you hear we live in terrible times—that all political options are unappealing and that prospects run from bad to worse—you are also likely to hear pundits, meaning to console, recall that the same claims have been made for millennia. Civilization, they say, rarely, if ever, lacks critics ready to add a dab of doom to their objections to the moral insensitivity that sadly passes as political necessity and political wisdom. But pundits-turned-historians will tell you that enemies eventually become allies, resentments regularly scab over, and tyrannies are soon upended. Pessimists persist, of course, and some among them in every generation are sure their contemporaries are the very first to have encountered the very worst. Still, I was surprised recently to read George Kateb's observation that "the canonical writers," from Plato forward, have been insufficiently pessimistic. Kateb complains that the canon has left us unprepared "to take in and comprehend" "the ferocious power" of the invidiously "hyperactive" political imagination. We must have a new and more emphatic pessimism, he proposes, if we are to appreciate how "the passionate sense of possibility" in politics—a gruesome "political aestheticism" that experiences its momentum as mission and destiny—inexorably leads to domination and devastation.[1]

This study of two versions of an old, deeply perceptive pessimism was just about done when I came across Kateb's call for something new. I had been arguing that the theorists who interested me, Augustine and Thomas More, had gotten where Kateb hoped the "inadequate" canon might have gone. The two acknowledged that the "hyperactive" political imagination was irrepressible—and terribly dangerous. They registered how grim public life could and would be. But students of history, religion, and political philosophy appear not to have sensed how sordid political practice seemed to the two. And scholars still accentuate the positive, latch on to the affirmative, and bring gloom down to the minimum, as the old song instructs. More has become patron saint of the politicians; Augustine, close to a Clinton Democrat.

A glance at Kateb's favorite pessimist, Hannah Arendt, suggests how this makeover takes over. In 1951, Arendt published an extraordinarily discerning and influential analysis of our "tragic era," from Dreyfus to the "death factories" and the Gestapo. She explained how and why "political systems make humanity superfluous." She accepted that the ideologically driven craving "to make the world consistent" would continue to give us ruthless, brutal regimes. But she refused to give tyranny, terrorism, fanaticism, and fascism the last word in her first edition. She reserved that for Augustine who had indeed averred that every person was created as "a beginning." To Arendt, "each new birth" suggested that meaningful political change was possible. According to Augustine, however, fresh souls were born into misery to be purged of their worldliness rather than to change this wretched world. He said as much in the chapter Arendt cited. He stressed that a new start was made at each birth, because he was trying to correct popular philosophers who believed in reincarnation, a "ceaseless to and fro of souls" that struck him as silly and sadistic. Would a good God cruelly bring souls back to life after they had been liberated by death? Augustine was certain that they were brought to life but once in this terrestrial city to experience, in their "hellish mortality," how truth and justice had been perverted, and to learn to yearn for both, for absolute truth and genuine justice, and for the beatitude of the celestial city.[2]

Each soul, each birth, was "a beginning," but Arendt has Augustine's certainty articulate what was left of *her* optimism. Theorists as prolific as Augustine and Thomas More can be made to say just about anything, because they said so much. For a time, in ways that were readily recognizable to their contemporaries, they were politically ambitious. They thought that politics might yield solutions to fundamental, moral problems. Both changed their minds, and either could be subpoenaed to prove that one old saw still has teeth: that if the young do not tend to optimism, something is wrong with their hearts, and if the old do not tend to pessimism, something is wrong with their heads. Historians, however, are right to call for inquests when parts of the deceased are resurrected to stand for the whole, when what Jean Elshtain calls "countervailing" comments are collected or assembled from More's or Augustine's texts according to collectors' needs. If a collector wants Augustine to herald new beginnings, advocate social reforms, plump for a benevolent political paternalism or, instead, for political pluralism, relevant remarks can easily be found. If a collector wants More to be a paladin for personal liberties, a meliorist of sorts, a purveyor of patently humane, Renaissance humanist political sentiments, a foil for Machiavelli, that More is on offer—in places. Such profiles in courage, ideal types, and cameo appearances can be enlightening. They may generate useful conversations that inform historical study, but historians, when possible, should supply contexts that make the best generalizations about characters and careers more plausible, balanced, and sturdier. I was moved to reread and write by sketches of Augustine and More that turned them into political progressives and that seemed only remotely related to the trajectories of their careers, careers that coursed through an assortment of remarkably contentious theological disputes, raced ahead with—then more or less without—political ambitions, persevered after disappointments, and imaginatively confronted everyday circumstance as well as grisly crisis. *Incorrectly Political* tries to repossess the conclusions to which Augustine and Thomas More came and to suggest how they arrived.[3]

It is tricky tracking the early stages of More's career. Unlike Augustine, who sensed that he had been groomed by God to overcome doubts, personal ambition, and arrogance—and who wrote to tell that tale—More mentioned little about himself while preparing to participate in public administration. We know he admired the Carthusians and that he dropped in on them—and may have been tempted to drop out of the Inns of Court and the practice of law. Yet More also admired less reclusive religious officials who dared to make a political difference, Cardinals and Chancellors John Morton and Thomas Wolsey.

More was not blind to the reign of self-interest in the realm's courts and councils. His early correspondence with scholarly friends and the first book of his *Utopia* acknowledged that public administrators were closed to good, new ideas. He was troubled by the "pettiness" of political intrigue. He conceded that flattery and "fierce hatred" rather than talent governed who governed, which factions and coalitions thrived, and whose reputations were wrecked. He lectured on Augustine's *City of God* at a parish church near the Guildhall in London while studying law. He would have known that similar observations led the legendary bishop to trade a promising political career for seclusion, conversation, and contemplation with friends and then later, as an influential diocesan, to reflect, in his *City,* on the failures and frustrations of

Christian magistrates. Yet More marched straight into the courts, into city government, and into the king's council.

Augustine swerved. If we may trust his *Confessions,* composed ten years after the facts reported, he had every reason to be pleased with his political progress when he was in Milan and at the imperial court in 386. Influential courtiers had hired him to tout their virtues and those of their friends, and a hardworking orator with powerful patrons could end up a provincial governor. But he grew disenchanted, he said; his familiarity with the rich and powerful bred contempt just when he was becoming more seriously, solemnly interested in Christianity. He learned of others who rather impulsively renounced their ambitions to become special "friends of God." But, according to the *Confessions,* his own retreat from political deceit was not impulsive at all. It was fitful and grudging—strenuous and, only then, suddenly done.

He admired Ambrose, governor of the Ligurian province before he became bishop of Milan. Augustine wanted to consult him, but the bishop was just then caught in one of the political crises that marked his pontificate from 374 into the 390s. Ambrose, in effect, became something of a contrast rather than a consultant and friend, and he functions as a contrast in the narrative that follows. For Augustine chose to avoid public service. Even when nudged into the African episcopacy, he only rarely and reluctantly intervened in the government's business. He took no pleasure in administering justice in the bishop's court or "audience." Pessimism had drawn him to Manichaeism before he left North Africa for Milan. Pessimism made him suspicious of political activism and distinguished him from Ambrose. And years later, responding to the Pelagians' optimism, he became more convinced of the pervasiveness of human decadence. He fluffed out passages from the Bible to prove it. Laws were unlikely to lead to lasting improvement. Laws "came in" that sin might be recognized as transgression (Romans 5:20). History, moreover, proved the ultimate insufficiency of laws and the regimes that made them. Neither could keep worthwhile intentions from unraveling. All that government could do was damage control.

For Augustine, it was obvious and incontrovertible: political cultures were driven by politicians' lust for dominion. Regimes, therefore, could never achieve the peace and justice that depended on obedience freely offered to those in authority, obedience based on reciprocal respect and affection, which, in turn, were founded on love for God. The government's damage control, nonetheless, was important, particularly in the early fifth century. Secessionists known as Donatist Christians were then harassing Augustine's parishioners and his allies among African bishops. Not surprisingly, the competition between the rival Christianities for basilicas and souls complicated the authorities' efforts to reach consensus. Augustine happens to be the source for nearly all we know about those complications, and he tended to editorialize and exaggerate to score off his adversaries. Relying on him, historians will more often be wrong than boring, yet the earlier critics of Donatism and several Donatists themselves have left enough to allow us to reconstruct something of those secessionists' positions. They argued that their churches honored the perseverance and more faithfully followed the practice of the very first Christians. They were more courageous than their rivals, they said; their ancestors' choices to resist persecutors in the early fourth century, their choices to stay away from churches whose long-dead officials had been less heroic, and their choices throughout the fourth and early fifth centuries to repudiate government efforts to end their secession constituted congregations of more perfect Christians.

Augustine scolded those "more perfect" Christians for having overlooked the fact that God had seen fit to convert their persecutors. Arguably, that meant the church would never again be as pure as it once was, but conversions to Christianity did mean the church might become universal, catholic.[4] Government's association with the churches extended Christianity's reach. Municipal, provincial, and imperial governments were God's blunt instruments in every age. Despite their officials' irrepressible drive to dominate, governments kept the world in some semblance of order. But for the catholic Christians, the biggest story of the fourth century was that coreligionists, as magistrates, were superbly positioned to protect their churches. And there were no better places on earth than their churches to struggle with the effects of sin.

Donatists, in Augustine's view, altogether misperceived, and thus misrepresented, that struggle and the challenges facing every Christian. The secessionists, that is, spoke as if perfection were possible if only the aforesaid political choices—joining the right church and resisting regimes that persecuted it and churches that criticized it—were made as they advised. He chronicled the inconsistencies between Donatist perfectionism and Donatist practice and looked forward, he said, to opportunities to discuss logic, exegesis, ecclesiology, and order. He was terribly concerned, though, that, increasingly in the early fifth century, his adversaries refused to argue and continued to out-number catholic Christians in Africa. He preferred persuasion. But, for his colleagues' and parishioners' protection and the Donatists' correction, he came to depend on the government's coercion.

Protection and correction preoccupied Thomas More as well, but he was more directly responsible for both than Augustine had been. Augustine appealed to government; More became the government. As noted, he learned early on that public service was usually compromised by political intrigue. The irrationalities of political behavior and the precariousness of acquired privilege were even more apparent to him soon after he joined the king's council—certainly by the 1520s. But just then Martin Luther's talk about the invincibility of faith and the invisibility of the "true" church seemed extremely dangerous as well as reprehensible. Evangelical anticlericals in England under Luther's spell "openly inveyeth agaynst good and faythfull thynges." Latter-day Donatists, they promised perfection. More heard them say that faith without "good endevoure" pleased God, perfected repentance, and redeemed souls.

He remembered that Augustine warned against perfectionists and tried arguing with them before appealing to the government to correct them and to protect his friends from them. Like Augustine, More seems to have believed that political intervention was never better than the best of a bad lot of choices forced on Catholics by the stubbornness and virulence of their critics. Still, perhaps more quickly than Augustine, he pitched his one-sided "dialogues" with antinomians and anticlericals—much as Augustine drafted a set of exchanges with leading Donatists—to acquire and retain political support. Hence, what has been said of More's efforts, to that end, almost certainly applies to Augustine's: "dialogue offers not so much a vehicle for, as an alternative to, reasoning with heresy."[5]

That literature, nonetheless, helps historians reconstruct the controversies More and Augustine confronted. One intricate, infinitely interpretable text by each, however, seems to soar from its polemical context and to enlighten readers about the predicaments they are likely to face. Thomas More's *Utopia* could be an indictment or endorsement of socialism, capitalism, asceticism, and cynicism. Although conclusions or closure on just about any count appear to cheat his fiction of its genius, I shall propose that *Utopia* takes a dim view of confidence expressed then and now that timely political counsel and incremental changes produce unselfish societies. But More also looks to be skeptical about sweeping changes and planned societies that purport to incubate virtue. To say, for the moment, that his *Utopia* is a story of a Shangri-La that aestheticizes social control only begins to explore its place in More's story and its importance for ours. Still, introductions are the proper places for beginnings.

Arguably, we should go no further. *Utopia* may have been just a joke. More was fond of riddles and amusements. In this instance, he had a man named Nonsense (Hythloday) describe and tout utopian alternatives to early modern European politics. His odd protagonist also professes how ludicrous it is to approach politics with expectations that leadership, counsel, or diplomacy might make meaningful differences, save for compromising the integrity of anyone who tries. Could this Nonsense be trusted? More wrote him into existence, after all, as his own political career was taking off. He was getting close to those closest to the king, would soon be among them and later become the king's Lord Chancellor. Besides, when More wrote *Utopia,* in 1515 and 1516, he was far from learning firsthand the perils of political celebrity. So, was the text a game or a guess? I suspect that *Utopia* rather was a repository for lessons More had already learned from having read Augustine's *City* and, likely, from having witnessed backroom maneuvering at Mercers Hall and in London's courts, traces of what he later lamented as the "dedly desire of ambiciouse glory." Nonsense serves notice that More will not be gulled by political colleagues who "frame[d] them self a conscience" and spoke of civic duty to camouflage self-interest.

But More elected to work among them, persuaded—as was Nonsense, if I am correct—that it was impossible to make improvements of consequence to "our dwellyng citie here." Yet persons of faith and conscience sometimes had to serve. They were imprisoned in public life. God was their jailer. History was his jail and plan, "so subtilly bildyed" that the incarcerated imagined they were free. Likely, the best of them would appreciate that their time could have been better spent repenting yet accepted that their churches had to be protected—the wicked and heretical, corrected. Nonetheless, most chose instead to "garnysh with gold and make . . . gloriouse" the penitentiary of this world. More, I suspect, "did" politics as a penance.

This is not to suggest that he was as consistently aware of that as he would have been sensitive always to the chafing of the hair shirt his son-in-law said he wore under his more status-appropriate apparel. And I cannot tell whether the prison metaphor occurred to him before he was confined in the Tower of London. Yet More seems to have learned from Augustine that God's peace could not be realized politically anywhere on earth, *hic nusquam*. Sentiments of that sort were certainly identifiable soon after he lectured on Augustine's *City of God,* where magistrates and martyrs jostle each other—with the one who summoned them urging the former to think like the latter. He urged all Christians to think like martyrs, be as pilgrims in the terrestrial city and keep their hearts and minds set on the celestial. *City* is the culmination of Augustine's political disenchantment. He would have been "a world-denier," Johannes Spörl guessed fifty years ago, had faith and circumstance allowed it. What he did deny, however, was that there could be significant political improvement in this world.[6] Governments were to be used, not meaningfully improved. For what Thomas More decried as "dedly" ambition and Augustine described as the sinister "lust for domination" kept politicians preoccupied with reputation and riches. They were demonstrably of Cain's kind—Abel was the martyr, and Cain, the would-be ruler—because politics amplified what there was of Cain in every creature. Augustine seemed surprised that the philosophers of antiquity saw civic duty and political passions as solutions rather than as problems. They had not learned from reading Plato how much ordinary people and princes mistrusted wise counsel and how hard it was to find.

Still, Augustine persisted in offering counsel. He flattered the influential to hold their attention and improve the chances that his advice would be well received. He came close, on occasion, to conflating their political and religious duties, yet his *City* is critical of pagan nostalgia for the time when, purportedly, their gods were the custodians of their governments, even as it puts Christian emperors in his God's good graces. The year 410, however, was shock therapy. It proved, above all, that political regimes were only instruments—and, being political, were not at all admirable instruments. I trust Augustine's sadness was as genuine as his relief when he repeatedly recalled during the long Donatist crisis that God had turned political authorities from persecutors of the catholic churches into persecutors for them. But he expected and got that kind of help from the government, and from his God. Nonetheless, he remained anxious about the false sense of security spawned by the church's collaborations with regional, municipal, and imperial regimes. He was reluctant to have Christian magistrates wholly dis-affected, but he urged them to reduce their emotional investment in what was politically possible. I imagine that Thomas More saw as much in Augustine's *City*.[7]

The very best evidence for More's "sighing for the celestial city"—Augustine's phrase—comes mostly from the final months of his life. Yet the sprawl of his previous polemical work shows, among many other things, his resentment at having been sucked into political service. Like Augustine, he accepted that government was a part of God's saving work. But, also agreeing with Augustine, he presumed that politicians' rare surges of selfless sentiment and good counsel could not save politics from itself "in this wepyng world," this "calamity to be bewailed." What then? I suspect Augustine and More looked for alternatives to mere survival, yet that suspicion is probably better aired during our stretch with the two than in an introduction, which, as an invitation, is already too long.

Chapter One

Augustine, Ambrose, and Ambition

Christianity?

Augustine was bishop of the coastal town of Hippo Regius for but a few years, and a fervently committed Christian for barely ten, when he preached an unexceptional sermon in 397 on confession. Confession, he explained, encompassed self-revelation, remorse, and repentance. All three were good for the soul. Candid disclosure of one's flaws and shortfalls made for modesty, and a sufficiently self-lacerating remorse saved the remorseful from God's more devastatingly punitive judgments. Repentance was the beginning of rehabilitation.[1]

At roughly the same time, Augustine was chronicling and confessing his misspent youth: mischief, intellectual arrogance, and ambition for reputation and for political influence. His *Confessions* are still widely read and considered to be the first Christian spiritual autobiography. Like all autobiographers, he imposed a "fundamentally anachronistic" perspective, which, as Carol Harrison says, "whilst informative, can be misleading." We must be mindful that Augustine, confessing in the late 390s, exhibits a more mature remorse and repentance as well as a more systematic understanding of the faith than his protagonist Augustine possessed during the 380s. And the latter was not simply the narrative's subject. It became an object of religious reflection and a way to suggest the transcendent was present or implicated in the concrete.[2] In the most often read and reread portions, the *Confessions'* midsection, Augustine detailed how he finally traded his contempt for Christianity for a budding commitment to the faith, hopes, and love commended in its sacred texts. At first he thought those scriptures unrefined and somewhat silly—harmless distractions for his credulous mother, perhaps, though too rudimentary and insubstantial for her learned son. The text has him probe and pass his twenties and turn thirty waiting for more compelling explanations of the origin of evil and of the reality and incorporeality of God, waiting among the followers of a third-century Mesopotamian master, waiting among the Manichees.[3]

Textbooks today variously call Manichaeism a cult, sect, philosophy, and heresy. Its dualism sometimes extended to a belief in two gods, and its materialism made malevolence a palpable force or monstrous mass lurking on earth.[4] Augustine claimed he became disillusioned the moment he met Faustus, a much-admired itinerant seer, celebrated among Manichees around the Mediterranean for his wisdom and erudition. Augustine long looked forward to his visit yet quickly discovered, he later said, that there was little to celebrate, save the seer's taste for fine wine and his way with words.[5] By 397, he regretted his discussions with Manichees nearly as much as he regretted his political ambitions, yet, in his final analysis, he believed that both his philosophical conversations and his pursuit of position were parts of God's plan to bring him to the Christian faith. At the time, though, he knew only that he had a filial duty to take seriously the trajectory his family set for his career.[6]

Patricius, his father, was a public official in Thagaste, a city of small importance several days journey from the North African coast. He supervised tax collection, occasionally attended to public works, and obviously wanted more for his son. He was not a particularly wealthy man, yet he had at least one household slave who escorted Augustine to the local school. When the schoolboy turned bishop, he was known to allude to his parents' "poverty" if that recollection served his sermon's theme, but the family orchards and fields appear to have yielded a reasonable return. Still, it took time to accumulate funds to send Augustine elsewhere for a higher education. And while Patricius saved, his son seems to have relished the leisure. His *Confessions* rehearse the pranks and pitfalls of his late adolescence. His parents must have been tempted to arrange an early marriage to anchor their boy to the conventional responsibilities of husband and father, yet marriage into any of the curial families of Thagaste would likely have kept their promising son among the provincials. More was possible. Even before he excelled in the study and teaching of literature in Carthage—and before his gifts of persuasion developed there, in Rome, and in Milan—he was thought to be a young man with excellent prospects.[7]

He was studying in Carthage in 372, when his father died. Apparently, by then, there was no difference between what Patricius had planned for his son and what his son expected of himself. Augustine started to teach rhetoric, continued to look for recognition, and set his sights on a career in public administration. In 383 he crossed to Italy and settled in Rome to acquire fame and influential friends. His mother hoped he might warm to the Christian faith. He had been a catechumen for some time, "under instruction," we might say, but he had not seemed serious about making a more complete commitment. He gave no thought to baptism, for example, even when he was taken seriously ill. Having recovered, however, he did make a significant change. He tired of Rome and moved to Milan, where the presence of the imperial court offered obvious opportunities.

Only later, composing his *Confessions*, did he reflect on his ambition for position and aversion to piety, writing in general terms about the preoccupations that keep persons from Christianity. He blamed what we might call "the high life," extravagances to which he became accustomed in the early 380s. And he blamed mortals' exaggerated opinions of what they achieved and planned to achieve. Distracted by it all, he and they were unlikely to understand just how badly they needed God's grace—and how it came to them from one who had descended and died so they might live.[8]

Augustine remembered that he remained suspicious of much that passed for Christianity. But he also recalled that he was intrigued by the humanity of Jesus and especially struck by how he lived, by accounts that emphasized his willingness to forgo material or temporal advantage to earn immortality. Others admired that in Jesus and tried to imitate him. Possibly, as historian Ramsay MacMullen imagines, their daily lives, "governed by a more insistent moral standard than could be found in any other non-Christian association," gradually drew Augustine to the faith, much as they drew pagans of various stripes during the fourth century.[9] Yet the *Confessions* reports only that he was baffled by what Christians said about their savior when they tried to explain how or why a word became flesh. If we may trust the text, Augustine and his friend Alypius talked about the obscurity of theories spawned to account for the incomparability, divinity, yet humanity of the faith's central figure. To Augustine, Jesus was a man, the closest a person could come to the truth but not "truth in person." Christians who spoke of Jesus' flesh as if it were a coat, put on and shrugged off—just to make the mysteries of the incarnation and resurrection seem sensible—made Christianity look ridiculous to Augustine, who only later learned that the ideas he had mocked were not those of most Christians, but of the few and heretical. He learned as well that God allowed heresies so Christianity's efforts to discredit them might enable it to grow. And it did indeed grow on Augustine. He soon gave up his opinion that Jesus was just an exceptional man; that, too, was heretical. He might have been told as much on his arrival in Milan on meeting Ambrose, the city's bishop and the religion's foremost advocate in Italy for the christology formulated sixty years before at the Council of Nicaea. The bishops then, and Ambrose subsequently, declared that Jesus the son and God the father were equal, consubstantial. But the Milanese Christians knew their bishop better as a pastor. Like Augustine, they were uninterested in christology.[10]

Augustine's first visit was a courtesy call. He and Ambrose apparently exchanged conventional compliments and not ideas. Ambrose had a wonderful reputation in Augustine's line of work, so the young orator from Africa naturally wanted to meet him. And what the *Confessions* tells us is indeed plausible: for a while after their first encounter, Augustine listened more to how the renowned bishop of Milan spoke than to what he said.[11]

That likely changed when Monica arrived to oversee her son's social and professional progress. To see that her son got ahead, she dismissed his concubine and arranged a good marriage for him in Milan. She worshiped in the city, and she met Ambrose, who impressed her tremendously. Augustine saw signs of it. His mother had fixed notions about what was proper and improper in the practice of her faith, he recalled, hence it came as a surprise to him when she abruptly stopped bringing food and wine to martyrs' tombs as soon as she heard that the bishop disapproved.[12] She asked her son to relay questions about Christianity in Milan to learn from Ambrose whether she should fast on Saturdays as the faithful did in Rome and Africa or to feast with the Milanese. (Many years later Augustine remembered the bishop's reply, recycling it in his recommendation that a correspondent follow local custom.)[13] Ferrying Monica's inquiries, he likely asked as well about the ambitions and uncertainties that kept him from making a more complete commitment to Christianity. Unless the *Confessions* misleads, his detachment was just then giving way to devotion, although the narrative will not allow us to measure displacements with any confidence. Still, it gives us reason to suggest, with a phrase borrowed from one of his later meditations on ambition and politics, that Augustine looked to his developing love for wisdom to temper his lust for position.[14]

He looked to Ambrose. To be candid and get counsel, he had to approach when the bishop was "completely at leisure," yet Ambrose was always busy. People crowded around him to solicit his help or simply to watch him study. Such was the price of celebrity and influence. By 386, he had been the mainstay of the Christian community in Milan for more than a decade, the bishop whose leadership other bishops in the region accepted in the 380s, and a powerful prelate, both trusted and feared at court. An anguished Augustine could only get so close, and it was not close enough.[15]

Ambrose and Power

Ambrose certainly ranked among that century's most politically engaged religious leaders. Augustine met him just as his own pursuit of a political career seemed near a successful end. Curiously, after the young orator became a bishop, back in North Africa, he wrote rather little about the man in Milan whom he admired. We have to look elsewhere to learn that Ambrose's advance started, as many then did, with a resourceful patron. Petronius Probus, like Ambrose, was a native of Rome. Thanks to family wealth and administrative skill, Probus accumulated prefectures in Gaul, Illyricum, and Italy. Ambrose was on his staff in Sirmium on the Danube in the late 360s and until Probus sent him as governor to Italy where, in 374, Milanese Christians were having difficulty reaching agreement on a candidate for bishop. Ambrose intervened to umpire the deliberations and ideally to break the deadlock. The story told later was that during the heated discussions a child nominated the governor-turned-umpire who, notwithstanding his wishes to the contrary, became the consensus nominee. He was elected, ordained a priest, and consecrated the bishop, in that order. And despite his protests, which were likely fashioned "for the cameras," to show his humility, Ambrose took to his new role quickly, seeming, seldom if ever during an eventful twenty-three year pontificate, to regret the apparent derailment of his promising career in imperial administration.[16]

Were the nomination and election rigged? Was Ambrose sent from Sirmium by his superiors "to seize" the church? Could the child who suggested his candidacy have been a government "plant," as Clementina Corbellini now imagines?[17] Or was Ambrose "the creature of a party," the favorite of the local Nicene faction, as Neil McLynn suggests, and not a pawn for Probus? Was the Milanese consensus stage-managed—rather than spontaneous—and stoked by the governor's feigned reluctance to accept?[18] The best contemporary evidence for these conspiracies is the opinion of Palladius, bishop of Ratiaria in what is now Bulgaria, who proposed that Ambrose owed his nomination and election more to the conniving of his friends than to the content of his character. Palladius' observation is admissible, but be aware that he was profoundly embittered, "rancorously resentful," Sergio Tavano now says.[19] Why? Ambrose opposed the subordinationist christology Palladius and other Illyrican bishops advocated and went to great lengths to discredit their anti-Nicene position within a decade of the Milanese "miracle" that started his own pontificate. The story is worth a synopsis because it seems to attest how politically adroit the winner could be.

Emperor Gratian was determined to resolve the christological disputes that divided the church for more than fifty years. He first solicited Ambrose's opinions, then asked Palladius to submit a written reply, and finally scheduled a general council in 381 to discuss the differences. Aquileia, the venue, was a commercial center on the Adriatic coast with a thriving Christian community in close contact with the faithful in northern Italy just to the west and with those in the Danubian region to the east. Palladius prepared to score for inequality in divinity, but developments further to the east preempted Gratian's council. Theodosius, who ruled the empire in the east, perhaps to establish his control over the church as well, summoned eastern bishops to deliberations in Constantinople. Ambrose, Gratian, and Palladius presumed that bishops would proceed west after a round of preliminary talks. They did not, and Palladius was the last to hear of it, arriving in Aquileia to find an assembly much smaller than expected and packed with Ambrose's partisans. As the emperor's delegates and fewer than thirty bishops looked on, Ambrose seized control of the deliberations from the local patriarch and pelted Palladius with accusations. Ambushed and alone, save for one subordinationist colleague, he tried to avoid debate over doctrine by claiming that a conference so constituted was not a legitimate council. But Ambrose repeatedly insisted that whoever subscribed to the christological "madness" condemned with the arch-heretic Arius at and after Constantine's council of Nicaea in 325 ought to be condemned. Predictably, the prelates present at Aquileia agreed, and Palladius, nursing a grudge, returned to his see.[20]

Political instincts that may or may not have been instrumental in getting Ambrose the see of Milan in 374 were certainly evident at Aquileia seven years later. Then and there, he demonstrated persistence, belligerence, and, of course, leadership. He forged the bishops into a united front before the conference and continued to lead them afterward. He and Milan were the center of the episcopal network that improved the church's economic position in most cities in northern Italy and thereby increased its political significance in the region. He urged other bishops to target affluent citizens for conversion, and his correspondence advised them how to do it. Well into the fourth century, people of means and local position in Lombardy and the Piedmont retained their attachments to the traditional Roman religions. That devotion, they would have said, was the stitch that attached them as well to Rome and its Senate, which had been notoriously slow to accept Christianity. Ambrose all but announced three related objectives: to curtail the public religious expressions of allegiance to Rome, to win over the souls and thus the wealth of the wealthiest of northern Italy, and to build and fill basilicas with the proceeds. Surely that would be the proper and providential culmination of what started seventy years before with Constantine's conversion.[21]

When Augustine paid his courtesy call, Ambrose was well on the way to realizing his objectives. The court, often in residence in Milan, brought many of the empire's most influential and affluent citizens to his churches. Equally, if not more important, Christians connected with the court gave the bishop access to privileged information. He was in an excellent position to play patron and to represent the interests of friends elsewhere in Italy. He commended candidates, embroidered reports of their virtues, and interceded for petitioners—for friends or for the friends of friends. Commenting on Ambrose's "immersion in court society," Neil McLynn concludes that he was "as poised and comfortable in the Milanese praetorium as in his own basilica."[22]

His influence at court was naturally closely related to his influence on the court. Petitioners asked him to solve their problems because he was successful in solving his own and those predicaments he identified as Christianity's. Augustine and anyone else who spent time in Rome must have known, for instance, that the bishop of Milan had blocked an effort by prominent Romans in 382 to restore the altar of Victory at the entrance to the senate house. Constantine, suitably cautious, left it standing in 312, rather than alienate pagans in the old capital. He never got around to taking the goddess down. That task fell to his son and successor in 356; not yet baptized, Constantius, according to Ambrose, feared that seeing her would "contaminate" him.[23] But Victory was back on site a decade later, when Emperor Julian, an "apostate" to Christians, engineered a short-lived pagan revival, and her altar managed to outlast that last pagan emperor, remaining at the senate house until Emperor Gratian had it removed in 382, shortly before he died. The imperial chancery had to decide with or for his younger brother, Valentinian II, whether Victory was to be restored. Ambrose assumed restoration was the thin edge of a perilous wedge, if only because it signaled that prospects were good for another pagan revival and for further resistance to Christianity. He bent every effort to have the petition rejected. He did not want to see the Senate's superstitions set in stone once again. He told Valentinian that, if his government appeased the petitioners and resurrected the goddess, the emperor was unlikely to find a bishop when he next came to church. Or, worse still, he might find an enemy in the pulpit.[24]

Enmity was not what Ambrose wanted. He thought of the government as a partner. His ultimatum to Valentinian notwithstanding, he hoped to cooperate with the court. There was nothing diabolical about political power, he noticed, although persons who exercised it seemed particularly susceptible to being seduced by the devil. Powerful persons, that is, while they often kept their inordinate desires for money and pleasure in check, nearly always succumbed to lust for more power, to their ambition. They must be closely watched, carefully counseled, occasionally opposed. The Bible suggested to Ambrose how valuable sovereigns might become: a second Solomon would consecrate "temples" to his God; another David, contribute worthily to the wider circulation of his faith. Yet sacred texts and subsequent history also proved how often princes found and fell down the slippery slope from compassion, honesty, and creativity in government to corruption.[25]

Ambrose's answer to ambition and corruption was humility, a sensible precaution and, he figured, a sure prophylactic. The powerful need only practice submission. Bishops might preach to them—as Ambrose did—that "he is blessed who glories in humility more than in power." But to be sure the faithful and powerful appreciated such counsel and sought that blessing, the bishop of Milan dedicated patches of his biblical commentaries to persuading them that power was a fickle mistress. She was certain to deceive and forsake those who lust for her and think themselves fortunate to possess her for a time. By contrast, humility is constant.[26]

Yet, despite what he wrote and preached about power and humility, Ambrose left tracks that lead in a different and, according to some historians, a contrary direction. Touting the hygienic effects of humility, he seems doggedly to have pursued power, opportunistically embraced it, and ferociously defended what he managed to get of it. We briefly touched on the possibility that his election as bishop was premeditated and pragmatic rather than impulsive or "miraculous." Frank Kolb stretches that possibility, suggesting that Ambrose, while he was governor, was inclined to give up his promising career in imperial administration because he suspected that, as bishop, he might dictate to the very people at whose pleasure he would otherwise have served as provincial administrator. Kolb also adds a strange twist to Ambrose's resistance to the Romans' petition to give Victory back to the Senate. The symptoms of a pagan revival undoubtedly concerned him, Kolb admits, yet this extraordinarily crafty politician, as bishop, reprimanded the emperor—whose regime in 382 may (or may not) have been on the verge of ordering the altar's restoration—because Ambrose wanted to establish as fact the principal part a powerful prelate ought to play in any religio-political ruling. Clues to motives are hard to decipher, yet some consequences of Ambrose's interventions were clear in 386, when Augustine observed that "the most powerful men respected" the assertive, activist, and effective patron and bishop of Milan.[27]

Ambrose had what we might call "clout." Gone was what Ernst Dassmann describes as "the reserve" that characterized the first Christians' attitudes toward political culture—"reserve," which in this application denotes a careful blend of deference and indifference. The faithful tended to make a virtue of necessity.[28] With Constantine's conversion, however, all that changed. Christians contemplated a kingdom of God on earth—or at least a Christian empire. At first the changes and outlook for further change were exhilarating. Even during the 380s, the faithful were excited about what the future might bring. Ambrose, as we learned, understood that ambition and arrogance attended the power that church officials had lately acquired, but, "he spoke with the accents of a man who knew that in the transformations taking place he was on the side of triumphant novelty."[29]

He spoke, that is, to fashion a new identity for bishops. Part administrator, part prophet, a bishop "on the side of triumphant novelty" must not expect imperial and local officials simply and selflessly to relinquish the reins. In the run-up to real change, indignant bishops play Jeremiah or Isaiah to instruct the powerful on the proper and pious uses of power. Occasionally a bishop's tone must be ominous and his bearing defiant. His prophetic persona will grate on some sensibilities. But Ambrose explained that bishops could not, at their discretion, either pronounce or withhold what God gave them to reveal. They must say their piece, though it may be more prudent to keep their peace, and they must say it or preach it "with authority."[30]

And Augustine knew that Ambrose was not all talk. He watched—and his mother, Monica, participated in—the bishop's conflict with the court in 386, which demonstrated he could withstand harassment and choreograph stunning protests that went well beyond preaching "with authority." Nothing prepared either the church or the government for what occurred. Competition between bishops and magistrates was to be expected. The competence of the church's courts were at issue, as was the alleged inviolability of its immunities. Resolutions were almost certain to irritate one party or the other, to sacrifice the interests of the church or those of municipalities, manorial officials, provincial governors, or perhaps emperors. Far-sighted officials proposed remedies in advance.[31] Yet there was no anticipating the difficulties that developed when, at Holy Week, Christians in Milan closely associated with the imperial court tried to take over and use a church just beyond the city's walls, the Portian basilica that was later dedicated to St. Lawrence.[32]

Ambrose was alarmed. The Christians who coveted the church had already appointed as their bishop one of Palladius' avowedly anti-Nicene acquaintances. He and they successfully importuned the court for the freedom to worship. They were sure to initiate new members at the Portian at Easter, to steal souls from Ambrose, despite the rescript against rebaptism in 379.[33] That prohibition had been Gratian's doing, but he had died. His brother and their mother ruled from Milan in 386, and they favored the local anti-Nicene party and its plans for the basilica and its baptistery.

To oppose those plans was to oppose the government. It could not then and cannot now be proven beyond a reasonable doubt that Ambrose orchestrated the opposition and asked his partisans to occupy the Portian while workers from the palace were hanging imperial banners there. We know, though, that, as the crisis intensified, he refused to call off the "sit-in."[34] The government thought the Portian was its church. Closest of all Milanese churches to the imperial palace, it was constructed with government money during the pontificate of an anti-Nicene bishop and functioned, *inter alia*, as the imperial mausoleum. Valentinian II's father was buried in the south chapel. The bishop's refusal to surrender any church would have been newsworthy; withholding the Portian, historian Marcia Colish confirms, was especially risky.[35]

To the argument that emperors owned everything in their empire, Ambrose offered his personal property, even his life. He tried to soothe the court, noting that churches dutifully paid tribute on demand. He granted that the church's lands were the government's to sequester. But "render unto Caesar," he explained, stopped at the church door. Churches belonged to God. Unsurprisingly, court support for the subordinationists triggered yet another of Ambrose's defenses of the Nicene faith, yet, on this occasion, he appended an expansive commentary on the limits of any government's proprietary interests.[36]

For the regime was ready to risk a confrontation. Armed soldiers surrounded the bishop's basilica; Ambrose feared the worst, and with good cause. The imperial garrison was stocked with troops from the Danubian region, subordinationists who swelled the ranks of the anti-Nicene faction in Milan conspicuously unsympathetic with those staging the sit-in and lockout. Ambrose was ordered to restrain "his people," yet he would do nothing that might put the Portian in the wrong hands and could do little without implicating himself as the squatters' leader. The court was short on incriminating evidence, and Ambrose preferred to keep it that way. Still, authorities tried to isolate him. Soldiers allowed persons to enter the Portian with supplies but let no one leave with information. Fines were imposed on the bishop's friends; some were imprisoned. The people within the Portian grew impatient and took down the imperial banners, nearly provoking what Ambrose feared would be a violent end to the standoff. He sent priests to the besieged basilica, giving the government what it wanted, that is, implicating the bishop in his most zealous partisans' defiance. More mild-mannered Milanese Christians—who were also ostensibly the emperor's loyal subjects—had a choice. They must abandon their bishop or betray their emperor, and the court must have left little doubt that the repercussions of the latter treachery would be swift and severe.

It gave Ambrose one last chance to relent. Still civilly disobedient and pas-sively resistant, he answered that he would neither surrender the church nor fight for it.[37]

A bloody conclusion to the crisis was still conceivable when, suddenly, the government blinked, lifting the siege and returning the fines it collected. Its soldiers' resolve had been sorely tested; some defected. Moreover, Valen-tinian and his associates knew that the Nicene faction had friends in Trier and in Constantinople who could have been expected to mop up a messy result and end the little independence left to them. Their plans for the Portian were set aside. Ambrose had gone about as far as he could have without becoming a casualty, yet he understood that the episode branded him. He wrote to his sister that the court thought him a tyrant and expected him to pay another day for the contempt he had shown for the emperor.[38]

Was he contemptuous? That is hard to say. Defiance does not always sig-nal contempt. Clearer by far were the bishop's declarations of the church's in-dependence. A more circumspect prelate might have hedged statements round with *politesse* and not have suggested that emperors were "sons" of a church in which bishops were fathers. Did he consider that the disadvantages out-weighed any advantage he could have gained reminding the emperor that he was "in and not above" the church?[39]

And what did Augustine think? Still hoping for a career at court, he may also have had misgivings about the bishop's behavior. His mother had none; he tells us that she kept vigil with Ambrose at his church the night before sol-diers lifted the siege. But the short report in the *Confessions* reveals neither what he thought at the time nor what he was thinking a decade later when he wrote so little about the sit-in and standoff.[40]

Augustine's silence is stranger still because the years between the basilica crisis and the composition of the *Confessions* were so eventful for Ambrose and for Christianity. Confrontations between Emperor Theodosius and the bishop of Milan in 389 and 390 concluded with what historian John Moor-head now calls "victories" for the latter, who first protested the court's in-sistence that a bishop of Callinicum on the Euphrates rebuild a synagogue destroyed by Christian thugs.[41] Descending from the altar for a private confer-ence with the emperor, Ambrose threatened to stop worship unless he re-ceived assurances that the Callinicum decision would be reversed. He got his way and returned to pray.[42] Soon after, Theodosius publicly atoned, as the bishop of Milan required, for having demanded reparations. Afterward, on hearing that a mob had murdered Butheric, the commander of the imperial garrison in Macedonia, the emperor precipitously ordered a retaliatory massacre of the inhabitants of Thessalonica; he thought better of it, sending a second message very soon after the first and lethal one, but his stay of execution arrived too late. Ambrose required that formal repentance be added to remorse before readmitting Theodosius to communion, and, well into the early modern period, special emphasis was given the emperor's humiliation and reconciliation whenever prelates wanted to echo the bishop of Milan and illustrate his dictum, "in and not above the church," to educate their Christian princes. Augustine, writing his *Confessions,* would have known that Ambrose's showdown with the government over the Portian in 386 was by no means the last time he forced the court to back off.[43]

But Augustine also undoubtedly heard about the miscalculation that complicated Ambrose's relationship with Theodosius. For a time, the former appeared to acquiesce rather than resist when Arbogast and Eugenius seized power in the west and located their headquarters in Milan. Arbogast had been Valentinian II's chief of security, so when that young emperor died in 392, he was understandably concerned how Theodosius, who shared authority with the deceased, would take the news. The surviving emperor was unlikely to accept a verdict of suicide, which meant that Arbogast would be held responsible and considered expendable. So he declared for Eugenius, a Roman rhetorician with a long record of public service and "a suitably civilized front for the regime of a barbarian general," as historian John Matthews now says, reflecting on Arbogast's perceived unsuitability for rule. Ambrose left Milan rather than meet with the usurpers. He later claimed that he had been loyal to Theodosius, yet the fact is that he failed to oppose the two whose coup was over within months.[44]

Theodosius criticized him. Ambrose replied that he would never have been so blind as to miss the signs of "heaven's consent," signs that God was on Theodosius' side. The emperor, after all, had earned celestial assistance, according to the bishop, because he lived so modestly and reverently. God could do no other than undo the enemies of so pious a prince.[45] Ambrose said that he could not imagine God disappointing an emperor who asked that prayers rather than processions, orations, or triumphal arches commemorate his conquests, an emperor who cared more for piety than for pomp.

Theodosius' request for prayers reached Ambrose shortly after the usurpers were defeated, and when he took it to the altar, he confided, he sensed a presence, a miraculous ventriloquism at the mass: Theodosius was expressing his faith with Ambrose's voice![46]

It would be rather preposterous to argue that Ambrose cut a tragic figure in this short, rapturous, yet servile suggestion of mysterious intimacy, but he certainly seems more calculating than heroic. He looks to have become a willing instrument and, as Neil McLynn claims, the "impresario" responsible for yet another of the public relations ploys that marketed images of a powerful imperial church and a pious Christian emperor. He was a powerful bishop who could, on occasion, play the pawn.[47]

A Word Peddler's New Purpose

When he first met Ambrose, Augustine was acquiring a reputation for public relations, but he would have us believe that he was disenchanted with his job and disillusioned with his clients at court. He was confident, soon after he gave it up, that he had mastered the art of marketing. His public appearances and addresses honoring the regime's most exalted officials established his notoriety, and notoriety attracted students. Students' connections meant more commissions and additional opportunities to toss words of praise conspicuously and generously, as if they were confetti, to turn the heads of those who might help him advance further in government. He imagined he was on the very threshold of promotion from public orator to provincial governor and, as he said, could have "sailed to the Sirens" had he not charted a different course.[48]

Perhaps he was put off, doubtful that any orator could make the feckless regime of Valentinian II look good. Long afterward he recalled that the boy-emperor was a powerless and pitiable figure whom Theodosius could have deposed with a flick.[49] It is anachronistic yet not at all unreasonable to suspect that the prospect of parading the virtues of the government's leading men was entirely uncompelling. What Augustine remembered ten years after the fact, however, was that he became troubled by the pride and deceit associated with his profession. Deceit and pride were the Sirens that charmed his ambitious soul; unless he decided to change course, they would wreck both his ambitions and his soul. Success fed ambition, he explained, and tempted him to assume that he controlled his destiny. Pride—and the illusion of control—disposed every mortal to expect others' submission and adoration. Only God could pass the litmus tests of success and control. If the *Confessions* are to be trusted, just as Augustine seemed master of his art and fate, he heard the Christians' God "thunder" against such expectations and "against the ambitions of this world," against the extravagances that fuel ambition as well as against the arrogance that results. Augustine's hearing, of course, improved soon after he became an ardently committed Christian and church official. He then specified that pride and ambition were Satan's snares. His autobiography made that quite clear, yet Augustine may already have sensed in Milan that there was something disgraceful about pride in one's position and about the way pride and position seemed always to require flattery, an ostensibly harmless yet dreadfully dangerous kind of deceit.[50]

But flattery was his business in the early 380s, though he had loathed lies ever since he read Cicero's *Hortensius*. He was not yet twenty and, training as a rhetorician, was told to study its style and disregard its substance. Yet the book, lost to us, lastingly impressed Augustine. He recalled its assault on philosophers' frauds and pretense as he pondered the arguments of the Manichees, Platonists, or skeptics and as he was drawn to Christianity's alternative answers. He never lost his intolerance for deceit. Living with philosophers' lies was unthinkable, yet he realized that he was making a living lying for politicians.[51]

Politicians' lies could have terrible consequences. Lies convicted Augustine's most politically prominent friend of treason. Lies complicated and ultimately thwarted appeals to overturn the verdict; lies cost Flavius Marcellinus his life.[52] Notwithstanding Augustine's loss, he somewhat sadly, it seems, gave ground on the issue of lying. He found in the Bible that Abraham had withheld the truth about his marriage to Sarah; Jesus in John's gospel (6:12) declined to tell all. So, given some circumstances, Augustine conceded, Christians might allow misperceptions to stand uncorrected. He stipulated that lies of that sort might still be sinful—sins of omission—yet he also allowed that disagreement about their status is possible among people of goodwill.[53]

Earlier in his career, before he wrote his *Confessions*, Augustine was less tentative in the first of his two treatises on mendacity and mitigating circumstance. Lies were somewhat defensible, he admitted, when they enabled

Christians to avoid greater evils. But they were lies, and lies were sins, and sins slay the soul.[54] Earlier still, Augustine may have been as severe. In Milan he was beginning to deplore the deceit that he and public relations specialists practiced. Everyone knew what they said was untrue, yet that widely held view gave him no comfort.

> How unhappy I was, and how conscious you made me of my Misery, on that day when I was preparing to deliver a panegyric on the emperor! In the course of it I would tell numerous lies and for my mendacity would win the good opinion of people who knew it to be untrue. The anxiety of the occasion was making my heart palpitate and perspire with the destructive fever of worry, when I passed through a Milan street and noticed a destitute beggar. Already drunk, I think, he was joking and laughing. I groaned and spoke with the friends accompanying me about the many sufferings that result from our follies. In all our strivings, such as those efforts that were then worrying me, the goads of ambition impelled me to drag the burden of my unhappiness with me, and in dragging it, to make it even worse; yet we had no goal other than to reach a carefree cheerfulness. The beggar was already there before us, and perhaps we would never reach it.[55]

Was it stress or conviction? Nothing is more natural than self-doubt before performances likely to make or break careers. Carefree beggars have a momentary, perfectly comprehensible appeal to careworn characters, fevered with "worry" and ambition. Historians have been tempted to leave matters there and to suggest that Augustine later moralized his experience of acute anxiety to create a crisis of conviction.[56] Moralization it may be, but if the orator's disenchantment was reported accurately, it would help explain his few words during the basilica blockade. He had no brief for either side. His admiration for Ambrose was more professional than personal. He cultivated clients at court but hardly respected them. He may hardly have noticed their reactions when the bishop prevailed at the Portian.

It will do, for present purposes, to infer that Augustine's "burden of unhappiness" was the result of both a crisis of confidence and a crisis of conviction. The plurals in the passage just quoted may be the closest we come to proof ("in all *our* strivings"; "*we* had no goal other than"; "and perhaps *we* would never reach it"). And the plurals resurface as Augustine narrates a later, lively conversation about "storms and troubles" of public life. The "we," this time, refers to friends contemplating early retirement. Alypius was almost certainly among them. He briefly served in Rome as an assessor in the treasury and, Augustine divulges, had been amused but very soon revolted by the bribery, mendacity, and intimidation around him. He, too, yearned for a life of leisure and literary study.[57] Another friend from North Africa, Romanianus, was in Milan to attend to "serious problems connected with his property," property that must have been considerable, for his resources, added to those of others, according to Augustine, might have allowed the community of scholars to remain undisturbed, *quieta* and carefree. It is tempting to think that this project was a response to the "storms and turmoil" associated with the Portian episode, but nothing we now know clearly links Ambrose's solutions to the problems at the basilica with either the dissolution of Augustine's ambitions or his scheme for a counter-cultural, communal alternative to the uncertainties of public life. The utopian arrangement he and his friends discussed seemed a serious prospect until those with wives or with plans to marry came to see that the enterprise was impractical. That was how Augustine accounted for its abandonment, which raises the interesting question: *cur ante non?*

Why had the chances for a quiet life devoted to reflection, conversation, and study not drawn Augustine and his friends from "the broad and well-worn ways of the world" at some earlier stage? Well-heeled Romanianus, arriving rather late, may have influenced them. Or perhaps Ambrose was a factor. His leadership could have been an impressive argument against seclusion. Our answering precisely is, of course, impossible. Nonetheless, it is a safe bet that without a crisis of conviction, retirement—though countenanced by Manichees, Pythagoreans, and Platonists—would have seemed reckless to Augustine. Lying to and for politicians repelled him. Searching for truth had attracted him ever since he read the *Hortensius.* In 385 and 386, he censured himself, public life, and ambition, but when the plans for his community capsized, he and his politically ambitious comrades were left "to return to sighs and groans and careers."[58]

How might things have been different had he gotten the extended interview with Ambrose he so desired? His crisis of conviction appears to have been brewing for years. Arguably, Augustine felt a tug toward truth, philosophical conversation, and leisure from the time he read Cicero. But his determination to change direction had not amounted to much and appeared rather flabby when he arrived in Milan. One subtle, albeit significant, change did mark that intervening decade: Augustine found Christianity more plausible than he ever imagined. Ambrose could have exploited that development and more swiftly transformed the younger man into what he eventually became, the standard-bearer and shaper of the medieval and early modern Christian traditions. But, as noted, the bishop of Milan was busy—*non vacat,* "unavailable," Augustine said. What the *Confessions* disclose, though, is that Ambrose was hardly the person to snatch anyone from the "storms and turmoil" of public life in 385 or 386. His bouts with the government amounted to a series of showdowns that kept him at the center of those "storms." Augustine only briefly and obliquely mentioned the basilica confrontation, perhaps because public display, which was very much his job as well as Ambrose's avocation, increasingly disgusted him. Still, he could see no way out. He settled into a routine that he called "vain and inane." Mornings, he met with his pupils; afternoons, with his clients and prospective patrons. His routine was a rut, he imagined, stretching from his time in training to his popularity and pandering in Milan.[59]

Peter Brown is probably right to suggest that Augustine "had lost his confidence" and was "disillusioned" when he arrived in Milan in late 384. He probably dragged his "burden of unhappiness" there, and the *Confessions* leaves little doubt that his successes in gaining the attention of students and courtiers did nothing to diminish it. And as the exposition nears his monumental decision to leave public life, Augustine is less discreet about his addictions to sexual pleasure and secular position; he feels trapped and writes about his "servitude."[60]

Ambrose was unavailable, so Augustine consulted Simplicianus, a presbyter in Milan and Ambrose's successor a decade later. Simplicianus told him the first of the two stories that brought the North African orator's crisis of conviction to a head. Its protagonist, like Augustine, was an accomplished rhetorician. Marcus Victorinus had been well known in Rome forty years before. He used his considerable skills to defend the pagans' cults and compose spirited polemics against Christianity. To that end, he studied Christians' sacred texts and was gradually won over. Simplicianus learned of it from Victorinus himself, yet his possession of newfound faith was not enough. He would not credit the conversion until he saw Victorinus in church. His public appearance, however, would undoubtedly displease pagan patrons and clients. Besides, he told Simplicianus, church walls do not make a Christian. But the presbyter persisted, finally giving Victorinus the courage of his convictions and drawing him within those walls.[61] Years later, during the basilica crisis, Ambrose was eager to keep some Christians in and others outside the walls of his churches. Maybe Simplicianus was at pains to show Augustine exactly what was at stake in that crisis: yet, more likely, he was trying to nudge him closer to a more fervent, institutionally based religious commitment. Until then, Augustine was a casual Christian; he might pass today as a religious individualist. Neither the walls at the Portian basilica nor the worship or community there—or anywhere—mattered much to him when he got to Milan. But by the late 390s, when he recalled the tale told by Simplicianus, his thinking had changed, due, in part, to a second story that had a more direct bearing on Augustine's disillusionment in 386.

Claude Lepelley calls it "a meditation on the vanity of political hopes."[62] After Simplicianus rehearses Victorinus' turns to Christianity and then into the church, the *Confessions* reminds us Augustine was still dragging his "burden of unhappiness" around Milan, enslaved by lust, if no longer by ambition. Without ambition, he nevertheless kept to his routine, in his rut, too "drowsy," he said, to climb out.[63] Ponticianus, an African acquaintance, employed at court, visited for some reason that Augustine had forgotten by the time he told the story. He was happy to learn his host was studying scripture. Their conversation proceeded from books to monks and edged Augustine closer still to quitting his career. Ponticianus spoke of relaxing with three colleagues in Trier, where all four were working for the government and where, after a stroll, two of the four paused at a humble cottage and found a Latin translation of Athanasius' biography of Antony of Egypt.

> One of them began to read it. He was amazed and set on fire, and during his reading began to think of taking up this way of life and of leaving his secular post in the civil service to be your servant. . . . Suddenly he was filled with holy love and sobering shame. Angry with himself, he turned his eyes on his friend and said to him: 'Tell me, I beg of you, what do we hope to achieve with all our labors? What is

our aim in life? What is the motive of our service to the state? Can we hope for any higher office in the palace than to be Friends of the Emperor? And in that position what is not fragile and full of dangers? How many hazards must one risk to attain a position of even greater danger? And when will we arrive there? Whereas if I wish to become God's friend, in an instant, I may become that now.

The one reading and the other were persuaded on the spot to forsake their secular ambitions and careers and to start a new life.[64]

They were already Christians. To become "God's friends" was to be like Antony, that is, to renounce their work in the world, to relinquish all they owned, and, for them, to trade career advancement and family life for an intense religious commitment and devout conversation. Ponticianus stayed in government service, but Augustine knew immediately, he said, which was the better of the two courses and the best of all. He admired the two who impulsively, disarmingly gave themselves "wholly" to God, and he wanted only the certainty (and consolation) that he would have the assistance and stamina to stay their course.[65]

Antony's reclusiveness and the purportedly peaceful, contemplative life in convents, together with the more active life of religious leadership, drew many into careers in the church. Especially during the fourth century, Charles Cochrane says, "the steady attrition of manpower" and "the loss to public service" distressed self-styled custodians of family values and of "organized society." Ambrose could have been counted as a loss at the start of his pontificate. The brain drain or "transfer of allegiance" suggests to Cochrane the failure of the Christian empire—from Constantine to Theodosius—"to effect any real amalgamation between ideals so incongruous as those cherished respectively by the church and by the state."[66]

That failure seems self-evident now but did not to Ambrose. He assured Gratian that, given a "firm faith," nothing was impossible. Goths could be beaten; Gratian's sword and God's shield would guarantee the empire would prevail over invaders and prosper thereafter.[67] But Augustine was far from certain that serving the government served God. He was on the verge of identifying that very equation with the arrogance he came to despise in 386, when he concluded that he could no longer lie to tout the virtues of emperors and consuls and no longer teach his students to embellish. Public orators were mere "peddlers of words." Let the Milanese find another vendor; Augustine was closing shop "to serve God."[68]

He vividly recalled quitting, but his recall, in the *Confessions,* returns us to the comments that opened this chapter, specifically, to our consideration of imposed perspectives and anachronism. How much of anyone's autobiographical account describes experience, and how much constitutes it? Sometimes it may be easy to ascertain when a narrator intrudes. For example, Augustine, an avid reader as an adolescent, would have been quite the child prodigy to have appreciated then, as when he later reminisced, how foolish and futile it was to study literature, to cheer Aeneas and cry for Dido! The adolescent Augustine almost certainly cheered and cried without seeing his enjoyment as *dementia.*[69] Should we also doubt whether the orator and budding Christian, in Milan in 386, experienced his political ambition as bondage and his retirement as emancipation? Was Augustine as close to "sail[ing] to the Sirens," as he subsequently said, when he grew disenchanted?

Doubts about his imminent promotion have since surfaced, yet, as Claude Lepelley suggests, the gathering of his family in Milan is explicable only if Augustine were as well positioned as he later reported. His mother was able to arrange an advantageous marriage. His brother and two cousins moved to the city. His son and several friends rounded the circle in 386, expecting him to proceed farther along in public life and into public administration.[70] Instead, Augustine retreated with his small company to the privacy of a friend's villa in the hills above Milan. And the dialogues he composed there, in Cassiciacum, satisfy in part our curiosity about the historicity of his experiences of disenchantment, bondage, emancipation, and redirection.

In two books of *Soliloquies,* we are invited to eavesdrop on his soul's conversations with reason which thinks it enough to retire and study, as did the celebrated philosophers, Plato and Plotinus. After all, those two said much about God that was true. But to have said something true about divinity was not good enough for the soul. To speak the truth was not necessarily to grasp the truth and comprehend it with conviction.[71] To that end, the soul must be properly disposed, Augustine wrote in another of his Cassiciacum meditations; the soul, that is, cannot yearn and pray for wealth or reputation, which slip away no matter how tenaciously one tries to hold them. The soul should pray for and cultivate the virtues that incline it toward the undistracted pursuit of truth. And for that, the soul requires serenity.[72]

There is no single, sufficient explanation for the shape Augustine gave his search for serenity in 386. His disenchantment with Milanese public life and with his professional obligations is as good a candidate as most, yet one should weigh other reasons as well: disappointment with Ambrose's disinterest in his personal struggles; nostalgia for contemplative retreats characteristic of the Manichaeism with which Augustine was familiar; fascination with the traditions of retirement and *otium* associated with "the philosophical life," especially with the appeal of living "in a state of continuous intellectual excitement." But, whichever of these plausibilities we elect to emphasize, the assumption holds that Augustine came to acknowledge that his Christianity could not be fully realized "without the severance of the restrictive ties that held him to his secular ambitions."[73] They restricted him from pursuing projects he considered, for a time, worthy of his best efforts. He would vindicate philosophy against the skeptics, discover the nature of the soul, prove its immortality, and reconcile its quest for Christian truth with the study of the liberal arts. Later, sensing that humanity's sinfulness severely limited what a soul might do, he set and kept on a course quite different from the one he charted at Cassiciacum. There, before his baptism in 387, he remained optimistic, schooled the younger members of his company in traditional disciplines, read philosophy enthusiastically, and engaged in lively discussions with Alypius. Augustine said he was content to have given up everything except life, serenity, and friends with whom, in retreat, he continued "to sigh after truth."[74]

It is hard to fit Ambrose into this picture. Serenity was not his strong suit. How then might he have influenced Augustine? James O'Donnell has a hunch that the next biography of the North African "word peddler" will abandon our old and, he believes, inadequate notion that Ambrose introduced him to fundamentally new ideas. O'Donnell says that, despite what he confessed, Augustine did not change his mind in Milan. He simply discarded misconceptions that the Manichees were circulating about Christianity, and he discovered that the Christians' faith, in the main and mainstream, corresponded with what he already believed (or wanted to believe). O'Donnell claims that Augustine's "leap" from the *Hortensius* into Manichaeism was much more "venturesome" than his "deeply conservative" conversion to Christianity. That seems right to me, and what O'Donnell has done—diminishing the intellectual content of Augustine's conversion—is consistent with the reconstruction offered here. What O'Donnell does with Ambrose, however, is not and seems implausible. He maintains that Ambrose showed Augustine how to rechannel the ambitions that the latter only seemed to renounce. O'Donnell's is a story of retrieval. Augustine "left Christianity in his youth to pursue a worldly career," experiencing from that time to Milan a tension between the piety of his mother and "the culture and class of his father." But, the story goes on, from Ambrose, he "discovered . . . it was possible to be a Christian *and* a gentleman." He learned to sigh after truth in a socially respectable manner, network effectively, fashion confessional and public personae tastefully at odds with each other, and "make [his] way in the world."[75]

The next biography of Augustine, if it meets O'Donnell's standards, will assume that its subject's various epistolary, literary, and ritual gestures structure rather than simply express his desires. Emphasis on such self-fashioning, however, tends to overstress the gravity of every utterance. Everything braces the subject's self-importance, conveying the image he self-consciously—or sometimes subliminally—wanted to project. Nothing was frivolous; the casual was calculated; the self-deprecatory was meant to mislead.

What, then, might the next life of Augustine make of his desire at Cassiciacum to relinquish self-control and to become "God's servant"? Must we mistrust Augustine's stated objective to become *in otio* more pious and less likely to lie his way to senatorial rank?[76]

Trusting him, we may understand more readily why he left Italy soon after Ambrose baptized him. If he were as interested in "mak[ing his] way in the world" as O'Donnell suspects, his departure for the relative obscurity of Thagaste would make little sense. Yet he returned with his family and friends to Africa where life was to be as it had been at Cassiciacum, though with a difference. Their conduct, Augustine hoped, might resemble, to some extent, that of the monks he admired, monks on the outskirts of Milan, who were patronized by Ambrose yet otherwise beyond the pale of public life.[77] An Ambrose might have set to work solving what he could only have perceived as the region's (and his religion's) problems. Nearby Madauros, where Augustine studied, was predominantly pagan.[78] Uncompromising Donatists, whom we shall meet soon, outnumbered Christians whose faith, practice, and polity were those of Ambrose and Augustine. Yet, whereas an Ambrose would have been drawn into the challenges and predicaments of local churches, Augustine, to some degree, shut out the world. His homecoming was uneventful, and when traveling, he skirted places with episcopal vacancies to avoid being detained and ordained. He no longer sought the celebrity that had been within his reach at Milan.[79]

The Bishop Looks Back

Yet Augustine seems to have been developing something of an obsession. Happy to have "left behind [in Milan] all worldly hopes," he repeatedly recalled how hard it was to surrender them. His *Confessions* made a point of chronicling irresolution, making Augustine a master of deferral. And thereafter he preached often against the kind of hesitation he had finally overcome.[80] Hence, it should come as no surprise that he left Thagaste for Hippo when he heard that a government official there, "a good Christian who feared God," needed help to overcome his indecision, needed help, specifically, to "reject all the passions and allurements of this world." Bishop Valerius of Hippo was then very much alive and beloved, so parishioners had no obvious cause to ask their visitor to stay and serve. Augustine thought it safe to go because it would be easy to return. To him, the official's request looked providential: conversations that led to his conversion were the perfect way to start a Thagaste-like community or "monastery" in Hippo.[81]

The outcome was unexpected. Daily interviews with the man who summoned him were having little effect when Augustine was "seized" (*apprehensus*) and ordained. The bishop needed help. Hippo was a busy port city; his diocese extended thirty miles in each of three directions from its center. With his approval, no doubt, parishioners "grabbed'" their gifted guest and prevailed on him to work among them as their priest.[82] Then (391) and long after his election as bishop four years later, Augustine was inclined to make some adjustments in his plans and his thinking about political engagement, inclined or compelled, that is, by his increasing acquaintance with the rough-cut commoners of coastal Africa and with the rival Christianities there. The world was more snarled than it looked to be from his seclusion near Thagaste. Yes, he renounced ambitions for a secular career, but, as priest then bishop, he worked among those who had not. Confronted by humanity's imperfectibility, he came to accept that the reign of Christ would not come on earth and in time and that, ostensibly, the peace of Christ was incompatible with Christians' contentiousness, not to mention, with the war within each person, the battle between flesh and spirit. The incompatibility posed quite a problem, but it also presented Augustine with an opportunity to redefine "peace" in terms of what Christians must hope for rather than what they might achieve, be it personal satisfaction or social reconciliation. Yet while he sometimes advocated a crisp, eschatologically realized dualism between privation now and peace later, he also developed more nuanced, ambiguous, realistic views about the possibilities of public life.[83]

He was not as politically prominent as Ambrose, with whom, as far as we know, he had not communicated since leaving Milan. Certainly no disrespect was intended. At Thagaste and probably at Hippo, he read Ambrose's exegetical work. It helped him compose his anti-Manichaean arguments in the 390s, which are said to agree with what Ambrose had offered in different contexts.[84] And it would have been natural for Augustine to assume that Ambrose's counsel had been critical at court in the early part of that decade, for the emperor issued a stunning series of prohibitions, putting paganism at a decisive and lasting disadvantage. Ambrose said that the rulings destroyed the cults.[85] But, far from the center of imperial government, Augustine learned that enforcement did not always promptly follow enactment. Still, even in Africa, one could appreciate that Theodosius was out to muscle the gods from places long reserved for them in forum and parlor and to intimidate (or worse) any opposition. He closed temples in the east and shrugged when fellow Spaniard Cynegius destroyed pagan shrines in Egypt. In 391, the emperor prohibited public sacrifices in Rome.[86] In 392, he forbade private cultic ceremonies, countenancing confiscation of the homes of those who still venerated domestic guardians or gods, lares, and penates. Local officials and their superiors could be fined for ignoring informants' reports of prohibited private worship. There was, by law, zero tolerance for incense, commemorative lights, libations, and loose talk. Even to yearn for a return to "superstition," for edicts repealing those of Theodosius, was impermissible.[87]

Yet informed onlookers got mixed signals. The emperor outlawed pagan worship but nominated pagans as praetorian prefects, knowing that their conduct in office would complicate, if not frustrate, enforcement of his prohibitions. Tatian, a pagan, was recruited from retirement to succeed Cynegius; from 388 to 392, his rulings against prelates were so severe that Theodosius had to intervene and rescind them. Still, he named Tatian consul for 391 along with Symmachus, whose appeals to have the altar of Victory restored were denied a decade before. The emperor promoted other pagans as well: Praetextatus, who had persuaded Emperor Valentinian I to relax restrictions on nocturnal pagan sacrifices, and Flavianus, who once threatened to turn Ambrose's basilicas into stables.[88]

Baffling, to say the least: Augustine joined the chorus of Christians praising Theodosius yet harped on his personal piety, not his political strategy.[89] Alluding to Cynegius' campaigns in Syria and Egypt, he credited Christianity's momentum and paganism's setbacks in the region more to its monks than to Theodosius' militia.[90] He seems to have divined what a recent, exhaustive study of Theodosius has set out to prove, namely, that the government attempted to control and contain, rather than to condone or promote antipagan excesses.[91] Yet the laws of 391 and 392 could only have encouraged Christians' optimism. "What was predicted has come to pass," Augustine mused, referring to the Old Testament's confidence that the worship of others' gods would eventually be undermined. He heard Christ speaking through the Hebrews' patriarchs and prophets and claimed his church was then in a position to attest to the omniscience of the one and the prescience of the others. For after "waves of persecution" had washed over it and swept many martyrs to their reward, the church was crowded and still growing in 403, largely due to its rivals' legislated disadvantages. How fitting! Christ had taken persecutors' weapons and turned them—imperial edicts, prohibitions, seizures, fines—on the persecutors.[92]

Augustine was pleased, in 404, with the developments of the previous decade. As noted, he knew the differences between pious imperial intent and provincial enforcement, yet something significant had changed. He began to publicize the change and, looking back, to probe its meaning. Prior to Theodosius, the pagans' cults and priests were clamoring for attention. Appease Neptune, and sail safely, they promised. Meanwhile, Christians read about the powerlessness of the pagan gods. Now, Augustine said at the start of the century, their reading and believing were at last complemented by their seeing. For how powerful could the gods be—how cunning their priests—when none could protect their cults' interests, prerogatives, and properties?[93]

The gods flat out failed to preserve the government's favors for their devotees. From the 390s, Augustine stressed that failure, less to make a political point, however, than to score a christological and soteriological one. He wanted to transform the public's ideas about the pagans' deities, priests, and daimons (deified heroes), long thought to impart wisdom and immortality. According to him, Christ supplied both. Augustine maintained as much, from the time Theodosius proscribed pagan devotions and, at length, in his *City of God,* where he labored the gods' lack of success. Christ was the proper and perfect mediator. He participated fully and equally in humanity and divinity. He knew the flaws and the faith of the faithful and could compellingly represent their claims on God's mercy. He also knew God's purposes intimately, for they were his own. And he could present God's gifts and grace abundantly, for those, too, were his. Hence, it made no sense to consult the pagans' priests or to leave offerings for their gods or to rely on their daimons. Their priests had no gods. Their gods had no gifts. And even if there had been gifts from those gods, the pagans' daimons had too little divinity to deliver them.[94]

This last bit of nonsense, suggesting the implausibility of gods, gifts, and daimonic delivery, declared the bankruptcy of paganism, as Augustine gauged it. Theodosius' prohibitions helped him make his calculations seem irrefutable. The Bible prophesied the end of idolatry; the pagans' gods were unable to prevent it. Recent history's lesson was that simple. Augustine cared little for the particulars, advising that new Christians be told of "turning points" as part of their training.[95] There was no need to discuss in detail emperors and their edicts. Perhaps he had Theodosius and Constantine pegged as secondary causes, as ciphers. In a slightly different context, he said that it was presumptuous to comment on a craftsman's tools when we could never practice the craft as competently as their owner. Did Augustine, here, undermine historical circumstance to underscore divine sovereignty?[96] Or was he wary of looking too closely at enactments and enforcement, because results were far less impressive than generalizations he might formulate about them? Pagans still served influentially in public office. "Shows and games" were held in honor of the gods, and Christians attended. Augustine grimly predicted that a Christian who was too weak to resist the seductions of the circus was unlikely to resist the temptations to apostasy, if Theodosius' laws were ever repealed.[97]

But what exactly does it say (and what have we so far said) about Augustine's reaction to the emperor's initiatives of the early 390s? One can hardly deny he was relatively content. Despite the pastoral duties that made him increasingly aware of human imperfectability and despite the reasons to question Theodosius' consistency, Augustine thought recent developments fulfilled the promises of the Hebrews' scriptures and proved the powers of the Christians' God. May we agree, then, that he "shared . . . the euphoria" and "jubilation" of some contemporaries? Robert Markus climbs to that conclusion from the incontestable premise that "the triumphant progress of Christianity . . . fascinated" Augustine. Markus is sure that fascination turned to "jubilation," "for a while" or "from the 390s for some ten or fifteen years" or "for a decade or more."[98] Goulven Madec disagrees. He thinks that when Augustine wrote about "Christian times" he usually referred to history from the incarnation forward and not to the results of recent political regimes. He never seriously contemplated possibilities for a "quasi-messianic empire" or celebrated Theodosius' "new order" as "an anticipation, and at least partial realization, of Christians' eschatological hopes."[99]

Markus and Madec are quick to exploit opportunities that the texts they cite supply. Imagine them at the same sermon at the turn into the fifth century: Markus dwells on and swells with its excitement about the "flourishing" condition of Christianity while Madec concentrates on its warnings that pagans everywhere badgered Christians, scoffed at the resurrection, and tempted churchgoers to find their pleasures elsewhere.[100] Rather than looking for consistency and building a consensus large enough to accommodate Markus and Madec, perhaps we should accept the inconsistency and say that Augustine sometimes crossed from contentment and cautious optimism to "jubilation," but that he also—and far more often— depoliticized the "flourishing" that made others euphoric. What looks to have been the most explicit, extreme, early instance of Augustine's depoliticizing begins with his observation that Christianity's "most glorious victories" fulfilled the promises of the Old Testament. Markus might inflect just this sort of sentiment. Augustine went on, however, to contrast the Hebrews' heroes with the early Christian apostles and martyrs. From the patriarchs and prophets, who were given kingdoms to rule or redeem, we learn, he explained, that political regimes were, and are, impermanent. God gives and takes away or topples them. From apolitical apostles and impolitic martyrs, we learn that the kingdom of heaven is superior and more desirable than any earthly "state."[101] Disturbances and disappointments in his time (and in our next chapter) led Augustine to amplify such lessons, as Markus admits. The Christian empire purportedly created by Constantine's, then Theodosius' edicts came to look like a "mirage," "a collective illusion." The Christians had enjoyed no swift, irreversible victory over their tormentors. Augustine prepared himself as well as parishioners and colleagues, instead, for "a long laborious guerilla war." Looking back at prophesies was one thing, plodding ahead was something else.[102]

Augustine was awed by the challenge. Shortly after he was made bishop, he terribly missed the leisure of Cassiciacum and Thagaste. The Christians in his care required counsel, inspiration, and arbitration. Pagan and Manichaean critics of Christianity needed answering. Catechumens more interested in saturnalia than in his sermons had to be reeducated—schismatic Donatists, refuted and reassimilated. That man of surpassing energy in Milan might have gracefully, effectively brought it off, yet Augustine was *mal à l'aise* among the politically powerful. He had neither the temperament nor the skill of Ambrose. Besides, senatorial classes in Africa still resisted Christianity; the schism that deposited rival churches in nearly every North African city and village made the faith (or faiths) unattractive to influential citizens who expected municipal solidarity and civic harmony from their religion. Augustine wrote about "dense fog" and "confusion"; "we can barely breathe here."[103]

The Crisis at Calama

Ten years later he was breathing more easily. Manichees, schismatics, pagans, and the Christians who still gravitated to them still troubled him, as did those of his sheep who were less given to straying yet who filled his calendar with their daily crises. Yet Augustine was a decade into his job and better at balancing its myriad challenges when, in 408, two appeals arrived from Calama, thirty miles southwest of Hippo and just beyond the precincts of his diocese. The author of both, Nectarius, was not a Christian, and his exchanges with Augustine demonstrated one of Christianity's failures. The new religion had not yet exploited the opportunities afforded by the legislation of Theodosius and that of his two sons, Honorius and Arcadius; paganism had been outlawed but not replaced, in one politically important way. Christianity had not yet forged connections between piety and local patriotism. Paganism promoted civic responsibility. Its Ciceros inspired civic duty. Its festivals celebrated cities' traditions and more conspicuous patrons. There was no Christian substitute for the pagans' rich mix of political fervor, piety, and pageant. Evangelical assurances of celestial reward were insecurely fastened, at best, to the services and sentiments cities required of their citizens. Nectarius knew the alternative: the pagans' preferred route, charted by Cicero, Sallust, and others, from political service and social responsibility to eternal reward and rest.[104]

But Nectarius was not writing Augustine in 408 to argue the point. He needed the bishop's assistance to spare his Calama clients considerable expense.

Christians of the city had reminded municipal authorities that an imperial decree prohibited pagans' parades. The local pagans responded by attacking the Christians. Several days of rage left the church in ashes and the arsonists dreading government reprisals. Possidius, the city's bishop, had gone to Italy to make sure some official response was forthcoming. While he was away, Augustine went to Calama, probably to survey damages. Unaccountably, though, he missed meeting Nectarius. He nonetheless promised the pagans he met that he would oppose the use of torture to identify the rioters' ringleaders and that he would oppose capital punishment for their crimes. He repeated those promises in the letters to Nectarius who was hoping for more. His clients were willing to pay compensatory damages, he said, but they feared Possidius would win punitive damages that would beggar them. According to Nectarius, the pagans of Calama preferred death to the disadvantages they expected.[105]

Augustine replied that it was a mistake to think of severely reduced circumstances as a fate worse than death. If Nectarius truly desired his clients' happiness, he should cease laboring so strenuously to save their estates and advise them to save their souls. Their properties were obstacles to entry to the celestial city. They ought to accept their losses as great gain.[106] Nectarius half heard and ostensibly concurred. He, too, believed that people here ought to attend to the hereafter. He elaborated his statement, certain that his correspondent would agree: "they live all the more with God for having lived usefully among their fellow citizens."[107] But, to Augustine, Nectarius' remarks seemed to have terribly inflated the importance of civic virtue.

Christianity did not disdain civic virtue, the bishop hastened to add. To the extent that Christian faith commended probity and diligence, it encouraged responsible stewardship and citizenship in this world while it prepared the faithful for the next. And such encouragement was no afterthought. Augustine had not meant to trivialize public service, only to ensure that it was not touted as a contributing cause of salvation.[108] He granted that Nectarius was determined to reach the celestial city and "live with God," as he alleged. The irony was that his determination destroyed his chances because it was expressed in and as a devotion to material prosperity, to the prosperity of his clients and that of their terrestrial city. Determination and devotion of that type, Augustine noted, were founded on a misguided trust in human enter-prise and political acumen. Nectarius, in other words, had the right resolve yet the wrong route. The "path" to celestial peace passed through "a true and sav-ing penitence," which, from Augustine's perspective, was impossible to culti-vate outside the Christian religion. That "true" and effective penitence re-quired the desire to please God rather than one's fellow citizens and the desire to "take refuge in his grace" rather than in a record of distinguished civil ser-vice. Nectarius read philosophers who let civil service stand for sanctity and cover for a multitude of sins; Augustine read Christianity's sacred texts to comprehend the meaning and importance of humanity's estrangement from God, the imperfection of its schemes for social control, and the ineradicable sinfulness of self-assertion.[109]

From what he learned, he concluded that Christian bishops were obliged to proclaim the imperfectability of terrestrial cities to the faithful and to guide them, as pilgrims on earth, to the portal of their celestial *patria*, "a better city" by far.[110] And at the portal, in their churches, their "disordered lives can be ordered with constructive results," as Eugene TeSelle suggests, but "on an in-terim basis."[111] Bishops, of course, were also to preach political reconciliation and to practice mercy. Nectarius was counting on as much, yet he was unable to persuade Augustine that the pagans' grief after the violence at Calama was a matter of conviction and not convenience: "now it is true, as you write," Au-gustine told him, "repentance wins mercy and atones for the offense itself. But it is only that sort that is undertaken by true religion with the future judgment of God in mind, not the sort that is displayed (or feigned) before human be-ings, just for the occasion, to free their ephemeral lives from immediate fear of trouble for the moment rather than to cleanse the soul of its misdeeds for eternity."[112] The pagans' remorse could only be construed as repentance if it pried them from paganism and prodded them to "true religion." This is the hard line Augustine drew when he later tried to stir the churches to "impose a rigid test of orthodoxy" against Pelagians who, like Nectarius, underscored virtue's role in religion.[113] At Calama, however, he would have been prudent to back off. The Christians and pagans there would continue to live within a stone's throw of each other and could only do so with difficulty if harsh penalties were assessed and clemency denied. Was it not wise to lay some foundation for social reconciliation with the pardons for which Nectarius asked? More "politic," perhaps, but Augustine believed that another of the bishop's duties was to weigh provisional peace in this world against perpetual peace in the next and to balance the benefits of relieving citizens against a greater good—redeeming souls. He was unswerving: "the profits we desire are souls."[114]

It had not escaped Augustine that souls and citizens were inseparable in the terrestrial city. But the attention he lavished on the former and the relief he denied the latter seem to substantiate the observation that Christianity cared little about rehabilitating the relationship pagans previously negotiated between religion and civic responsibility. Obviously, the correspondence with Nectarius could be read differently. Robert Dodaro imagines that Augustine therein identified "religious sources for civic virtue" and insisted on Christian theology's superiority to the pagans' political philosophies. In Dodaro's view, the bishop intimated that the philosophers were unrealistic. They assumed that citizens' shared sense of honor was a solid basis for good government, but Augustine's plans for the polis were sturdier, says Dodaro, because Augustine was more realistic. He knew that self-interest ordinarily trumped honor. Hence, the pious and politically optimal course was to cultivate "aptitude[s] for reconciliation" by promoting regular confession of dishonorable sentiments and behavior. So it was best to think the worst of citizens and to have them think ill of themselves and develop "a compassion for other sinners that arises out of a recollected experience of moral weakness commonly shared." In Augustine's "politics of conversion," compassion fashions society.[115]

True, Augustine's first reply to Nectarius coupled Christianity with public safety and prosperity. Acknowledging his correspondent's noble desire to secure Calama against cycles of vengeance and violence—to have it "flourish"—the bishop specified that citizens would "flourish forever" if their community were somehow assimilated into the celestial city. He mentioned that possibility years later and in another context, allowing that Christianity might stifle the urge to return evil for evil and thus "establish [and] consecrate the commonwealth."[116] But neither then nor responding to Nectarius did he elaborate. Both propositions were hypothetical rather than programmatic. We may infer, therefore, that tentatively, and from time to time, he contemplated the conversion or "consecration" of this world's cities or empires. Yet we ought to conclude that consideration of humanity's resistance to measuring success in terms of sanctity swiftly deflated his confidence. He immediately followed his comment on Calama's forever flourishing, for example, with a grim discussion of further punishment. God might "flog" them further, or, worse, permit them to go unpunished, unregenerate, unrepentant, and unredeemed. God might grant the relief Nectarius requested, an amnesty for his clients here, only to deal with them catastrophically hereafter.[117]

For Nectarius' clients were perfect specimens of the enduring problem that made municipal assimilation or consecration ultimately unimaginable. Desperately attached to their earthly possessions, they were forgetful of the celestial patrimony of which their advocate wrote. Or possibly they believed, as did he, that virtue was sufficient to acquire it. Either way, they had not embraced the central tenet of the religion they assailed, the contention that Augustine put concisely in a sermon on John's gospel: love for God and love for gain were antithetical. If Nectarius and his clients were smart, they would fear prosperity more than poverty. They would deplore the chasm between Calama materialism and Christian altruism.[118]

For his part, Nectarius was much given to mending things. He promised that the pagans of Calama would repair what they destroyed. Once the punitive damages were waived, he predicted, the city would come together, and the result would be *securitas* for all.[119] Augustine countered that security born of the kind of forgiveness that his correspondent was proposing could only encourage further outrage. Amnesty authorized enmity. The government's part in God's plan was to punish and thus deter wrongdoing.[120] That was a more dependable way to political security, Augustine alleged, though he was most interested in another sort of security, and an extraordinarily more important one. He preached the security founded on faith in God's sovereignty, sustained by living well, and accompanied by contempt for the settled state, mended fences, public safety, and prosperity of terrestrial cities so highly touted by antiquity's political philosophers and civic-minded citizens like Nectarius.[121] Their religion played a central political role by maintaining civic order and municipal solidarity and by inspiring civic virtue. It taught them social survival skills that paved their path to peace and, reputedly, "the road to heaven," making all things, from empire to Elysium, possible. Augustine's religion, by contrast, "cast in the sharpest possible light the intrinsic limitations of political life."[122]

Chapter Two

Limitations

Augustine's Court

Augustine seemed to have sensed the limitations of political life in Milan as early as 386. Ten years or so later, writing his memoirs or *Confessions,* he clearly signaled his disenchantment with the rituals and pageants of politics. He remembered becoming less politically ambitious when he learned that he must lie well to succeed and find a place among influential men prepared to reward him with reputation, influence, and position for what they knew were lies.[1] Ten years after that, he again remarked on the limitations of public service when he explained the relationship between Christianity and civic virtue to Nectarius in 408 and 409. What happened in Italy and to Rome in 410, as we shall see, only convinced him that he was correct. But he continued weighing the possibility of using local and imperial government to assist the churches and their officials. We will have a chance when we discuss the duel between Donatist and Catholic Christianities, in the next chapter, to illustrate the assistance that seemed to Augustine appropriate as well as necessary and to probe his resolve to procure it. In this chapter, we will chronicle his growing realization that defeated ambition in this world prepared Christians to appreciate how important it was to hope for their place in the next. Understanding how the empire's recent humiliations fit into God's plans was critical—understanding its limitations, that is, and the reasons for its apparent disintegration. But this chapter will also document what Augustine learned from his disputes with Pelagians, specifically, how crucial it was to comprehend the limitations of any person's ability to avoid corruption, cultivate virtue, achieve justice, and hold together what was everywhere disintegrating. We might usefully start with a visit to Augustine's episcopal court or "audience" to show how his awareness of limits and possibilities affected his practice.

Augustine was ambivalent about the "audiences." Emperor Constantine licensed them in 318, probably to spare devotees of his new religion the bias they almost certainly would encounter when summoned before pagan justices. Decades later, when many more Christians staffed the government's tribunals, the jurisdiction of the bishops' courts was scaled back. Augustine sometimes sounded as if he would have preferred to have those courts phased out completely. He was none too happy as well that fellow Christians, as government magistrates—and following standard Roman legal practice—tortured and severely punished people who appeared before them, witnesses as well as suspects.[2]

But the episcopal courts or "audiences" were popular because, as historians now tell us, government courts were notoriously slow and corrupt. Citizens generally could count on cheaper, speedier, and more reliably impartial judgments from their bishops.[3] Besides, the apostle Paul had urged Christians to avoid the embarrassment of public litigation. Augustine agreed: it made sense to keep the contentiousness of Christians under wraps—to be discreet. The faithful were supposed to be unstintingly generous to their neighbors. Personal faith, ideally, led to social reconciliation. But it was not an ideal world, as the bishops well knew. Their religion's projected moral standards were seldom met, and, as pastors and justices, they continually had to deal with the shortfall. Augustine wearied of umpiring the quarrels in his diocese. They occupied time he would otherwise have spent happily and, he believed, more advantageously on study. Litigants, moreover, were horrid creatures. They answered questions dishonestly, preventing him from arbitrating fairly. They shocked him with their questions, wanting to learn how "to work the system," to work around the laws, persuasively perjure themselves, confiscate properties that belonged to others, and dodge their creditors.[4] Possidius left an airbrushed account of the bishop's court in Hippo, but Augustine told a different tale. He complained about the discourtesy and dissembling. He grieved that, even when plaintiffs and defendants were honest, episcopal justices necessarily faced a disagreeable choice. They must either find in favor of one party and alienate the other or propose acceptable compromises that, in effect, set aside the truth of someone's claims.[5]

But one of the letters lately discovered by Johannes Divjak suggests that Augustine was more optimistic. He wrote Eustochius, a layman learned in law, to ask about the legal standing of certain slaves. He wanted to know whether fathers might sell their sons into perpetual servitude. What were the respective rights of tenants and their landlords to an estate's slaves? When could a landlord legally enslave a tenant or a tenant's sons?[6] This inquiry may have been contemporaneous with another Divjak discovery in which Augustine lamented slave trafficking to Alypius and looked for remedies; the volley of questions for Eustochius, therefore, may indicate Augustine's interest in expanding his court's competence, as Kauko Raikas now claims. Or perhaps some pending litigation preoccupied him. Claude Lepelley cleverly connects the dots to sketch a complicated hypothetical "cause" from the bishop's questions. Episcopal courts recorded the emancipation of slaves with some frequency; conceivably, Augustine was looking for ways that he, as a judge, might be more aggressive and win slaves their liberty.[7]

Was Augustine what we would now call a "juridical activist" bent on making as well as enforcing law? Or was his letter to Eustochius a rather routine inquiry? It reports that owners counted on bishops to counsel slaves to submit, and it shows that Augustine thought that his audience was an appropriate venue for such conversations, so, plausibly, he was asking about the law to guard against urging submission on persons wrongfully enslaved. If there were something more to it—if Augustine meant to "widen the secular and juridical dimensions" of episcopal practice—one would expect that letter to have recommended new law instead of looking for explanations of the old.[8]

Augustine could be assertive, as when he tried to have sentences for capital crimes commuted. Arguably, such interventions were more pastoral than political, but government officials referred to them as "usurpations."[9] Macedonius, Christian layman and vicar of Africa, averred that naïve bishops, as advocates, were hardly friends of his court. They trusted that every criminal's remorse was unfeigned. When, in 413 or 414, Augustine entreated him to reconsider the sentences of several criminals in his custody, his reply was curt and condescending. He held that the church's soft line on crime was endangering society. Bishops' meddling was politically imprudent, he said, wondering whether their appeals on behalf of offenders were religiously defensible. The church, to Macedonius, looked to be overreaching.[10]

Augustine responded somewhat defensively. He said he was trying to help the courts' officers as well as its prisoners. If justices expected God to be merciful to them, they should show mercy to others. Recidivism was regrettable. Despite magistrates' best efforts, wickedness would persist. But God's patience would also persist, and justices ought to become executors of that patience as well as forces for order. Their well-intentioned severity (*benigna asperitas*) was good for society and for the safety of its Christians. Augustine's correspondence with Nectarius about Calama shows his appreciation for penalties intended to deter vandalism of the churches and terrorism in general. Yet whenever possible, and when solicited by bishops, magistrates must exercise patience, bearing with the malice of those they hope to correct and add to the number of the good. For, should they lose patience, punish to revenge rather than to reconcile, and ignore the bishops' appeals and advice, they would surely add themselves to the number of the wicked and malicious. Augustine told magistrates that, with the church's assistance, they could be both dutiful and devout.[11]

Bishops would press magistrates to be benevolent but also help them be socially responsible. On matters of crime and punishment, the church and government ordinarily might find themselves at cross purposes—justices tasked to end felons' lives; bishops, to amend them—yet, for Augustine, collaboration was possible and desirable, although only on the church's terms. Pardons would buy time for bishops to participate in the rehabilitation of the criminals for whom they interceded and to see to the compensation of their victims.[12] The church's part in compensation and restitution would be informal. Bishops would try persuasion from their pulpits and not coercion in their courts. The glimpses we get of Augustine's audience suggest he preferred mediation to draconian measures. True, he once interrogated a Manichee and had him driven from the city without waiting for complainants to come forward. Yet, late in his career, gently chiding a young, rash, and rancorous colleague who issued sweeping reprimands and compassed whole households in his censures, Augustine recalled that he dared do nothing comparable during his pontificate and had actually been quite restrained.[13]

And we seem to catch him proposing an alternative to litigation and intimidation when he tried to assist farmer Faventius. This episode, together with Augustine's distaste for court business, suggests a *modus operandi* more to his liking. Faventius' landlord had registered complaints and arranged to have his tenant taken to a provincial court, where, Augustine guessed, the odds were good that a verdict unfavorable to Faventius could be purchased. Eager to oblige the landlord, a constable snatched his tenant from sanctuary before he had a chance to ask the municipal magistrate for the customary thirty days to settle his affairs in preparation for the trip. Augustine protested. He did not refer explicitly to the jurisdiction of his court or to that of any other. He merely raised the expectation that, during the month Faventius was denied, he, Augustine, might have negotiated an amicable, equitable resolution and reconciliation. We have only his version of the affair and no way to determine whether that expectation was unrealistic. But from what he said (and what he did not say about resolving matters in the church's court), it sounds as if he preferred to avoid litigation and to undertake what we might now call shuttle diplomacy.[14] Obviously, we cannot rule out the possibility that, as time passed, Augustine would have been more favorably disposed to integrating the bishops' courts and functions with those of municipal and imperial officials. And it might have been a more attractive option, had the empire just then not seemed to be disintegrating.

Augustine saw that coming. Military setbacks, political intrigue, and treachery since the late 370s had diminished Rome's glory. Tribes from beyond the Danube were for many years ready and nearly able to put the lie to all talk of its eternity. The poets had lied apparently when they promised *imperium sine fine,* an empire without end. Boundaries had shifted before, of course, but the surrender of something greater than a garrison or colony looked to be inevitable as the century turned. Still, all was neither lost nor in jeopardy. Augustine was less apocalyptic than others.[15] Troubles in Italy, after all, had not prevented Emperor Honorius from assisting the African Christians against paganism. An imperial legation crossed the Mediterranean in 399 to complete the suppression of the pagans' worship. African bishops cooperated enthusiastically and monitored the progress of that initiative in their cities and on the estates in their dioceses into the next century. Campaigns against heresy also required their collaboration with government authorities. There seemed to be possibilities for effective partnerships in public administration. Yet Augustine's court work, his appeals for amnesties, and his other overtures to provincial officials now seem to be quite modest. His episcopal audience was far less conspicuous than one would expect if he aspired to the influence Ambrose exercised. He was uninterested in becoming a government agent. The government's usefulness against paganism and heresy, as welcome as it was, did not tempt him to triumphalism. The empire was Christian, but it was not Christianity.[16]

"In the Face of Evil Days"

The year 410 probably gave Augustine a fresh perspective on his first encounters with the Goths in Milan. Battles, truces, and new alliances brought them there in great numbers during the 380s. They and their friends at court precipitated the two basilica crises that preoccupied Ambrose, the second while Augustine was reevaluating his political ambitions in 386. Doubtlessly distracted as he pondered his future, the young African orator would nonetheless have known better than we do who those Goths were. Their chroniclers, trying to tidy up a venerable past for subsequent Ostrogothic and Visigothic kingdoms, suggested that Gothic tribes were ethnically homogenous, but historians now tend to emphasize the polyethnic character of their tribal confederation. They did, however, have a common language, which had been given literary form by subordinationist (Arian) missionaries earlier in the fourth century, missionaries whose brand of Christianity Ambrose so deplored. Augustine was wise to that much and would have known more about the crises and court intrigue that put both the government and church in jeopardy.[17]

Emperor Theodosius was impeccably orthodox—by Ambrose's and by Nicene standards—yet he routinely employed the Goths against his enemies, notably, the usurpers Maximus and Eugenius. The regent he appointed on his deathbed, Stilicho, half-barbarian by birth, relied on the Goths as well. Secure in his position and influence in the West over Theodosius' younger son Honorius, he had difficulty making good his claims to influence in the East where Honorius' brother Arcadius, listening to others, found the Goths useful as well. One of their leaders, Alaric, a veteran of Theodosius' campaigns, realized the pivotal position of his people and negotiated with both East and West for pay, rations, and territory. He settled in eastern Illyricum for some years before invading Italy late in 401. Stilicho turned him back and, within a year, turned him into an ally, hoping to have Alaric's army join, if not lead, an assault on Macedonia, and eventually Constantinople. But that expedition had to be postponed. In 405, Italy was attacked from the north. The Goths were waiting across the Adriatic when Stilicho was again distracted. A renegade soldier from Britain seized power in Gaul, styled himself Emperor Constantine III, and contemplated stabbing into Italy from his new capital in Arles. Meanwhile, Stilicho's rivals at court arranged for the regent's overthrow and murder in 408 and, to assure their safety, made it clear that his troops were unwelcome by massacring their families settled nearby. Learning of Stilicho's fate, Augustine wrote to ascertain how the events in Italy might affect the government's cooperation with the church on his side of the sea. Had he heard about the atrocities when he referred to the new regent, largely responsible for the coup and deadly purge, as a sincere Christian?[18]

On his death, Stilicho's soldiers defected to Alaric, who followed developments and still waited across the Adriatic for orders. Why he invaded Italy without them is no mystery. The newest additions to his ranks, eager to avenge their slaughtered families, depleted the West's defenses. Besides, the court in Constantinople, at peace with Persia, concentrated on refortifying its other extended frontier in the Balkans. By contrast, Italy was poorly protected, and Honorius replied coarsely to the Goths' demands for pay and land along the Danube. Alaric's army made for Rome in late 408.

News of its campaign soon reached Africa, causing Augustine "great grief." He compared hardships in Italy with those in North Africa where violent elements among the Donatists terrorized ordinary Christians as well as church officials. But he suspected that the best way to take some sting out of all early fifth-century ordeals was to compare them with adversities recorded in Hebrew scripture. For the Old Testament, without assuring an end to misfortune on earth, promised God's kingdom would survive and ultimately "consume" the empires that held it captive. Augustine also sensed that there could be consolation prior to the ultimate "consumption." Hostages might lead captors to Christianity. It had been known to happen. As for other casualties, their consolation must come, in part, from their trust that God would not be punishing them unjustly, that their misery was God's sentence on their sinfulness, that God, their judge, was also their redeemer and would not forsake them during their ordeals, and that posterity would never forget their courage. And victims should be told of and consoled by the certainty of their eternal reward and their persecutors' punishment. Obviously, the world was again, as it had been before Christ: bloody, *plenus sanguine*. Augustine, like his prolific contemporary Jerome, concluded that Rome had not before, and could not then, save that world. The politics of empire was too much a part of it. The Christian empire's place in God's plan was already diminished, in their view, before its old capital fell to Alaric.[19]

Augustine may not have known all the details of the Goths' "conquest." We do not learn from him, for example, that Alaric paced for eighteen months between Rome and Ravenna, the city to which Honorius retired. The Goths' hesitation probably puzzled the Africans, if they knew of it, and is hard to explain now. Was Alaric deliberate or just directionless? Peter Heather has him besiege Rome for leverage in his negotiations with the court and has Honorius dither. The western emperor could not decide whether to talk terms or remain intransigent. He delayed, and delays allowed factions to develop among the Goths. (Was that Honorius' intent?) When a rival attacked Alaric en route to another round of negotiations near the marshes of Ravenna, the Goth's commander returned to Rome and turned on it. "The sack was incidental," Heather concludes; "the fall of the empire's capital city actually represents a Gothic failure."[20]

Alaric's army filed into Rome in August 410, and was gone in three days. He contemplated crossing to Sicily and, from there, to Africa, but died soon after the sack, failing to extort any favorable terms from the government. His brother-in-law removed the Goths to Gaul in 412. The Romans lost what they had—prestige and pride—without the Goths getting what they wanted, the two unable to adjust their ostensibly compatible needs to assimilate and be assimilated respectively.[21]

Or so it seems. Edward Gibbon's somewhat less subtle verdict passed into early modern textbooks. The consensus was that decadence caused the empire's decline and fall, that no approach to, or appeasement of, the barbarians could have saved Rome from itself. Its senators preferred debauchery to defense. They spent lavishly on their palaces and praetorian games yet were stingy with their soldiers. As recently as 1981, historian Pierre Chaunu could still hold that Rome was perfectly decadent and that no subsequent civilization approached the lows to which the city and empire descended.[22] Augustine had a different but related take on decadence. Dissolute Christians had disgraced their churches, he reported; they flaunted their bad habits and compromised their religion. Rome was humbled during nominally "Christian times," he explained, because God could hardly let the Christians' indecency go unpunished. Ambrose tried to discipline his diocese. Augustine mentioned the efforts to maintain sobriety and decorum at gravesites in Milan, and, on returning to Africa and becoming bishop, he, too, urged that the heavy drinking and unruly conduct at the church's festivals be curtailed. He appreciated that pagans' old habits died hard. Their former cults had encouraged them to couple boozy sociability with supplications to their deities. It was no wonder, then, that they took the anniversary of a martyr's death as an occasion or excuse to get drunk. Still, Augustine also weighed the probable costs of strict censures and prohibitions: the recent converts might slip away from the faith. Nonetheless, he insisted that the time had come for the pagans-turned-Christians to abandon their old pleasures and more fully to subscribe to the discipline of their new faith.[23]

They objected and argued that the Roman church long indulged behavior similar to theirs. Augustine admitted that Rome was something of a wreck in the late 390s. It was an administrator's nightmare, he suggested, too big to police effectively. Immigrants and petitioners and pilgrims streamed into the city every month, flooding its churches with all sorts of Christians. Some from one fringe of the empire cherished customs and practices vastly different from those of others from a different fringe or frontier. Furthermore, the resident population was unmanageably diverse as well. Augustine believed the bishops tried to be responsible without becoming ruthless, yet he conceded that the old capital was an embarrassment. Embarrassments also, and telling signs of the church's decline and decadence, were the drunkards of Africa (*ebriosi*) who continued to use the unruliness of Rome to justify their own indiscipline.[24]

But, to Augustine, greater embarrassments still were the Christians who attended their pagan neighbors' spectacles, participated in their pageants, and identified with their civic religion. He was distressed by what he took to be the pagans' idolatry, their seduction of "his" parishioners, and what was shaping up as an unbecoming competition. For their part, the pagans must have found his distress jarringly unpleasant. It surely put the municipally advantageous "trend towards coexistence" under considerable strain in the early fifth century. What might have happened at Calama, for example, had Augustine been more obliging in 408? Did he forfeit the chance for a quick consolidation after the crisis there by "tribalizing," in effect, pagans and Christians who might otherwise have come to some consensus about civic virtues and civic duty?[25]

Nectarius' bid for reconciliation was rejected in 408, but resistance was not the exclusive property of either "tribe." From 410, pagans provoked Augustine by blaming Christians for Rome's fate, suggesting Alaric's expedition would have been less eventful had the empire not forsaken its gods. The Christians' god, they said, was a poor, powerless substitute for their deities who had long protected the old capital; to Augustine, however, such nostalgia was nonsense. Where were the city's supposedly formidable protectors, he asked, when Nero reduced Rome to rubble? Proof that paganism had little connection with material prosperity and less with military security packed several of the sermons Augustine preached within a year of the sack of the city. He treated the topic so often that he was accused of picking at scabs and preventing wounds from healing. The refugees from Rome in Hippo and Carthage begged him to stop.[26]

But his message seemed exceptionally important to him; his evidence against paganism's civic religion seemed irrefutable. How could its gods have been expected to save Rome, he asked, when they had failed to save Troy? How foolish of Aeneas to have transported their images! How absurd of his descendants, recent Romans, to trust them to be powerfully present against Goths early in the fifth century, when the gods and images had been unable to save themselves from Theodosius at the end of the fourth! Theodosius, Ulysses, Nero, and Alaric destroyed what had been precious to Rome's deities. Either the gods were infinitely patient or utterly powerless. In Augustine's view, they were nonexistent, and he imagined the sack of the old capital as a last straw, which would break the back of paganism. It was an offense or "scandal" from which the city's and the empire's civic religions could never recover.[27] But that "scandal," as Augustine scripted it, had a happy ending: the pagans should repudiate their old religions and gods, acknowledge the Christians' God, and accept that hardships had been staged, in part, for their benefit. They expected their pieties and deities to save them; their disappointment, according to Augustine, ought to incline them to sweep the shards of those expectations into the rest of the debris from Rome's "fall" and to rebuild their hopes on firmer foundations, on the scripture's promises, which, he said, had no bearing whatsoever on political security and material prosperity here, now, or soon. "Heaven and earth shall pass away." Cities were built to topple. Lives, laws, and empires lasted only so long. They served at God's pleasure, so to speak. Hope for something more lasting could be a solace as well as a source of inspiration; however, it satisfied one's deepest religious needs only when its object (and one's objective) was an eternally enduring place of perfect justice, peace, and love.[28]

That was Augustine's line. He assumed it would trip up countless Christians as well as pagans, and not just Christians who subscribed to the pagans' civic pieties. For there were those among the faithful who figured Rome's sacred graves would save the city. To them, the Goths inside the gates must have been particularly vexing; to them, Augustine addressed words of criticism and comfort. Their hopes for Rome had been misplaced, he scolded, as had their confidence that the apostles Peter and Paul would save the city simply to protect their bones and tombs therein. Yet the Christians' faith, Augustine surmised, should make it easier to find peace in the promises of their creator and redeemer. And their faith should enable them to comprehend an intended lesson of the humiliation and hardship they experienced, namely, that the meek and not the politically shrewd, ambitious, or hopeful might find God "in the face of evil days." The press of events was meant to wean pagans from paganism but also, Augustine emphasized, to wean Christians from their attachments to this world.[29]

He described "scandals" or offenses as training exercises (*exercitationes*). They trained Christians for their eventual departure from this life, and Augustine sounded in some sermons like a drill sergeant, toughening tender recruits: "Fix your hope on God. Yearn for eternal rewards. Expect them! You are Christians; we are all Christians. Christ came into the flesh, but not for the delight of it. We ought to bear with, but take no delight in, the present moment. We know what jeopardy we now have. Adversity is obvious, but prosperity deceives. Beware the sea, even when it is calm."[30] He suggested that Christians were tested in the best of times; even when seas were calm (*malacia*) and no immediate danger presented itself in the "press" of events, they should be wary and learn to cling to God with faith and hope. Augustine alleged that both were God's gifts and that, once received, they fastened the faithful to their redeemer. Without faith in God, the most virtuous citizens and public officials would come undone and were damned, however much their political resourcefulness or righteousness might exceed the civic dutifulness of faithful Christians.[31] Augustine acknowledged that faith might shade into awe. Reflecting on God's dramatic sacrifice of his son, Christians had been known to marvel at Jesus much as onlookers admire wirewalkers (*funiambuli*). Hope, therefore, should accompany faith. Hope was forward-looking, and the Christians' "training" in adversity assured that it would "fix" on what was promised in God's Word and not on what was perishable in the world's cities.[32]

Augustine preached as if it were possible to maintain that kind of concentration or "fixation" through times of prosperity and adversity, in calm and rough seas, yet he knew that fugitive feelings of desolation during bad patches and self-congratulation during the good were bound to distract the most hopeful among ordinary Christians. He knew also, though, that examples of steadfast hope abounded in the cloisters. Monks were heroes to Augustine. He wrote often to and for them, but he could not stop interpreting history for the many more Christians who remained helplessly caught in its changing currents. He advised them repeatedly to cope and to hope—never more urgently than in his most widely read sermon on the "fall" or "destruction" of Rome, his *De excidio*. It begins with Daniel confessing his sins, implying that those overtaken by tragedies in more recent days, unlike Daniel, had been tempted to forget their shortcomings when they looked into what went wickedly wrong and incurred God's wrath. Daniel in captivity blamed no one but himself. He did so again at the start of Augustine's sermon, to advise Christians, who were wallowing in their sense of self-righteousness and in their status as victims in—and after—late August 410, that they must admit their complicity, self-satisfaction, and sin to appreciate the saving purpose of that season's scandal.[33]

Augustine insisted in this sermon on the fall, as he had before, that Christians take their suffering as a test rather than as punishment. Before the sermon proceeds very far, Job joins Daniel to make precisely this point. Christians fail the test if they expect some political or military deliverance from their troubles. Ten years before, Augustine all but told them to forfeit any hope that a political or military messiah might save the faithful from their enemies and embarrassments. He said that an impulse to dominate fueled all political ambition and that political ambition fouled every leader's or would-be leader's good intentions. That emperors could secure lasting peace was, for him, the longest of long shots. A much safer bet was that public officials would join the raft of scoundrels seeking power over their neighbors.[34] Another Theodosius might have those virtues that Christians admired and be penitent for his political sins, yet that second Theodosius or Constantine would not deter the next Alaric. It was a mistake to expect the powerful and pious to do more than damage control. Christians simply had to cope with adversity, hope for eternity, and, like Job, keep their "heart[s] from evil thoughts and tongue[s] from cursing."[35]

The sermon is a blend of exhortation and consolation. Jean-Claude Frédouille thinks it offers Augustine's "ultimate consolation," namely, the assurance that jeopardy and adversity here and now avert suffering hereafter and forever. The bishop broke and brokered the fall of Rome with that assurance, and he was certain nothing could rival its consoling powers as long as the world remained "under the condition of change." Prayers at the apostles' tombs in the old capital proved just as ineffectual as the pagans' civic religions, he said. Poets echoing Aeneas' remark that Rome's power was eternal, *sine fine,* sounded absurd to him after 410. Improvements made to Rome's high walls shortly before Alaric hardly cheered or consoled residents after him. Neither walls nor prayers nor poets nor cults stood between them and misery. In Augustine's judgment, however, misery "under the condition of change" was part of the Christians' training, and grief deflated worldly expectations and "false" consolations that retarded progress in their training.[36]

Grief occasionally led nowhere. The aggrieved might keep hoping for economic recovery. They might blame others for their ordeals, refuse to confess their sins as Daniel did, or refrain from cursing as Job did. By contrast, hopeful yet grieving citizens of the celestial city offered their contrition and "broken spirits" as sacrifices, much as martyrs offered their lives.[37]

Augustine approved. The humble and hopeful, he preached, "put off" asking for explanations: God wants them to bear up but not necessarily to figure out why they were afflicted.[38] Yet in this same sermon, the bishop proved again that he was unable to leave off explaining why Rome and the empire were humiliated. His reasoning was much the same as it had been and would be in similarly distilled remarks, but this sermon, delivered in the summer of 411, is rightly described as his most pessimistic. Elsewhere, he doubted whether the devastation of 410 was all that extensive. This once, however, he entertained the possibility that it was. If God had been more vengeful than ever before, it was because the results of a century of politically patronized, financially favored Christianity had been so disappointing. Pagans, schismatics, and ordinary Christians were so busy storing up treasures on earth that they had neither the patience nor the will to reorient their expectations.[39]

To the pagan critics of Christianity, 410 was unlike previous calamities. The one concession Augustine made to that assessment may have been regretted as soon as it was uttered. Without minimizing the misery of recent events—save to say that Rome was no Sodom and was still standing—he continued to suggest that previous mishaps were of the same or greater magnitude. He knew, however, that his evidence for that observation left something to be desired. Sometime in 414, he prevailed on Orosius, a priest from Spain who had fled from the Goths, to compose a history that should answer pagans' censures. Completed by 417, the work occasionally incorporated Augustine's explanations and directives that Christians be patient and "bear up." Yet it looked more consistently to a brighter side of early fifth-century developments. It even proposed that some political recovery was at hand. The Goths' hegemony was a passing phase. Rome was, and the empire would be, saved by its Christians' faith. According to Orosius, the most recent difficulties fit a pattern. Misfortune befell the empire when Rome martyred the apostles Peter and Paul. Galba rebelled in Spain; Vespasian rebelled in Syria. Both insurrections, though, were easily suppressed. The implication was that the Christians' God was a benevolent sentry, letting pass just enough trouble to chafe or jolt and edify.[40]

Admittedly, then, the Goths jolted apologists for the Christian empire by having so easily overrun its old capital. But Orosius was consoled by the empire's expanse, by Christianity's continuing influence, and by the common rituals, customs, and laws that seemed to bind Rome back together. Correspondences, that is, suggested durability, if not permanence. But Augustine was unimpressed. He concluded that, "under the conditions of change," no set of customs or laws conformed or could ever conform to God's laws. And no reform would change that. Political changes might make the regime of a terrestrial city less oppressive, but no more godly.[41] Augustine could not quarrel with Orosius' observation that Rome had been saved, yet he disagreed with him about the character of that salvation. Rome was spared, but not because it was or would be possible to realize a divinely just disposition in its time or territory. True, Christians on pilgrimage on earth could conceive of what God's justice required. "Genuine" justice was imaginable, yet, Augustine averred, Christians would never be able to fashion institutions to administer it or to have their cities declare for it. Augustine, in other words, was nowhere near as fond of Rome as the poet Prudentius had been and, as Goulven Madec says, not as "infatuated" with "providentialism" as historian Orosius was. Augustine's "deep pessimism" about the powers and prospects of humankind never congealed into a political theory or doctrine. But his simmering pessimism made him suspicious of Nectarius' civic idealism and more skeptical than Orosius about Rome's rebound. Confidence in the persistence of political virtue and in the strength of humanity's best instincts seemed ever more capricious to Augustine after 410, the year two refugees from Rome, Pelagius and Caelestius, started toward Africa.[42]

"The Enemies of Grace"

They were not as bullish as Orosius about the empire—after Alaric, few were—yet Caelestius and Pelagius were confident that, after baptism, Christians could choose to change their lives and behave impeccably. The remission of sin in their baptisms, directions given with God's law, the goodness of created nature, and examples of exemplary conduct in their sacred texts were sufficient to break humanity's bondage to bad habits.[43]

Pelagius, a Briton who had been living in Rome for nearly twenty years, likely counted Caelestius among his partisans, although the latter may have also learned from Rufinus the Syrian that souls were free to pick their perversion. Others at the time accounted for evil by shifting blame back to prior existences or to inherited disabilities. Caelestius and Pelagius, however, underscored the importance of human freedom and responsibility. At first they saw Augustine as an ally and looked forward to closing ranks with him against the fatalism of their Manichaean critics. He seemed to be suggesting in his *Confessions* and in his anti-Manichaean treatises that individuals were capable of strenuous effort and striking results. And a good thing, too, for, according to Pelagius, it was absurd to assume that one could reap celestial returns with an ordinary life. Those who behave unexceptionally (*omnium ritu*) ought not to expect exceptional rewards.[44] But Augustine was increasingly uncomfortable with such talk about merit and reward. He wrote more about perseverance and, later, about predestination than about the virtues that Pelagians thought people could and should cultivate and practice. Contesting Caelestius' and Pelagius' confidence in such cultivation—and the claims for human nature and ability, which became the defining characteristics of Pelagianism—Augustine soured still more on the prospects for human perfectibility and for meaningful political reform in the second and third decades of the fifth century.[45]

But initially, on hearing that the two refugees from Rome had come, Augustine was courteous. He complimented Caelestius' intelligence and called Pelagius a "friend." Maybe he hoped to draw them into North African anti-Manichaean circles. Or was he mindful of their influential friends? During the 390s and into the fifth century, Roman Christians had warmed to the Pelagians, perhaps because they distinguished between an authentic, muscular Christianity and the tepid confessions of faith that, after Constantine, seemed convenient rather than earnest and inspiringly comprehensive. Pelagius was his patrons' "spiritual trainer," trafficking in encouragement, exercising the elites so they might compensate in their private lives for compromises their churches had made to accommodate new converts and for the imperfections of their empire.[46]

Pelagius soon left for the East. Caelestius remained and planned to be ordained a priest in Carthage, but objections were raised there to his views on original sin and infant baptism. He was heard to argue that newborns were as Adam had been before disobeying God and that nothing, therefore, would be gained by baptizing them. He figured that sins were products of choices, and newborns had yet to make any. Augustine also learned that Caelestius presumed good, godly choices were pillars of a Christian life, erected and sustainable without direct divine assistance. But his statements to that effect are preserved in and with Augustine's rebuttals, and it is hard to imagine Augustine lifting sentences from Caelestius' texts and depositing them, without distortion, alongside his replies. Still, in general, Caelestius could have replied to his critics as reported, namely, that the human will was itself "a grace." For Augustine repeatedly insisted on the contrary: if divine grace and human will were so defined or identified, he asserted, sin would conquer grace every time a person chose wickedly.

In Palestine, Pelagius would later deny that he had encouraged Caelestius and was apologetic when confronted at a council in Diospolis with his own previous remarks on human freedom and responsibility. He had been indiscreet and reckless, he conceded, yet he had not started out to question the validity of cherished doctrine or the value of the church's sacraments. To Augustine's dismay, those apologies and disclaimers saved Pelagius from censure. He was sly, slippery, and acquitted. Caelestius was transparent, arraigned, and condemned. Augustine was unhappy with half a loaf, because he believed both refugees from Rome were committed to the proposition that nature, law, and biblical exempla supplied all the grace necessary to choose virtuously, accumulate merit, and win celestial rewards.[47]

In Augustine's judgment, the Pelagians' commitment to that proposition made them "enemies of the grace" that God supplied *ab extra*, from beyond the created order. But Pelagius, after having been exonerated, was warmly received in Jerusalem by Bishops John and then Praylius. Caelestius returned to Rome to appeal his conviction at Carthage. Augustine and his episcopal colleagues in Africa also approached Pope Innocent I, to have him uphold their verdict against Caelestius and condemn Pelagius—despite Diospolis—for overstating the powers and independence of human nature and for limiting the scope of divine grace. Perhaps the Africans hoped that papal criticism might prevent the Pelagian persuasion from becoming a popular religious movement in Palestine. But it would also have seemed strategic to Augustine and his allies to strike a blow against the Pelagians' "new heresy" at its point of origin, where Innocent was immensely respected by its patrons.[48]

Early in 417, Innocent assured his African colleagues that he and other Christians in the old capital thought themselves well rid of Pelagius. They wanted nothing further to do with his errors.[49] But Innocent died soon afterward, and Zosimus, who succeeded him, was satisfied with Pelagius' professions of orthodoxy. The new pope was also influenced, it seems, by Bishop Praylius' friendliness to Pelagius in Jerusalem. So Zosimus scolded critics of Caelestius and Pelagius in Africa for irresponsibly and falsely having accused the two. The African bishops were incensed and asked the imperial court at Ravenna to intervene. On that front, Augustine and his colleagues prevailed. Emperor Honorius, in effect, set aside the new pope's judgment and issued a rescript against the Pelagians in early spring of 418. He branded them the aggressors. Disregarding Zosimus' sentiments and Praylius' patronage, the court at Ravenna condemned both Caelestius and Pelagius for disputing matters already decided by their church. The charges explicitly referred to troubles in Rome, suggesting, as did Zosimus' decision to reverse his predecessor, that Innocent had understated the Pelagians' strength in Italy. In Africa, though, Augustine and his colleagues were not fretting about the difficulties faced across the Mediterranean by Innocent, Zosimus, or Honorius. More than two hundred bishops assembled in Carthage in 418 to declare against the "new heretics" and for the depravity of human nature, because they thought that the Pelagians' perceived indifference to sin endangered the church's work in their own precincts.[50]

The Carthaginian council's position was that one's appreciation for "the true forgiveness of sins" as practiced in the churches was predicated on understanding the depth of human depravity. And to comprehend that, Christians must acknowledge the gravity of Adam and Eve's fall from grace, the universal and devastating consequences of original sin, and the necessity for infant baptism. But even before the council formulated its positions in May, and before the court at Ravenna had proceeded against the Pelagians in late April, Zosimus grudgingly conceded the influence, if not also the coherence, of the Africans' position. He called a moratorium of sorts. No final verdict would be formulated without further consultations with his colleagues in Carthage. But such gestures were late in coming. They are now called "clumsy" and "meaningless."[51] At the time, they had the effect of alienating Zosimus from all concerned parties. By contrast, Ravenna's intervention tipped the scales decisively. The pope had no choice but to follow, "caught in [the] swing of feeling against the Pelagians" engineered from Carthage and almost certainly given momentum by rioting in Palestine and Rome associated with Pelagians' dissent. Three surviving fragments of Zosimus' subsequent circular indicate that he resigned himself to do his part to see Pelagius' heresy was condemned *per totum mundum.*[52]

Several Italian bishops resisted and were dispatched to the East. Among them, Julian of Eclanum appears to have been emboldened by Zosimus' death late in 418 and continued from exile to assail the doctrines that, in his view, Augustine and Africa had imposed on Rome and Ravenna. Julian claimed that Augustine was sadistic to maintain that all were corrupt, including newborn infants. The emperor must have been bribed to have agreed. As for Zosimus' capitulation, it was unforgivable yet predictable, once the government tipped its hand. Hence, the episode and its unfortunate effects for the Pelagians, in Julian's judgment, could only be explained by the fact that the Africans had cheated; they shamelessly practiced the corruption they preached.[53] Julian may have been right to cry foul. Even so, the skill and persistence with which Augustine developed the doctrine of grace that isolated Caelestius and Pelagius is impressive. He offered his definitions of grace and nature, passing them off as the long-cherished definitions of the church—making the Pelagians appear to be equivocating and innovating when they introduced or elaborated their own. To have that strategy succeed, to have his views about the gratuity of grace and the insufficiencies of human nature prevail, Augustine had to assure that the Pelagians were seen to fail. Or, to be more accurate, one should say that Augustine had to see to it that Pelagius' remarks on human nature's insufficiencies would sound so tentative that they were construed as unconventional claims for its sufficiency and dignity. Here is Augustine explaining Pelagius' acquittal at Diospolis to Innocent:

When the bishops at Diospolis pronounced Pelagius a Catholic, we trust they did so for no other reason than that he confessed his belief in God's grace. He allowed that Christians, through determination and effort might live uprightly, yet he specified that such allowance did not deny the need for divine help, the need for grace. . . . If those bishops took him to mean the 'grace' that comes with human nature, which the wicked have as well as we, and took him to repudiate the grace by which we are sons of God and Christians, they would not have listened to him patiently but rather banished him from their sight. But for this reason those episcopal judges are not to be blamed: they heard the word 'grace' and understood it to mean what the church traditionally means by it. They were unaware of what Pelagians write or say about grace in various other places.[54]

Augustine allowed how easy it was to mistake Pelagius for an orthodox Christian, exonerating the bishops at Diospolis while also formulating a tradition (*ecclesiastica consuetudo*), familiarity with which alerted authorities from then on to the Pelagians' heresy.[55]

That "tradition," then, was designed to distinguish the heretical from the acceptable. The choices Christians then made would place them on one or another side of the divide. If, with the Pelagians, they assumed divine law and human nature were "graces," they might try to become more disciplined by exploring hitherto untapped reservoirs of resolve, for their *natural* resources. Pelagius presumably would have approved. He confided to a friend that whenever he wrote about ethical dilemmas he "typically showed the character and power of human nature and what it was capable of accomplishing." He stressed the autonomy of the will even when discussing the importance of humility.[56] But Augustine learned from experience, he said, how hard it was, unaided, to be humble and chaste—and how impossible to remain continent and to give up worldly ambitions without ongoing, transcendental, comprehensive help from divine grace. Afterward, he became aware how offensive God found human self-sufficiency. That was when and why he instructed Christians to stop searching for personal strengths and start confessing their weaknesses. God demanded that much by law, he said, and supplied it by grace.[57]

From Augustine's perspective, Christians might choose to rely on their strengths or to confess their weaknesses and rely on God's grace, but not on

the "grace" Pelagius and Caelestius identified with "the power of human nature and what it was capable of accomplishing." To rely on that "power," Augustine explained, was to build on sand. The foundation for his objections to
the two heretical refugees was laid two years after they first landed in Africa as
he was responding to a catechumen's questions that were only indirectly related to the Pelagians' position. He told his correspondent then that a truly
happy life depended on a decisive change. One must stop striving for one's
own good, which of course seemed always to change with circumstance, and
find the good that never changes, to find and become faithful to God. The
goal was "perfect participation in that unchangeable good of which [one's]
faith was now a pledge." Participation by expectation: that was the objective
Augustine formulated after he read the Platonists and developed during his
subsequent confrontations with the Pelagians. He learned from the Platonists
that the soul moves toward a complete union with God—a union not to be
realized on earth because each soul was distracted by its body and by sense
perception. Imperfections attached to all souls, so souls must attach themselves to the cross of Christ. Persons who aspire to a worldly perfection of any
sort predictably made less sense of the way of the cross than they did of their
own earthly and unstable ambitions. They could make no sense of the grace
bestowed and promised in the New Testament and through the cross, because
grace "belonged to eternal not temporal life." That was the lesson of the cross
for catechumens, Augustine emphasized, given to help the faithful understand their fate. To that same pedagogical end, earthly goods go as rewards to
the wicked so that faith should not take such rewards as its due. Christian devotion had nothing on earth to hope for. Its lot was to yearn for higher things,
especially for the righteousness or justice of God.[58]

Unlike the changeable standards for human righteousness, the standard
for eternal righteousness was always the same: love of God expressed in love
for neighbors, for no ulterior terrestrial purposes. To illustrate, Augustine
borrowed from the Apostle Paul's letter to the Romans, which criticized the
Jews for establishing their own standards for justice. They did not submit to
God. Pride and envy ruled them. They were "icy" and "hard" and "cast off."
From 412—and increasingly thereafter—Augustine believed the Pelagians'
efforts to make themselves holy would end similarly.[59]

He admitted to Julian of Eclanum that self-assertion sometimes produced a good result. But virtues, he went on, were not determined by actions

or consequences. Instead, an agent's aims determined whether actions and consequences were virtuous. One might do well for the sake of honor or fame, as did the ancient Romans, and the results would look to all the world to be desirable, even admirable. Romans enjoyed peace, prosperity, and the enormous expanse of their domain. Yet the virtues that served those ends, Augustine argued, had not been true virtues, any more than refraining from theft was a virtue, if one held back for fear of getting caught. The only virtues worthy of the name aimed not at temporal, but at celestial advantage.[60]

Julian's position, as Augustine reported it, was different. Virtues were qualities of mind—prudence, justice, temperance, courage—directed toward what human will desired. They were virtues, however one intended to use them. Julian did admit that virtues were somewhat diminished by the pursuit of "spindly" or slender rewards, but Augustine's counter-arguments took no notice of the concession. He insisted that the prudence of the greedy is contemptible when it plots to increase their gain. The temperance of the greedy who live frugally to avoid expense and hoard their wealth is miserly. The courage of the greedy who undergo torture to save their goods is sordid. Qualities are not virtues unless, guided by faith, they enable Christians to live courageously and justly. If one's qualities are not employed to acquire the happiness that faith promises will be immortal, they are "in no sense true virtues."[61]

Augustine hammered his point home, doubtlessly at the expense of an adequate, accurate report of his opponent's. But Julian seems to have been as much a moralist as Pelagius, whose spiritual exercises for the laity were nearly monastic. Indeed, Augustine generally underscored and heaped scorn on the Pelagians' perfectionism. They looked to achieve; he hoped to endure. The perfection "possible within the limits of this life," he said, was a perfection by anticipation. And admission of the imperfections of public service, political righteousness, and civic idealism was, if not the precondition for that "perfection," one of its constituent characteristics.[62]

Augustine heard the Pelagians say sinlessness was achievable, if only because it was commanded of Christians in the Bible (Matthew 5:48). He heard them say that such perfection was a matter of choice, that persons determined to do well could do well and become better and make the best of God's creation, counsel, revelations, and remissions in order to please Him. Augustine's counters were not always cogent. He suggested that sinlessness was conceivable—nothing was impossible if God willed it—yet not exactly achievable. He elaborated smaller perfections and degrees of perfection that imply progress in perfection was possible. He confirmed, for instance, that one could be a perfect student without becoming a perfect teacher, that one might be perfectly compassionate and love one's enemies without preparing or resolving to suffer their insults. Such "perfections" were subject to change, and the changeable, Augustine declared, was imperfect, far shy of the "perfect participation in that unchangeable good" available with faith and as anticipation, given the limitations of this life.[63] Faith, hope, and love bring Christians close to God, so there was "no need to arrange for long voyages," Augustine advised: "to one who is everywhere, we come by loving and not by sailing." Tempests and temptations made voyages treacherous, yet nothing was said about Christians' strenuous seamanship. Pelagius' Christian, "making himself holy," worthy, and seaworthy, was far from Augustine's mind and metaphor. "Let your faith board the wood of the cross and you will not be drowned," he promised; "you will be borne up by the wood."[64]

All during the controversies with Caelestius, Pelagius, and Julian, from 412 deep into the 420s, human nature was the problem for Augustine and the possible solution for his opponents. He was convinced of its mutability, depravity, fragility, and insufficiency. They were sure he falsely interpreted Genesis to prove his point. His rejoinder was that the apostle Paul usefully wrestled with and pinned the meaning of that episode in Eden, where "by one man sin entered the world." Paul, not he, clarified how *in quo omnes,* in that original sin, all sinned, *peccaverunt.* Sharing Adam and Eve's nature, we share its faults, Augustine explained; humanity bears the consequences of its progenitors' disobedience. The more Caelestius, Pelagius, and particularly Julian insisted that one becomes sinful by imitation rather than through propagation, the more Augustine's writing was suffused with a certainty and urgency: "born under the power of sin," the faithful can only be "borne up by the wood" of the cross and should be dissuaded from relying on themselves or relying on a "grace" that, in Augustine's opinion, did not deserve that name.[65]

He complained that the Pelagians more attractively packaged their enthusiasms for human nature by underestimating the power of sin and reducing the role grace played in curbing it. For their part, Caelestius and Pelagius seldom missed the chance to couple Augustine's notions of "the power of sin" and pollution of nature with the Manichees' debasement of the material world. Julian's criticisms were apparently the most scornful. He berated Augustine for filling the world with "children of disease," "guilty from their origin." Augustine's replies show the quality of his craftsmanship in the simplicity with which they relate the power of sin to the pardon in baptism. "[S]in in paradise changed human beings for the worse," he observed, "because it is far more serious than we can judge. It is contracted by every child that is born and forgiven only in one that is reborn." Forgiveness comes with baptism, yet a "carnal concupiscence that resists the law of the mind" remains, although without being counted against subjects as *their* sins. "It does them no harm unless they consent to its promptings." Guilt seems gone but only seems so. Human nature is still impaired, feeble, and susceptible to those terribly damaging "promptings."[66]

The question of consent was obviously critical, and one can understand why the Pelagians were perplexed. Original sin so weakened nature's resistance, in Augustine's view, that consent would be more a matter of time than of choice. Sooner or later, the Christian was bound to go bad. How, then, could consent be called freely willed? And, equally to the point at issue, this human condition or predicament was hard to reconcile with the goodness of God. Would a benevolent father bind his children so? Augustine dodged such questions. He put them alongside other imponderables that occur to finite minds on the lower slopes as they gaze at the summit and attempt to comprehend God's infinite wisdom. The enormous discrepancy between what we can know and what God knows was an answer of sorts, yet Augustine also introduced considerations that, in some measure, justified the ways of God to humans, whose consent to "the promptings" of concupiscence placed them in harm's way. Heirs of Adam and Eve, he said, had no right to expect their bodies to obey them, when their first parents had so disastrously disobeyed God. The symmetry between crime and punishment was all that finite minds might fathom. Their punishment perfectly fit their crime. The disobedient were to be disobeyed.[67]

Hence, humans were "handed over" to inordinate desires. They were "overtaken" and "possessed," "the law of sin" inscribed in their very nature— "in their members." As if he were anticipating the Pelagians' replies to his description of defeat, Augustine added that the very efforts to resist or to break captivity once it had been decreed smacked of ingratitude and disobedience, insofar as God's mercy (and Christ's cross) were forgotten.[68]

Julian argued that Augustine was wrong about the routes into and out of captivity. Humans inherit death—not sin—from their first parents, he noted, identifying Augustine's mistranslation of the *in quo omnes* passage in

Romans 5:12. They choose their bondage freely and may choose emancipation as well, because they were "handed over" to their wickedness (Romans 1:28) by God's patience and not by God's power. For Julian, the implication is clear: the creator awaited his creatures' recovery of their determination, their discipline. But, for Augustine, the creator was more emphatically the redeemer. Only God could recover what God took away when humanity was "handed over," namely, the will and ability to resist the sin within.[69]

God showed the way out of captivity but not, as the Pelagians trusted, by giving humanity its laws and God's law. A treatise on the Christian life composed under Pelagius' influence saw no way around the reply Christ was alleged to have given ("obey the commandments") when asked how to obtain eternal life (Matthew 19:17).[70] Yet, to that, Augustine responded by citing the apostle Paul's opinion that the law had been given so sin might abound (Romans 5:20). And that was said to apply not just to the law of Moses but to natural law as well, which could be construed as an instinct or aptitude for righteousness. Augustine, to the contrary, conceived of it as the defining characteristic of humanity's decadence, as "the law under which persons, behaving reasonably, added personal sins to original sin."[71]

He may have been disingenuous, equating sinfulness with reasonable or rational behavior, and meant *ratio* to refer to the cunning that came, as an accessory, with one's corrupted nature. He knew moral philosophers often referred to the "law" dictating the practice of virtues as "a natural law." The fiction that conduct corresponding to that law was "natural" yet also agreeable to God would be rather harmless, he said, were it not for inferences that could be drawn therefrom, notably, the idea that unbelievers pleased God simply by being humane, by acting naturally. Augustine never tired pointing out that faith corrected nature, making it possible to behave humanely and virtuously.[72] If the Pelagians had their way, a release from captivity might be obtained without faith in what the church claimed for the cross. To Augustine, the cross was crucial, as was the humility he thought Pelagians sadly lacked. Preaching the cross of Christ brings salvation to those who would agree to abandon their efforts to establish and measure righteousness with natural laws or the civil law. "Just as Christ is the end of the law"—the law of nature and laws of Moses—"so he is the savior of corrupt human nature." The cross and Christ are "the end" to which all laws tend, Augustine confirmed, quite simply because natural and human laws demonstrate their own insufficiency. The laws were given so sin might abound.[73]

No wonder Macedonius and other Christian magistrates needed help making sense of what Christianity required of them. Nectarius, trying to relate piety to local laws and local patriotism, would also have had difficulty with what Augustine told Caelestius, Pelagius, and Julian. Nectarius read philosophers who referred to reason as a remedy, as the way to overcome asocial sensibilities and to cultivate an appreciation for the value of the polis and public service. The Pelagians were his kind of Christian. Their emphasis corresponded with the meritocratic features of his civic religion, specifically, with his trust that civic virtue earned citizens eternal rewards. But the meliorism that informed both Nectarius' and the Pelagians' social programs was alien to Augustine.

It may be inappropriate, though, to suggest that Pelagians had a social program or platform. Caelestius was known to express socially reconstructive sympathies, laying the groundwork for what might well have been a radical redistribution of resources when he urged affluent Christians to renounce their possessions. But Pelagius proposed nothing quite like that, he said at Diospolis, and surviving Pelagian pamphlets do not mention Caelestius' counsel. Feeding the poor seems not to have entered very often into the Pelagians' calculations. When they advised against accumulating wealth, they were probably thinking of property as an encumbrance and of renunciation as something promoting personal piety rather than social equity. On that count, Augustine and a Pelagian could have agreed; he and Nectarius could not.[74]

But, to Augustine, the most pertinent and objectionable part of the Pelagians' analysis was its apparent naturalism and optimism: Caelestius, Pelagius, and Julian underestimated the fallen, fissured condition of the personality. The consequences of disobedience in Eden were genetically passed to everyone, Augustine argued, so everyone was subject to inordinate desires. Reason itself was sorely afflicted. Everyone was guilty and justly punished; the world was a penal colony.[75] The fortunate were saved by God's mercy, yet their societies were too dreadfully disordered to be made sound and less (or more than) punitive. The proper role for governments, therefore, was damage control. Public officials punish wrongdoers and, ideally, somewhat deter wrongdoing. Christians, then, must resign themselves to live in a world that was always changing, though forever on the verge of disintegration. What might appear, for a time, to be social reconstruction and political rehabilitation or recovery, inevitably exploited some for the sake of others. Such settlements were trivial at best, tyrannical and arrogant at their worst. And they should never be thought to represent God's justice on earth. If Augustine seemed to be badgering episcopal colleagues and ordinary Christians, it was because he feared they might be easily misled by the Pelagians' optimistic and meritocratic sentiments or by their exemplary manners. Their occasional bursts of charm ought to carry no weight. Their idealism, moralism, and meliorism inflated egos, yet lost souls. Augustine was certain that, although they recalled that humans were creatures, Pelagians forgot what it meant to confirm that creatures were sinners.

Chapter Three

Using Government

Augustine and the Donatists

Secession

Government could be useful. As long as the good and the wicked shared the same universe, the former must be protected against the latter. That was why Possidius, bishop of Calama, after the pagans attacked Christians there, left for Ravenna. He sought to have Emperor Honorius approve punishments that would deter similar assaults. Recall, though, that the conflict in Calama started when Christians provoked their pagan neighbors by an appeal to local magistrates to enforce imperial prohibitions of pagan parades and public displays. To repeat, government could be useful. After Church authorities at Diospolis acquitted Pelagius, African bishops, displeased with that result and fearing the feisty Caelestius might prevail on the papacy to reverse the Carthage judgment against him, sent a delegation to the emperor. Augustine's friend Alypius, bishop of Thagaste, was dispatched to Ravenna to ask the court to condemn the Pelagians. He was an excellent choice. He had been among the ambitious provincials who clustered around Augustine during the late 380s in Milan. He was there, as was Augustine, to learn tact, to learn to cultivate clients and important benefactors. Well connected and schooled in the ways of the world, the two returned together to Africa and, soon after, found themselves serving the church. But they did not forget how to get the powerful to oblige them, and the powerful obliged in 418, opposing the Pelagians, just as, acting on earlier requests from the North Africans, they opposed Alypius' and Augustine's other adversaries there, secessionist Christians known as the Donatists.

This chapter examines those requests and discusses the conditions that seemed to require them. We want to watch Augustine contemplate whether, how, and why the government could and should be useful to the church. But we will see that, although he grudgingly approved of asking municipal and imperial officials to compel or coerce the Donatists to return to the unity of the universal, "catholic" church, he developed apolitical, sacramental alternatives to ensure religious conformity and to build religious community.[1]

There is no denying that the Donatists were at a disadvantage. Their bishops were "locals," as Peter Brown says, and knew less about "the wider and more ruthless world of imperial bureaucracy." But it does not follow that Augustine, who had recently returned from Italy, looked to improve his political position as well as to shield catholics from Donatist critics. He was learning to live without political ambitions, as Claude Lepelley now says, and he "had no wish to substitute the power of the church and the bishop for that of state officials, whether at imperial, provincial, or municipal level[s]." But bishops were patrons, and priests and laypersons in their dioceses depended on them. Augustine clearly understood as much and intervened with public authorities to protect his and his friends' catholic congregations.[2]

To protect them all, he initially planned to refute then reconcile the Donatist Christians. But they were ahead in the polls, so to speak, and generally avoided debates. Their support in the countryside has been described as "massive." Donatist bishops competed successfully with catholic counterparts in cities of every size. Donatists' basilicas, in places, were larger than those of the competition and more often filled to capacity. By the late fourth century, their numerical superiority in Numidia was widely acknowledged, and some of that number in Proconsular Africa were educated and articulate defenders of their faith and discipline.[3] Bishops Parmenian and Petilian were effective apologists. The grammarian Cresconius occasionally made Augustine's thrusts and counterthrusts seem awkward. Tyconius, a tremendously skillful Donatist exegete and rhetorician, told tales of two cities that likely inspired, and certainly influenced, those of Augustine. Donatists were not all louts or bumbling rustics, and their leaders were smart enough to know how much a majority party might lose from public confrontations with an incomparably able opponent, with Augustine, who had been exhibiting his gifts for some time against the Manichees.

Soon after returning to Africa, he took on Fortunatus, publicly drubbing him for having suggested that incorruptible divinity might somehow dwell in a sinful soul. The soul was "from God" and, in some respects, "of God," Augustine explained, although it was not God.[4] The Donatists agreed. They lost no love on the Manichees and were quite comfortable with the African catholics' theology. But, from the 320s, they gathered that their moral and evolving ecclesiological positions were wholly irreconcilable with the ministry and sacraments of the catholics' church. The Donatists believed that catholics had betrayed their Christianity by conduct unbecoming. A first betrayal during the last great persecution allegedly stained all catholic priests from that time forward. They were soiled (*sordidi*), Donatists said, necessarily sinful, and thus unable to absolve others' sins. Even if it were not imprudent to debate the accomplished Augustine in public, apologists for the Donatists' secession must have doubted whether anything useful could come from conversation with a soiled, sinful, faithless colleague.[5]

The story of how African Christianity split into supposedly soiled and sanctified sides got more tangled with every telling. Who did what to whom is still contested. Of course, rivals tried to tidy up the tale, reclassifying victims and villains to win spectators' sympathy and government support, and the competing, partisan accounts complicate the historian's task. Perhaps, after nearly seventeen hundred years, one can only say with certainty that as yet undetected personal animosities fueled the earliest controversies. Ordeals make enemies; persecution ordinarily prompts or exaggerates resentment and envy among the persecuted. And, in the early fourth century, persecutors put Christians through a terrible ordeal. It ended in Africa when usurper Maxentius declared toleration and, soon after, more emphatically, when Constantine converted to Christianity. But by then, 311, Roman authorities had been harassing prelates, closing churches, and confiscating sacred texts for well over a decade. Christians who lost their property or freedom suspected more fortunate coreligionists of having collaborated with government officials, and once toleration seemed sure, suspicions unfurled as accusations. To many, collaboration—specifically, handing over the church's sacred texts (*traditio*)—was unpardonable, but neither the policy nor practice of the church immediately reflected that sentiment. Bishop Mensurius of Carthage was known to have cooperated with hostile authorities during the persecution, yet he died in 312 without having to defend himself. Indeed, he remained on friendly terms with Secundus of Tigisis, the leading prelate in central Numidia, who only later came to Carthage to sanction several colleagues' secession from alleged collaborators (*traditores*), among them, Mensurius' deacon and successor Caecilian.[6]

Secundus is a perplexing figure. Apparently he could be indulgent as well as unforgiving. Earlier, back in Numidia, he helped elect Silvanus to the see of Cirta, despite the latter's admission that he had assisted persecutors. To be sure, that assistance had not included the surrender of scripture; Silvanus was evasive when local magistrates came for it.[7] But not so, the bishops Secundus assembled to consecrate Silvanus. A few conceded they had handed over their texts, but Secundus would not censure them. Their confession and Secundus' ostensible indifference make it hard to understand why he, they, and other Numidian prelates were soon so categorical that *traditio* discredited sitting bishops and disqualified candidates for episcopal appointment. Conceivably, the earlier occasion accounts for the tolerance. Cirta was the center of attention; the nominee, immensely popular. There could have been little doubt Silvanus would get his see. His religious fervor—he vandalized a nearby pagan shrine—sat well with many Numidian Christians. Secundus and the bishops with him were unlikely to cross constituents in still uncertain times. Later, with North African affairs in a more settled state, they turned with the tide against bishops and would-be bishops reputed to have collaborated during persecution.[8]

Numidia, by most reports, was a sad, unruly place, particularly as one moved farther from the coast. Inscriptions and other evidence from excavations suggest socioeconomic decline during the third century and into the fourth. Absentee landlords raked in profits from vast estates but returned little to the working poor and indigent who were left in the province after "the middle class" was "taxed out of existence." W. H. C. Frend wrote about the investment and impoverishment, inferring that the Donatists' determination was directly related to the poverty, powerlessness, and anti-imperial sentiments he put in the foreground of his study of Numidia. Leaders like Secundus and Silvanus, on Frend's reading of the region's xenophobia and economic grievances, courted popular support and grew fanatically opposed to those who collaborated with imperial agents.[9]

To the east lay Carthage, regarded by Romans and residents alike as the empire's thriving African capital. The Numidians also acknowledged its importance and may have been offended when Christians there failed to consult them in 311 before selecting a successor to Bishop Mensurius. Caecilian was chosen and consecrated but not well liked in some quarters. Optatus of Milevis chronicled the ensuing crisis. Partial to Caecilian, he supplied an inventory of his protagonist's enemies that reads more as a rogue's gallery, a set of inordinately ambitious church officials, shameless embezzlers, irascible aristocrats, all accusing Caecilian and a bishop who had consecrated him of having collaborated with persecutors. When the accusers summoned Secundus and perhaps as many as seventy other Numidian bishops, Caecilian offered to have himself reconsecrated—and by them—yet they refused. They set one altar against another, Optatus said; the Carthaginian secessionists, with the blessing of the Numidian rigorists, left the traditional church. Their new church in town appealed to Constantine to have Caecilian removed as bishop of the old and thus to reunify the Christian community. The emperor and the bishops to whom he referred the matter, though, found the accusations unjustified and condemned the African secessionists. But the condemned did not fold. With the election of Donatus as their bishop in 313—and due largely to his resourcefulness and vigor—the *pars Donati* prospered in Carthage, elsewhere in Proconsular Africa, everywhere in Numidia, and in parts of five other provinces on the continent.[10]

Donatus lived into the 350s. If he drafted defenses of the secession, none survives. Still, from what his successors and their critics, including Augustine, tell us, we can make good guesses about the line he likely took. He almost certainly identified his partisans as a righteous few living among an unrighteous many, Caecilianists and all the Christians in communion with them. He claimed that Caecilian and his early allies had cooperated with the persecutors and that their cooperation wrecked the ministry of their church, the *pars Caeciliani*. Caecilian was improperly consecrated. Hence, he had no power or authority to bestow on bishops he consecrated and on priests he ordained, all of whom, therefore, were powerless. They were, in effect, imposters. The sacraments they administered were worthless. The upshot: the Christians in the African catholic church were misled and ill-served.

Emphasis on the plaguelike effects of collaboration was unique to North Africa. *Traditio* was only infrequently an excommunicable offense elsewhere. And when other rigorists pondered its criminality—in the Nile delta, say, or around Rome—they were less likely than the Donatists to pull their oars decade after decade for secession. They were less obsessed, that is, with contagious contamination. "Obsession" is not too strong a word. Only in North Africa did a century of speculation about the reprehensible consequences of collaboration tear the catholic church apart. Why?

Replies to that question have fairly consistently concentrated for the last half century on the social contours of the secessionists' new church. The religious division was said to express the protest of an indigenous, economically deprived, and politically powerless population faced with Romans' cultural hegemony and a military occupation. Discontented Africans flocked to the Donatists who railed against *traditio,* against the empire's accomplices. They were soiled; their critics were sanctified. Stress on socioeconomic disadvantages may explain why "backwoods" Numidia soon became something of a secessionist stronghold. Such stress is worth sifting, but beware exaggeration. Caecilian's foremost enemies were members of the Carthage elite. Affluent Carthaginians offered Numidian bishops hospitality at the height of the crisis. Lucilla, the principal hostess, and her wealthiest friends, furthermore, were known at the time to have had far more than bit parts. They almost certainly financed the municipal unrest. And the first Donatist bishop of the city was one of Lucilla's retainers. The explanatory power of economic disadvantage can be overstated.[11]

As can the explanatory power of political grievances. From the start, the Donatists understood that the new government in Rome was anxious to reunify the west. Schism in Africa jeopardized what Constantine achieved by defeating Maxentius and distracted the court from its campaign against Licinius who ruled in the east until 321. So, early on, the African dissidents proposed unity, but on their terms, which included Caecilian's disgrace and removal. Later, after their terms were rejected, the Donatists would come to think of the emperor and his court as hopelessly corrupt. Government, to them, meant only one thing: persecution. But the first Donatists were the first to appeal to Constantine. Preoccupied with his rival Licinius, the emperor issued edicts favoring the Caecilianists. He scarcely imagined that, once proscribed, Caecilian's critics might survive and spread. When they did, he reconsidered and urged, rather than forced, reunion on the African Christians.[12]

Thereafter, periods of relative calm were punctuated by conflict and persecution, which became particularly acute during the late 340s and from the late 390s. Catholics' embassies to the imperial court identified their church

with the preservation of peace and public tranquility. In 403 Aurelius of Carthage echoed generations of catholic bishops as he blamed Donatists for disorder: "if they think they have some truth to convey, let them do it reasonably
rather than disruptively," *contra publicam quietam.*[13] But as time passed it
seemed to the Donatists that their truth could only be conveyed disruptively.
They subscribed to the increasingly unfashionable idea that resisting the
powers of this world was a religious duty, as was commemorating the resistance of others by ostentatiously, sometimes riotously, observing the anniversaries of their martyrdoms. To catholic Christians, it seemed dangerously
provocative to celebrate defiance so conspicuously. The government, after all,
had turned Christian, and it was not always easy thereafter to distinguish
martyrs from rebels and criminals. Moreover, Augustine later suggested, the
motives of the secessionists' first martyrs were suspect. After running up debts
and making a mess of their lives, they feigned religious fervor to attract a
magistrate's attention and, as self-styled but insincere prisoners of conscience,
to escape their creditors. In spite of Donatist efforts at disinformation, Augustine could tell, he said, that their "heroes" figured they would live through the
persecution to begin new lives. Others, he complained, opportunistically
schemed to turn a profit in prison, trading on their celebrity to solicit gifts
from star-struck benefactors.[14] The imprisoned put on a rigorist's face and
preyed on guileless Christians' sympathies, which, catholic bishops and public authorities alike feared, could get out of hand. For veneration of the fourth-
century African martyrs had been known to lead to violence against those
who condemned them. Officials tried to dispose of casualties' bodies and thus
contain, *post mortem,* idolization and possible insurrection. But the plan
sometimes backfired. The remains of more than one victim were reported to
have miraculously resurfaced only to be entombed or exhibited as a rallying
point for subsequent defiance. Reports inspired and provoked as well. Typically, they congealed into legends emphasizing the virtue of political defiance
and the venerability of the defiant, putting God squarely on the side of the
government's inveterate enemies.[15]

Tales of dramatic deaths, "resurrections," and fanatical devotion prolifer-
ated and circulated widely during the century. Self-destructive Donatists imi-
tated the martyrs they revered. They courted death even when magistrates no
longer obliged them with death sentences. They hurled themselves into fire,
water, and air—over steep cliffs or at armed bystanders, who were expected to

do in self-defense what the government authorities did less often as the century came to a close. To be sure, persecution continued into the fifth century. Donatist bishop Petilian took the measure of measures taken against his church, understanding they were intended to frighten rather than annihilate.[16] The Catholics were reluctant to have the government prefer supply what the least squeamish secessionists appeared desperately to want, namely, more martyrs. Yet when Donatists could no longer look forward to martyrdom, their apologists looked back, assimilating current confiscations, incarcerations, and forced exiles to the executions and suicides of the 340s and, earlier still, to the suffering of Jesus and the apostles.[17]

Augustine thought differently. He compared the Donatists' ordeals to those of Dathan and Abiram whose insubordination led to their annihilation. Their fate and that of their rebellion against Moses and Aaron "was an example to warn us" against schism, he insisted, reproving more recent, fourth- and fifth-century dissidents for their defiance of government and catholic church authorities.[18] But defiance was not the rule. Ordinary Donatists ordinarily conformed to custom. Crispin, Donatist bishop of Calama, leased an estate from the emperor's agents in 401 and asserted what appears to have been a landlord's widely acknowledged prerogatives or proprietary rights when he insisted on his tenants' rebaptism. Augustine objected. True, he had praised Pammachius, a catholic, for converting his tenants in Numidia and conceded to Celer, a landlord in his diocese, the right to have on his estates preachers whose doctrine and sermons offended catholics' sensibility. Crispin of Calama, however, had started rebaptizing tenants into the secessionists' kind of Christianity, thereby "plung[ing] them into an abyss."[19]

Augustine's application to Celer was modest. He only wanted to confer with the offensive preacher, ideally, to win him over. Augustine's proposal to Crispin was rather more radical. The Donatist bishop and landlord likely thought his catholic colleague half-serious, if serious at all. Augustine was suggesting rules for a debate that could result in tenants making fundamental choices independently of and inconsistent with those of the owners of their farms and vineyards. The rules were simple: after listening to different arguments drafted by him and Crispin, the latter's *coloni* could choose their Christianity. The implication was that any landlord's leases and lawful influence were less important than each tenant's preference. Augustine supposed that he could out-argue Crispin and that auditors would prefer catholic Christianity, but he had to know the proposal would seem socially irresponsible. He now looks to have been improvising, chiefly because so little had been done to limit the Donatists' influence since Emperor Julian—"apostate," according to the catholics—gave the secessionists back their basilicas when he reopened the pagan shrines in 362. Within two years, Julian was dead, and the improvements in the pagans' position were reversed. Donatist bishops, however, remained formidable. Augustine was growing impatient; the catholics' position in Africa, deteriorating.[20]

Protection and Correction: Augustine and the Failure of Argument

It probably galled Augustine that Crispin got and kept his lease, despite some Donatists' involvements in a failed African uprising only a few years before. We shall have more to say of that shortly, but the catholics who had remained loyal assumed that the imperial government would not let religiously or politically secessionist sentiment go unnoticed and unpunished. Ideally, from the catholics' perspective, local officials might extend prohibitions against heresy to penalize ostensibly orthodox Donatists as well. After all, they had been resisting reintegration for nearly ninety years. They cherished the memory of martyrs whose motives, often subversive, were always suspect, and they harbored grudges against prelates, against whom no reliable accusations were registered at the times of their alleged crimes and collaborations. Predatory secessionists, Augustine fussed, had been cruising through the century and trawling for converts until they hauled in packs of overzealous faithful who only lately, he noted, had turned on the government after taking to task the catholic church. Was he overreaching, then, when he told Crispin in 401, three years after the uprising had been suppressed, that if he wished, he could have him fined and deprived of his possessions? Was Augustine hoping—or actually planning—to stretch the old laws, in particular Theodosius' edict of 392, to cover his Donatist neighbor's "tyranny"?[21]

Donatists were apprehensive. Legislation against heretics applied to Manichees, Marcionites, and Arians but not to them, they argued. Their sacraments were those of the catholics; their doctrine was as well. Soon after Augustine threatened him for rebaptizing his tenants, Crispin had occasion in the courts to test whether the equation of secession with heresy would hold. Possidius, the catholic bishop of Calama, held him responsible for violent episodes provoked by some rambunctious Donatist clergy under his supervision. Possidius sought to use the old laws against heresy against Crispin who defended himself successfully, at first. The preliminary ruling was that secession or schism was not heresy; but that verdict was overturned on appeal. And Emperor Honorius, shortly afterward, in decrees of 405, explicitly branded the secessionists as heretics. The edicts provided for the confiscation of Donatists' properties and fined officials slow to seize them. Secessionists, as "new heretics," were forbidden to leave or receive legacies. Rebaptism was outlawed. Landlords who permitted Donatists to worship on their estates were penalized; officials were told to exile clergy who objected.[22] A Donatist preface to a fifth-century copy of a chronicle of the edicts' effects maintained that the ensuing "persecution of Christianity" was comparable to Constantine's initiatives to suppress secession. But Augustine claimed that African Christians of all stripes welcomed Honorius' measures because the militant Donatists' strong-arm tactics made all secessionists unpopular.[23]

Augustine also challenged the Donatists' contention that their doctrine and sacraments corresponded with those of the catholics. Catholic Christians did not rebaptize, he pointed out; "if the baptism that counts for us does not also count for you, how can we be of one and the same religion?" To the Donatists' objection that first baptisms were bogus when administered by Caecilianists—by catholic clergy—and that therefore the Donatists' *re*baptisms were actually first baptisms, Augustine replied that baptism, just like circumcision, was unrepeatable. Its effectiveness did not depend on the perceived or imagined virtues and vices of the priest administering it, but on God's power to make good use of even the basest parts of creation.[24]

To the claim that the Donatists' christology and doctrine generally looked right, Augustine answered that their discipline had gone terribly wrong. They rushed to judgment instead of waiting for God to separate wheat from the chaff, good Christians from bad. Donatists were so sure that the bad infected or contaminated the good—and so sure they could tell the difference—that they presumed to gather as the good and to select out and segregate themselves from the evil, to create, in effect, the sanctified and the soiled. Thereby the secessionists or segregationists not only mistrusted God's will and power to protect the elect—the wheat, the good, the sanctified—but they substituted their judgment for God's.[25]

Augustine was a resourceful polemicist, but is he a trustworthy source? Should we accept his reports of the Donatists' selectivity and growing unpopularity when there seems to be no other evidence of declining numbers? Indeed, one could infer continual growth from the count of bishops at a conference in Carthage in 411. Writing at a "time of serious trouble for the [catholic] church," Augustine tended to exaggerate.[26] Of one thing, though, we may be certain: however popular and perfectionist the Donatists were, Augustine celebrated and exploited—while they deplored—the advantages that Honorius' edicts gave catholics. The year 408 might have led to realignment; Donatists imagined that everything would be new after the recent coup. Their catholic critics anxiously put together a case for continuing on the course the emperor set three years earlier. His edicts resulted, they said, in many conversions. If the laws were abrogated or unenforced, new converts would fear for their safety, and local magistrates could not protect Augustine and his allies from Donatists' reprisals.[27]

Loath to relinquish the advantage, Augustine came to welcome the catholics' partnership with the government and to accept that coercive measures taken to correct the Donatists were, in essence, part of the government's proper role to protect the catholic or universal church. Local congregations had already experienced the Donatists' fury. Who but municipal and provincial public authorities might deter further violence? That seems reason enough to couple correction with protection. The last few pages here have likely established *that* Augustine welcomed government intervention, to those ends—a fact he was not always eager to advertise—but we shall want to examine more closely *to what extent* and *why* he embraced politicians as partners, while reminding himself and his friends that they were, in some respects, poachers as well.

What triggered his thinking kindly about government intervention? He was not always eager for it and initially campaigned for the reintegration of African Christianity without appealing for partners or poachers in high places. He stated that he preferred to "fight with arguments," and his letter to Crispin of Calama in 401 illustrates the preference. It only briefly mentions magistrates, courts, and fines before sketching rules of engagement for a point-counterpoint, for the submission and circulation of arguments, which, he trusted, would net him and his church the loyalty of Crispin's tenants. Fear, force, and fines seemed less effective than persuasion to Augustine, who believed that apologists for secession could not dodge the preposterous implications of their reasons for seceding and that coercion would have Donatists pretending to convert and conform just to avoid the penalties for refusing. Rather quickly, however, he acknowledged that "fighting with arguments" would be a far more daunting task were the emperor not "to decree that anyone who preached catholic truth or chose it be protected." So Augustine warmed to the use of force, he tells us, after his catholic colleagues had. Early on, they favored coerced correction. He was wired differently and took some convincing. Still, we know no more on this count than Augustine allows us to know, and he wrote for a purpose, which, I suspect, was something less than full disclosure. He was explaining why, after having held out for preaching, persuasion, and choice, he endorsed vigorous enforcement of the edicts of 405, the persecution of the Donatists. His explanations to moderate Donatists, government authorities, and posterity are plausible, yet somewhat self-serving. He said that he had resisted peer pressure until he discovered that conversion by intimidation worked. He found that recent converts were sincerely committed to catholic Christianity and grateful for having been forced "to come to their senses." And, in this application, "coming to one's senses" did not only refer to the catharsis resulting from the legislated likelihood of suffering—some rude, yet desirable awakening—but to the Donatists' emancipation as well. For their bishops had been the first bullies on the block. They coerced conformity, keeping secessionists together by threatening anyone who contemplated defection, Augustine accused, and by retaliating against those who defected. When the catholics welcomed the government, their bully, into the struggle, they only intended to protect themselves. They were interested in rescuing the misled, not in avenging Caecilian or subsequent victims of the Donatists' libels.[28]

Conceivably, what he did not want understood by moderates, magistrates, and posterity was that he knew "fighting with arguments" was failing. Fear had proven to work better than "fighting" of that kind, however dexterous he might be in debate. He admitted that the results of the discussions with Donatists left something to be desired. Their calls for sanctity now and for separation had a proven appeal. Augustine invited Christians to consider an alternative, patience and hope, insisting that they could never become all that God meant them to be, as individuals or as a church, suddenly, by secession. His brisk candor about human imperfections and imperfectability was not as effective as he anticipated. He finally endorsed government intervention when his invitations and appeals to commonsense, common experience, scripture, and recent history fell on deaf Donatist ears.[29]

Augustine first seemed sure, for instance, that he had shown a Donatist assertion of some, if not central, significance, to be indefensible: no one could claim that the pure conscience of a priest or bishop made the sacraments he administered valid, because no one, he argued, could judge accurately the conscience of another. People can see others' faces but not their own. One can probe one's conscience, but not that of another. Artful dodgers were skilled at managing their memories, letting sins pass unacknowledged, or suppressing their regrets and hiding their worst transgressions. Conscience was no match for a conscientious dissembler, though ordinary people were known to put good faces on bad consciences as well and as adroitly. Donatists looking to be baptized by a pure priest and utterly convinced that they ought to refuse baptism from any other will either delude themselves or cease looking. When they find an ostensibly pious priest, they imagine the little they see is what they get. Or, when they learn how easily they have been or can be fooled, they doubt the sacraments as well as their priests. Deception, self-deception, and paralysis! To Augustine, these were the only options, once the secessionists invested so much, ecclesiologically and soteriologically, in the personal holiness of their clergy. He thought that his rejoinder, on this count, was irrefutable, and he may have guessed their century-long dissent was close to an end when Donatist grammarian Cresconius seemed to give ground, granting that some quirks, sins, and scandals go undetected and that the laity could not reasonably be expected to know all about their priest's personality and piety. Yet scrappy Cresconius argued on.[30]

His part of the argument survives only in specimens Augustine supplied to refute them. That Cresconius' positions are fully, fairly represented in the *Contra Cresconium*, therefore, is unlikely. But readers can retrieve a keen sense of Augustine's frustration. He was troubled by the failure of his first arguments and by what he took to be the absurdity of Cresconius' counter, which instructed laypersons unable to swear to the caliber of their priest's conscience to rely instead on his good report, his *bona fama* or reputation. Augustine was quick to point out that reputations were easily and deservedly shattered, that public knowledge or *fama* was no more, and sometimes much less, reliable than private information. Secessionists collectively could see no more deeply into a conscience of a cleric than could any individual intimately acquainted with him. Cresconius was unconvinced. It was enough for him that priests from whom he received the sacraments were not condemned by Christians known (and notorious) for their intolerance of immorality, specifically, by his fellow Donatists, who seceded from more indulgent and inclusive Christians and whose separation, intolerance, and suffering suggested, certainly to the secessionists themselves, their superior sanctity.[31]

That suggestion only demonstrated to Augustine how badly the secessionists misunderstood sacred texts and recent history. Psalm 101 warned in no uncertain terms that false accusations led to the persecution of the accusers. But the Donatists continued to accuse Caecilian, even after impartial judges acquitted him and declared those accusations false. True, Jesus' Sermon on the Mount promised those punished for the sake of righteousness that they would be blessed and vindicated, but, as the psalmist indicated, anyone persecuted for lies and libels, as were the Donatists, rightly, rather than righteously, suffered.[32] So it happened that "the sect of Donatus, restricted to Africa alone," became "an object of scorn to the rest of the world." Augustine was astounded, he said, by the secessionists' inability to read in their fate—and in the Bible—the judgment of history and of God against their secession.

> If their predecessors, when they effected the schism, made true charges against their colleagues, they would have won their case in the church overseas, whence authority spread to those parts of the Christian faith, and those against whom the charges were made [the Caecilianists] would be outside. But now when the latter are found to be in communion with the apostolic churches . . . while the former are outside and severed from that communion, who does not understand that the ones who had a good case were those able to win it before impartial judges?

History substantiated their verdicts and the psalmist's decrees: those who falsely accuse and unfairly condemn colleagues, and thus "rend the peace and unity of Christ," will be persecuted for their trouble and for the trouble they cause.[33]

"Outside and severed": Augustine thought of Donatism as a provincial religion. The same could be said of the religion of Jesus' earliest disciples, yet Christianity had developed into something different. Augustine in Italy, at the crossroads of empire, saw what became of it and watched as Ambrose of Milan exercised influence far beyond the precincts of his diocese. If Donatists were right, the labor of centuries should be undone, and, by antagonizing authorities, they would irresponsibly ensure that government in the fourth century would complete the work of previous persecutors, thin the ranks, and whittle Christianity to but a sliver of what the prophets predicted it would grow into and what the apostles worked to make it. But to every argument of that kind, it seemed, the Donatists had an answer. They could hardly contest their minority status within the Christian world at large, so they gloried in it. Had not the Bible celebrated a select and saved remnant—the few chosen when many had been called? So if truth were measured with statistics, the few in this world of unbelievers must count for more than any many (*in paucis est veritas*). Augustine granted that Christians were few by comparison with the world of unbelief, but scripture suggested that many would come to Christianity. Nowhere did scripture urge any to leave it for something smaller. Indeed, the secessionists' arguments for separation and selectivity were compromised by their own sect's history. They alleged that strength and certainty lay in small numbers, but anyone in Africa could name factions that had declared independence from them and had survived, for a time, as smaller or miniature Donatisms? If one followed the Donatists' logic, one would have to admit that fractions of their fraction possessed a greater truth and sanctity than the sect from which they split.[34]

Maximian was responsible for the intramural Donatist schism that Augustine most often cited to make his point about fractions and sanctity. Primian, the Donatist bishop of Carthage, expelled Maximian, a deacon, who soon attracted quite a following. We know neither the offense alleged nor the reason that more than forty bishops protested the deacon's dismissal. Within three years, by 394, they deposed Primian and nominated Maximian bishop. Several years later, the two sides were close to agreement, but, according to Augustine, reunification further undermined the Donatists' claims to truth and sanctity. They welcomed Maximianists back without requiring their rebaptism, though they had been far more abusive than had the catholics. During the early 390s, catholics had not been loudly critical of secessionist leadership, yet their sacraments were thought to be contemptible, compromised by a century-old crime that likely never happened. But to Augustine's (feigned?) surprise, the sacraments administered by the Maximianists, still spiteful right up to their recent reconciliation, were accepted as valid and effective. The Donatists rebaptized catholics but took back their more recent enemies and more virulent critics without hesitation and sacramental reinitiation. "The branch" welcomed the "twig" but sneered when the catholic and universal church—to Augustine, "the tree"—endeavored to have its Donatist branch back. Augustine was indignant. If Donatists cared more for purity than for peace, why would they hasten to readmit renegades, whom they once thought ruthless? But if they cared more for peace than for purity, why would they resist reconciliation with catholics who were generations removed from Caecilian and the supposed scandal that set off the firestorm?[35]

Augustine's indignation trenchantly made his point: the Donatists cared neither for peace nor purity. He trusted he could demonstrate as much by belaboring the secessionists' endorsement of their wickedly belligerent elements, above all, the brigands he knew as circumcellions. For an apologist looking to interest government authorities in correcting the Donatists and protecting their catholic critics, dramatizing the Donatists' occasional support for, and general indifference to, the circumcellions' atrocities might be an excellent use of one's time.

Thugs

Who were the circumcellions? A government edict specifying assessments against them in early 412 suggests that they were something more than a loose confederation of criminals and less than a terrorist network. They could be found with and fined as Donatists, yet their association with the *pars Donati* seems to have been unplanned at first. In 340, they were a nuisance. They assailed creditors and landlords, apparently as advocates of the dispossessed. At that time, the two "leaders of these saints," Axido and Fasir, about whom nothing more is known, annoyed Donatist as well as catholic bishops. Only later did these "saints" acquire another name, purportedly for hanging around (*circum*) local shrines (*cellas*), mostly but not only in central Numidia.[36] By then, opportunistic Donatist bishops had turned to the local gangs for help with work that required ruffians and would have passed then as "discipline." Historians variously describe them, at century's end, as militant migrant farm workers and as practiced revolutionaries. Their apparent animosity toward the affluent made them the perfect partners for many Donatist prelates, who, although propertied, imagined themselves economically and politically disadvantaged.[37] Augustine was unsympathetic. He thought of circumcellions as the Donatists' enforcers, as soldiers in a war that gave the lie to all secessionist talk of peace and purity.

> Were we not holding you [Donatists] hostage in our cities, we would be driven off by the vicious assaults of *your* circumcellions who fight furiously in the troops organized on your say-so. . . . Say not then that 'it is far, far from [y]our intent to compel Christians to [y]our [Donatist] faith.' When you have power, you do it. When you do not force faith, it is because you cannot, inasmuch as you fear the laws or the mob that would resist your initiative.[38]

Yet the evidence also signals that circumcellions were more than enforcers and soldiers. They took their Christianity seriously. They were prepared and sometimes eager to die for it. The intensity and trajectory of their dedication must have perplexed contemporaries, much as the strange combination of socioeconomic grievance, political ill-will, and suicidal religious devotion among present-day martyr-murderers puts them beyond the pale of comprehension. Chronicler Optatus of Milevis said the circumcellions were "crazed" (*insanientes*); Augustine thought them "fanatical" (*furiosi*). We are told that they targeted catholics and creditors but lusted for martyrs' deaths. They and the other would-be martyrs, about whom we have already heard, waded into crowds of pagans, smashed their idols, and menaced armed men likely, lethally to fight back. And these circumcellions threatened to murder government officials who declined to have them killed. One lucky magistrate, accosted by them, promised to oblige, bound them over, talked of execution, but fled once they were restrained.[39]

Augustine's stories about these self-destructive thugs are historically useful, but not altogether truthful. He wrote to bring the government to the barricades and embarrass Donatist moderates, painting the grimmest possible picture of the circumcellions' cruelty to shame them. The circumcellions disgraced Donatism, he said, and the Donatist church officials who dared to shelter them were accomplices, no better than the thugs they were encouraging.[40] Senselessly, to Augustine's mind, the Donatists attributed their survival and, from the 390s into the next decade, their revival, to violent extremists. Ingratitude was out of the question, he imagined the moderates maintaining, and he criticized them for circulating complaints against catholics' violence while applauding their circumcellions. "Their feet are swift to shed blood," secessionists said of their catholic persecutors, quoting to them the thirteenth psalm, which Augustine applied to the Donatists' enforcers. Their thugs were monstrously effective. "So many places" were stained with the blood of the Maximianists, he reported, because they defied the Donatist bishops of Carthage. "So many places" were stained with the blood of catholics, beaten in their basilicas. One of them, the bishop of Bagai, had been bloodied at his altar, dragged from his church, and left for dead. What Augustine said of that battery also characterizes his graphic, blow-by-blow description of it: both were *incredibile.* To their credit, he admitted, Donatist moderates regretted the circumcellions' rage. But Augustine wanted more than regret. Donatists of all stripes, he thought, ought to disown *their* circumcellions.[41]

The Donatists' premise that guilt passed by association should have dictated their severing all ties with the circumcellions. For nearly a century, secessionists insisted that catholics shared Caecilian's guilt. As a consequence, the catholics' sacraments were said to have been compromised and their churches hopelessly corrupted. Caecilian's sins had passed to the catholics' bishops; those bishops' sins passed to the priests they ordained, and the priests' sins passed to their people. Augustine pointedly wondered what the circumcellions' sins had done to the secessionists' bishops, priests, sacraments, and churches.[42] For most Donatist prelates were unwilling to disown their thugs. Several secessionist bishops retained and, in effect, "owned" them. Primian of Carthage turned the thugs against the Maximianists. Optatus of Thamugadi in Numidia, encouraged their participation in Primian's purge and was said to have recruited them in 397 when he and Gildo, an African imperial commissioner, rebelled against Rome.[43] For Augustine, Optatus was the preeminent secessionist villain. To pour oil on the government's fears, Augustine conjured up clones of Optatus, each captaining a squadron of scoundrels. The threat to Roman rule was real, but the conjuror's rhetoric made the Donatists' rage much more menacing. The insurrection of 397 was, in fact, quite brief. Gildo and Optatus were finished by 398, the government quickly extinguishing African resistance. Yet Augustine fanned the embers long after, trying to embarrass Donatist moderates, inflaming authorities against the ongoing secession, coaxing historians to think that "the circumcellions blazed into activity" at the century's end.[44]

Yet there are skeptics. Not all mobs and militants spawned by anti-Roman sentiment, economic inequality, and religious fervor were Donatist and circumcellion. Hans-Joachim Diesner suspects that circumcellions' participation in the insurrection has been overstated. Emin Tengström thinks Augustine's case for pervasive Donatist complicity was based on rumor and innuendo and thus seriously flawed. There is even some question about Optatus' (dis)loyalties. But Augustine had no patience with Donatist defiance, which was second nature since the time of Constantine and Caecilian, he argued, and *their* circumcellions were their *arma*. It was nonsense for the Donatists to claim that thuggery had nothing to do with their religion. They armed themselves with companies of thugs and, unwittingly, armed Augustine with sturdy arguments against them.[45]

He repeatedly jumped at the chance to club them with their criminal associates. The propaganda advantage was too good to miss. The Donatists thought that suffering made for sanctity; if so, persecution sanctified the circumcellions' catholic victims. The Donatists alleged that persecutors were always unrighteous; if so, associating with the circumcellions degraded Donatism. Optatus of Thamugadi was Augustine's premier example of a fallen Donatist in a degraded, intolerant church, in a fallen world: tyrant, rebel, swindler, and thief, his career undermined the secessionists' claim to be the party of purity and peace. If some comparatively minor offense of Caecilian had corrupted his friends and North Africa's catholics ever after, as Donatists alleged, then what did Optatus' tyranny and treason do to Donatists who had yet to condemn him?[46] But, for Augustine, of course, neither the "if" nor the "then" held true. They were parts of a polemic designed to show that conclusions derived from the Donatist premise—guilt by association—might substantially injure the Donatists themselves. Their premise was idiotic. The spiritual paternity of no single prelate determined the legitimacy of his church or the validity of its sacraments. Neither Caecilian nor Optatus had such influence. To assume otherwise was to put one's hope in man when it was God who kept churches on or off course.[47]

Obviously, Augustine could not stop "fighting with arguments." Yet he must have given up hope, during the first few years of the fifth century, that colloquy might result in the Donatists' capitulation. From then, he used the circumcellions' belligerence, Optatus' rebellion, and alleged Donatist complicity less to score points in the give-and-take of conversation or written controversy and more to make emphatic and effective his justifications for government intervention. Donatists, by breaking out and staying outside the catholic church, had become extraordinarily dangerous enemies of order and empire. Augustine did not want public-spirited civilians or their officials to forget that. He told the government that it defended order and itself whenever it acted against the African secessionists.[48]

Earliest Donatists offered similar observations nearly a century before when they put Caecilian at the center of the controversy and demanded his dismissal. But, as noted, they got nowhere with the government. Caecilian did not then seem to be the enemy of order that his enemies made him out to be, and their relentless pursuit of his conviction irritated the emperor. Worse still, they impugned the impartiality of Constantine's closest clerical consultants, Bishops Hosius and Miltiades.[49] Yet by the 380s, détente of some sort had been achieved. Parmenian, who succeeded Donatus as bishop of Carthage in 362, was less confrontational than his predecessor. The same was said of his catholic counterpart, Genethlius. Yet when Primian succeeded Parmenian calm gave way to a storm that wrecked chances for a reconciliation. And, at roughly the same time, the early 390s, Petilian, Donatist bishop of Cirta, by then called Constantine, renewed the campaign against catholics, displaying his genius for generating resentments. Despite the schism within their Donatist ranks, though, Petilian and Primian might have gained ground on the catholics, had they not been matched against Aurelius, Genethlius' successor as the catholic bishop of Carthage in 393, and, to the west, Augustine of Hippo. Of course, the added factors of Gildo's and Optatus' insurrection and speedy defeat further discredited the Donatist cause. And catholics were fortunate as well that Augustine proved to be so good at deploying both the rebellion and its disintegration to make sure of the discreditation. He peddled the peril at century's end so effectively, one might argue that Honorius' anti-Donatist edicts of 405 were largely his doing, and he saw to it that they remained in force after Stilicho's death, which, Pietro Romanelli suggests, gave the Donatists "new vitality" in 408. The secessionists' attacks produced at least one prominent government casualty, and that, perhaps in part, convinced the emperor that he should remain on the catholics' side.[50]

That the Government Should Be Used

Honorius dispatched notary and tribune Marcellinus in 410 to reach a settlement favorable to the catholics' church. A conference was called for Carthage, to be held the following year. Finally, Augustine would get a chance to expose his adversaries' sloppy thinking and win a monumental, maybe a final, victory. He would not defend the purity of his church—it was a school for sinners and not a sanctuary for saints—yet he certainly could underscore its preference for peace. He was inordinately irenic himself, agreeing to the delay requested by his secessionist "brothers," pledging to respect their episcopal standing if only they returned to the catholics' church, and proposing joint pontificates with the catholic bishops in towns where other arrangements proved impractical.[51]

For their part, however, Donatists were looking for a chance to reassert their superior sanctity and recover momentum. At the conference, Marcellinus was the government, so, understandably, they tried to take the issue of government interference off the table. But they failed. They could not seem to avoid revisiting Caecilian's purported collaboration and the government's part in his phony acquittal. They could not help returning, that is, to the origins of the schism to establish their purity and catholics' corruption. Augustine knew that the Donatists, condemning catholics, inadvertently condemned the government as well. They said that catholics were culpable for associating with Caecilian and implied that emperors and their agents in Africa were guilty for continuing to associate with those catholics. Then the secessionists insisted that catholics were damnable, again, for relying on government and coercion to achieve religious conformity. The Donatists held that their rivals had made two unholy alliances, one with Caecilian and another with the rulers of this world whose ancestors crucified Christ. Nero was then the paladin of persecution; catholics created new Neros every time they asked government officials for counsel. To Donatists, the coalition between church and "state" developed into a grisly beast with a catholic's tongue and butcher's hands.[52] Augustine answered that recent emperors were not Nero's heirs, but heirs to the apostles who had been sent to spread the gospel and to "plant" the church everywhere. Back then, God used itinerant preachers and prophets, but the Bible promised that God would someday use kings—imperfect and impeachable, to be sure, but useful all the same. That day had come. To

Christianity and its universal church, God gave a universal empire, with growth and for growth. Augustine trusted that nothing could be inferred from recent history with greater certainty.[53]

The Donatists were not so certain. To them, coercion was not the only thing that made the alliance between catholics and imperial commissioners unholy. Secessionists thought the empire was idolatrous: cults had survived Christianization. Catholics who came over to Donatism were treated as if they were pagans because the leaders of their former church had gotten too close to the rulers of this world to be effective gatekeepers to the next.[54] Donatists did not deny that Constantine had brought sudden and sweeping changes or that Theodosius had contributed to paganism's decline. But both regimes had been unprepared to acknowledge the justice of the secessionists' cause, so both, in their estimation, were terribly flawed. The Donatists consequently claimed that, to the extent catholic Christians adored the two emperors, turned their churches over to government care, and called it all Camelot, they were wickedly, politically idolatrous. Donatus' reply in the late 340s to an embassy sent from Rome succinctly made that point by articulating a counter: *Quid est imperatori cum ecclesia;* what does the emperor have to do with the church?[55]

Yet, as Augustine often underscored, the secessionists themselves occasionally appealed to the government against the catholics. He said as much, of course, to make the Donatists seem ridiculously inconsistent. But he may have been as surprised as historian Émilien Lamirande that they did not protest Marcellinus' mission more vigorously. They could not have welcomed the interference so soon after Honorius had shown his hand in the edicts of 405, which proscribed their worship. Lamirande is less persuasive, however, when he claims that Augustine's silence was equally surprising. Catholics risked little for what might have been an end to a century-long schism, a resolution and reconciliation on their terms. Augustine was game.[56]

Procedural issues dominated discussion at the first two sessions of the conference. Augustine dominated the third and final meeting, answering point by point the Donatists' brief for secession. Marcellinus, having heard the rival churches' delegates and reviewed documents related to the charges against Caecilian, judged they were unwarranted. That meant secession was unwarranted as well. The conference adjourned a few days before the start of summer in 411. Early in 412, the government issued a new edict that made it a crime to be a Donatist. Basilicas fell to the catholics faster after penalties that formerly applied only to secessionist clergy were assessed against the Donatist laity as well. Enforcement may not have been all that Augustine wished, but the government clearly indicated a resolve to quash Donatist dissent.[57]

Augustine approvingly reported the resolve. He had been pressing for government help for years and answering criticism that came his way when he argued for intervention after having preferred persuasion to legislation and coercion. Donatist Bishop Vincent of Cartenna in Mauretania complained of that change. He, too, objected to the circumcellion militants and to his Donatist colleagues' hawkishness. He belonged to the small dovish faction of the *pars Donati* named for his predecessor in Cartenna, Rogatus, which, after Gildo's rebellion, survived as a rather superfluous caucus.[58] Augustine replied courteously, conceding that the edicts of 405 brought out the worst in some catholics. They sought personal profit from rival Christians' misery. That displeased him, he said, yet a good shepherd must use a rod to steer stray sheep back into the fold. Catholics who use force vengefully and dishonorably are no argument against the proper, pastoral uses of force. Augustine cited biblical precedents for coerced conversion: wedding guests in a parable compelled to come to the celebrations after having ignored the invitations; the apostle Paul thrown from his horse and blinded that he might see.[59] God was known to have drawn creatures close to him by fear. And, Augustine explained to Vincent, as he had explained to others his justification of coercion, many who were drawn from Donatism to catholicism by the fear of losing their property or freedom effusively expressed their gratitude. True, the letter to Vincent refrained from endorsing a general reliance on government threats and sanctions, yet it opened with a claim that Donatists had grown too arrogant and agitated to be reached in any other way.[60]

In another letter written roughly at the same time Augustine supplied perhaps his clearest comment on his adversaries' combativeness.

[I]f you don't like us because you are being forced into unity by the imperial decrees, well, you have brought this about yourselves. Whenever we were happy simply to preach the truth and let each person listen to it in security and choose of his own free will, you have always prevented us from doing this by your violence and terrorism. Now don't start shouting and getting yourselves worked up.

Study our words patiently, if it is possible, and bear in mind the behavior of your circumcellions and your clerics (who have always led
them on); then you will see what has stirred all this up against you.
You are complaining simply because you yourselves have forced all
these orders to be imposed upon you.[61]

Forsaking the unity of the church was bad enough, Augustine held, yet demands that others "overthrow the faith"—demands that were costumed as
appeals for purity—were supremely destructive of both souls and society. Secessionists resisted friendly persuasion. They would not "let each person listen . . . and choose." Enemies of choice, they were "enemies of charity," and
could only be reached by catholics reaching out to the government.[62]

To Augustine, schism was sacrilege: none should tear asunder what God
put together. God gave creation a universal church and eventually gave that
church a strong right arm, the loyalties and legislation of the rulers of this
world. Force had been a factor in the growth of Christianity from the start.
God unhorsed the apostle Paul; the wedding guests in Jesus' parable were
compelled to attend. Government was something of a newcomer, to be sure;
no wonder, then, Christians in Africa struggled to come to terms with its role.
Augustine took stock of the situation: stubborn secessionists and useful magistrates. The former should expect some reckoning. The latter were "the rod"
of discipline. Emperors commissioned provincial and municipal authorities
to enforce the decisions of episcopal courts. Augustine expected those officials
to enforce prohibitions and penalties stemming from the conference umpired
by Marcellinus.[63]

The penalties prescribed the following winter were intended to suppress
the "dour fanaticism" of militant secessionists and, ideally, to put an end to
the ordinary Donatists' simmering antipathy that, in Augustine's judgment,
perpetuated the schism. The schism divided parents from children, husbands
from wives, siblings from one another, he said; rivalries between churches in
each village wrecked homes. Augustine attributed the tragedy to Donatists'
lack of charity. Destabilization and sacrilege were due, he argued, to their in-
sistence that their fictional account of Bishop Caecilian's consecration war-
ranted lasting enmity in Africa.[64]

Biographer Possidius tells us that Augustine was distressed by the domestic disharmony from the start of his pontificate. Historian Frend adds that
Augustine was tempted, early on, to appeal for government intervention, de-

spite his later disclaimers. Frend has him biding time until Gildo's failed bid for regional autonomy and particularly Optatus' complicity "freed" him to interest the imperial court and local courts in "courses which, in his heart, he may have approved previously."[65] Plausible as that may be, Gildo, Optatus, and the circumcellions seem peripheral to Augustine's growing impatience with what he perceived as general, Donatist arrogance. Arguments were perfect weapons, but only if rivals consented to listen and deliberate. But Donatists preferred to complain. They compared themselves as wheat with the catholics' chaff, quoting Jeremiah 23:28, "what is chaff to the wheat." Pronouncements of that sort exasperated Augustine: how should one respond to such shameless excuses (*impudentissimae*) uttered to stop all commerce with the catholics and with the truth?[66]

After the conference at Carthage adjourned, Gaudentius, Optatus' successor as Donatist bishop of Thamugadi, afforded Augustine a memorable opportunity to level criticism at the catholics' critics and to defend his trust in government. For Gaudentius locked himself and his congregation in a tower, threatening self-immolation if soldiers sent to seize his basilica did not back off. The troops' commander wrote to Augustine, who wrote to both the besieging and besieged. He reemphasized the gratitude of many Donatists-turned-catholics for the coercion to convert. Urging unity and charity, he warned that obstinate opposition ought not to be confused with courage. His reply to Gaudentius contained nothing substantially new, yet the suicide threats seem to have rattled him.[67] He all but insulted the intelligence behind the effort when Gaudentius collected biblical examples of heroic, to-the-death defiance. The list proved little; not every scriptural protagonist was imitable. The apostle Peter was called "blessed" one minute and diabolically insolent the next. Should Christians be inspired to suffer by the humility and hardship recorded in the sacred texts, they ought to assure, as Gaudentius had not in 420, that they were suffering for the right church.[68]

Augustine was dismissive. Years had passed since the council at Carthage. Marcellinus was dead. Many Donatists had defected. Pelagians preoccupied Augustine when he sent Gaudentius "the most heartless of [his] writings in defense of the suppression."[69] But Augustine would have had a ready response to Peter Brown's characterization of his letter to the self-imprisoned secessionists. He would have described them as incomparably more "heartless." Their counterfeit Christianity robbed the faithful of immortality, for it lacked charity or love, which the apostle Paul put above all. That larceny and the

Donatists' encouragement of militants "to draw down violence" on Maximianists and catholics alike proved who was truly cruel. Secessionists spoke of peace, but it was blood-spattered (*bellifera pax*), Augustine said, coining a term to cover the hawkish sanctimony he typically ascribed to his rivals.[70] He claimed that Gaudentius only appeared to be defending his basilica; he was actually the aggressor. He defied the edicts and was at war with the government. He was at war with its authorized church in North Africa and with God. The soldiers at Gaudentius' gate were a regrettable necessity. Augustine acknowledged that their presence was undesirable, but not unscriptural. Why else did God deliver rulers of this world into the hands of the church if not to have their power put to good use?[71]

Were alternatives to the soldiers exhausted? Were there alternatives? Augustine tried persuasion. African councils urged compliance with government edicts. Catholics looked to bring the weight of the churches *transmarina* to bear. They appealed to Rome on occasion but generally tried to keep disciplinary decisions in their hands. Augustine, Aurelius, and other local catholic bishops knew they were implicated in an imperfect system of enforcement, as historian Serge Lancel says, and were obliged to cope.[72]

Coping with Pelagianism, as we saw, also prompted appeals to the pope and the emperor. That "new heresy" spread from Rome, after all, and "infected" far more than North Africa. But Donatism was a local problem. The government commissioners closer to it, in Africa, seemed the catholics' best possible partners; provincial administrators saw as well as local bishops that government edicts and emperors opposed the secession. That the apostles experienced the same type of political opposition in the first century might have given a few fifth-century Christian magistrates pause, as the Donatists evidently intended by emphasizing the parallels. But Augustine's response, familiar to us now, likely satisfied catholics in government. Times had changed, he replied, as had God's ways of testing, correcting, and protecting the faithful. Once the enemy of the church, government had become its partner.[73]

Probably the church's partners in government were equally, if not more, receptive to another of Augustine's observations and explanations, one more politically relevant, it seems, to the partnership's usefulness. Augustine equated the government's intervention with its self-preservation. "Rulers of this world defend themselves," he observed, "when, possessing the precepts of the apostle Paul, they suppress secessionists."[74] Optatus' participation in Gildo's rebellion seemed to illustrate the maxim; Augustine often and exuberantly described that collaboration to dramatize the dangers posed by Donatism to peace in Africa. Donatists, too, he sometimes added, realized that government played a necessary and self-interested part in resolving religious rivalries. When faced with Maximianists, a sect from their sect, they turned to Numidian justices for help. They must have gathered, as did he, Augustine surmised, that government neglect would lead to endless rounds of mutual incrimination. One side, boldly off-putting, called a council to accuse and condemn the other; the other, once accused and condemned, condemned its accusers in a second council, and so on. Government, as God's umpire, was the way to call a halt.[75]

Emperors, from the time of Constantine, accepted the challenge. Edicts from the courts of Honorius and Arcadius, Theodosius' sons, showed the same general orientation as those of their father, suggesting to catholic bishops that the government was becoming more proactive in criminal matters and reasserting its jurisdiction over some civil matters as well. Augustine's objections to relinquishing the authority of his "audience," if he had any, have not reached us. Besides, we have heard him begrudge the time that he spent with squabbling neighbors and parishioners. He preferred to work with words, many of which he composed to get the government to appreciate that its interests coincided with those of the catholic church. Sometimes he overstated "the state's" chances for ridding the world of evil, yet he was, for a time, optimistic that the government might rid North Africa of Donatism.[76]

He knew his history. Wicked emperors made bad laws. Julian returned basilicas to the secessionists. Governments, of course, were known to have persecuted Christianity in the new religion's first few centuries. Christians were then called on to suffer, with Jesus as their model and "commander." Beliefs were tested; martyrs, attested and ever after esteemed. Augustine only rarely warned that times of such trouble might return, as we shall see in the next chapter. Yet that possibility must have occurred to him more often than he wrote about it. The anti-Donatist campaign was not likely to be helped at all by mentioning governments gone wrong. Instead, Augustine emphasized good rulers who had been "on the side of truth and against falsehood." The secessionists who chose to suffer when good governments legislated against their sedition suffered not for righteousness and certainly not according to Christ's model or command, Augustine said; instead, they suffered for their arrogance, impudence, and intolerance.[77]

Magistrates "on the side of truth" were not unequivocally good. Martyrs who suffered for righteousness were exemplary but not unexceptionably good either. "We are all sick," Augustine said shortly after the conference of 411, where secessionists spoke often of their sanctity. Augustine preached about the sinfulness attributable to all persons this side of the grave.[78] He preached as an apostle of imperfection. Mulish perfectionists, be they Pelagians or Donatists, expected too much. Priests need not be impeccable to make the sacraments work, to forgive the faithful. Priests could no more be without sin than public officials could be free of the drive to dominate that put them in politics and put politics, as we shall see, beyond the pale. Frog princes were always frogs. "We are all sick," yet princes used their power to compel the Donatists to convert. Catholic priests and bishops used princes to restore unity to the African church. God used all three, the princes, priests, and bishops, as parts of a comprehensive ministry of reconciliation. Augustine tucked them into his sermons on protection, correction, and forgiveness.[79]

Tyconius, a lay theologian condemned by Bishop Parmenian, was one Donatist Augustine read with interest and some admiration, in part, because he conjured up a city of the saved who flee from the city of the damned who rule. They flee temperamentally, that is, for they cannot escape persecution. When Augustine adapted Tyconius' striking image for his own new tale of two cities, he accommodated the partnership that he and his associates in Africa contracted with public officials. Why flee rulers inclined to protect the catholics and, on their bishops' signals, to correct their critics by legislation and intimidation? To Augustine, though, this was never more than a marriage of convenience. Tyconius' two cities were not merged in any significant way. The city of the saved was not something that the terrestrial city would or could grow into. It was not ahead but above. It was part of the earthly city, yet apart from it by virtue of the "lucid mind[s]," "fervent love[s]," and "genuine mutuality" of the faithful.[80] Augustine accepted that magistrates might count as citizens of the celestial city. They could be pious as well as useful. But the systems they served could not. Augustine recalled that King Solomon, whose peace was nearly perfect, composed Ecclesiastes simply to explain that nothing was "solid" or "stable." There could be no perfect politics, no perfect polity. A holy society in this life was unimaginable.[81]

Chapter Four

Used But Not Improved

Augustine's *City of God*

Martyrs

Apparently, the holiest Donatists—martyrs all—were convinced that political culture was unholy. For them, the proof was in the persecution. The persecuted *pars Donati* being blameless, persecutors were without excuse, save, of course, that they were playing roles God had assigned them in the imminent overthrow of the established order. Overthrow? Donatist martyr Isaac heard a ghostly voice say so: "woe to the world, for you are perishing." But Isaac perished first; dying in prison before the world came to an end and after he relayed a few other messages of doom to those who tormented him. He reported, for example, a vision in which he soundly thrashed "assistants to the emperor," whom he also called "assistants of wickedness." An enraged emperor then grappled with him until he clawed an eye from its imperial socket. That dream or vision circulated with various prophecies and stories featuring the Donatists' opposition to—and their spiritual triumph over—public authority. Every stroke the martyrs received attested their virtues and the authorities' viciousness, vulnerability, and ultimate defeat. Isaac died in 347. His voices and visions were added to the literature that functioned as something of a "myth kitty," from which Donatist martyrologists continued to draw to prove that the sufferings and deaths of venerable victims, from Jesus Christ forward, won them a glorious crown more precious than any earthly official might wear. Martyrs were the real winners; persecutors, the losers. Politics, by the early fifth century, was a lost cause.[1]

Bishops in communion with the catholic or universal church drew different political lessons from the voices and visions of their martyrs, the retelling of which amounted to a celebration of catholic Christianity's virtues. In some respects, they did little differently from the Donatists. Church authorities in Africa and around the empire sponsored building projects at martyrs' burial sites to set in stone Christianity's defiance of a persecuting society. "Churches rose over the tombs" to commemorate the heroism of the interred. The faithful flocked there to mark anniversaries of their martyrs' deaths and to "bridge . . . in their devotion and imagination the gulf which had come to divide their world from that of the persecuted church."[2] But bridge building of that type was tricky after Constantine's conversion. The empire having embraced Christianity, it might not do to have Christians overimpressed with the virtues of the defiant. For "fostering the martyr spirit against the compromising forces of the world," Carol Harrison says, could promote as well the idea that imperial or municipal politics, even then taken as the art of compromise, were anathema to the new official religion. Precisely that idea or anathematization was what the Donatists wanted to get across.[3]

Catholic bishops had something different in view. Augustine's challenge was to celebrate the martyrs' courage and to have his church's developing cults achieve coherence without demonizing public authority. Devotion to martyrs' memories and memorabilia (relics) was proving irrepressible during the fourth century and into the fifth, and it remained so long afterward, as supplicants looked for signs that neither God nor their faith's heroes had deserted the world. An eleventh-century chronicler referred to the recovery of martyrs' bones as "relic resurrection," claiming that people heard heaven's "voice" in the stories of their martyrs' visions and victimization as well as in sermons of the bishops who possessed the relics or remains.[4] Augustine and his colleagues also noticed that their authority was related to the relics, remains, and stories of suffering that the supplicants revered. The Donatists' bishops, he said, had not listened to their martyrs and had misled their parishioners. Martyrs were humble; leading Donatists were arrogant. Martyrs were patient; Donatists, impetuous. Martyrs were apolitical; Donatists, antipolitical. Passion narratives blaming the martyrs' fate on an irretrievably evil empire were scandalously self-serving and overstated the diabolical character of public administration. Augustine was determined to make sure heaven's "voice" correctly registered just as the Goths were creating new Christian martyrs.[5]

Soon after Alaric's sack of Rome and for the next fifteen years, Augustine wrote his compendious *City of God* to explain the tragedy. It was a tourniquet of sorts to stop the hemorrhage of all hope. But the *City* also suggests that Christians had hoped for too much from the empire and from Peter, Paul, and other martyrs buried in Rome. Troops and tombs were unlikely to preserve the churches and their relatively recent, altogether agreeable, political settlement forever. Augustine took the Goths' aggression and Rome's humiliation or "scandal" as shocks administered under God's supervision to disorient the faithful of the city as well as those far from the epicenter.[6] But the *City* was also written for pagan critics of Christianity who expected too much from the Christians' disappointments and the empire's setbacks, pagans who anticipated a revival of their old religions, once the Christians' tombs and relics proved powerless to protect the capital. To be sure, Alaric's Goths spared many of the faithful—and a number of persons feigning faith—who sought sanctuary at the sacred gravesites and shrines in Rome.[7] The tombs, therefore, did protect some, yet many Christians were among the casualties. Why did God allow that to happen? The answer was in the Bible, but survivors trying to make sense of the suffering would need help finding it in what was said about the Hebrews' perils and Jesus' promises. They got that help from Augustine, who instructed them how to judge history by scripture and advised them not to judge scripture by history.[8]

His *City* begins as a dirge, rehearsing the failures of the pagans' deities to protect their shrines and worshipers. Poor Priam bled to death at one of Troy's altars. Juno and Minerva could not save his city. Gods elsewhere were terrible sentries. History showed them as ineffective as mannequins in a world of war. Cities and empires were wiser by far to rely on brawny soldiers and sly strategists. The Christians' God, by contrast, was supremely sovereign and effective but had never promised victory and security. Maybe many Christians were prepared to accept such a disclaimer, yet if their faith and church were to escape permanent scarring from pagan critics' coupling of Christianization with the recent devastation, Augustine would have to address all the speculation about God's purposes. Why 410? Why the "scandal"? Why all the Christian casualties? The questions persisted, so once he established how ludicrous it was to think that the pagans' gods were staging a reprisal (and comeback), avenging Constantine's conversion to Christianity and Theodosius' insult to their shrines, Augustine contemplated, then rejected, the possibility that God had orchestrated the early fifth-century massacres to appease his wrath, that he required the martyrs' sacrifices as repayment for what he had given to all Christians—as the substitutes for something unspecified that all Christians had not yet given in return.[9]

Augustine tackled the issues of appeasement and payment as he approached what would become the midpoint of his *City*. He repudiated the idea that the Christians' God had somehow to be appeased; nonetheless, he acknowledged that Christians' piety *was* a kind of repayment. Martyrs showed admirers how to meet the price, not by surrendering their lives but by making "invisible sacrifices" with contrition that battered and bruised their hearts.[10] Later in the *City*, and more prosaically, Augustine defined the "best sacrifice" as pure thoughts, clear thinking, and a life well lived. That much was expected, yet not to show there was something in creation worth salvaging. Self-discipline, clarity, contrition, and righteousness were payments through which ardent yet ordinary Christians experienced "true felicity." Their ordeals or payments were likely less gruesome than those of the church's celebrated martyrs, though the Goths, Vandals, and others picking apart the empire during the fourth and fifth centuries might keep the faithful guessing about that. In any event, Christians ought to have learned from the martyrs (certainly they would learn from Augustine's *City*) that suffering, grief, humiliation, inward sacrifice, repentance, and rehabilitation were in their best interests and not to assume that they were in God's.[11]

Martyrs were wonderful instructors. Their selflessness, discipline, and suffering suggested that inward or "invisible sacrifices" would be struggles. Their reported calm and courage signaled that redemption could be experienced in repentance. What ordinary Christians learned from them put their own lesser ordeals in perspective and led them to expect a touch of heaven on earth. That expectation kept devotees coming to the martyrs' tombs and shrines. But many of the Goths' latest victims were unburied. No churches rose over their remains, the whereabouts of which were unknown. Nonetheless, they were interred, after a fashion, and could be visited in Augustine's colossal *City*. It had been drafted, in part, as a monument to them, yet also to urge that martyrs be emulated and not venerated, to console Christians perplexed by Rome's fate, and to assure them that the martyrs' humility and tenacity—as well as their own—would not go unrewarded. The faithful should be sure that "the city of God esteems as all the more honorable and distinguished those martyrs who resisted so persistently and to their deaths the impiety" all around them.[12]

It was inconceivable that Christian martyrs would cling to the things of this world and choose security in time and for a time instead of fellowship with God forever. But it was quite conceivable that ordinary Christians would prefer a course contrary to that of a martyr. That preference excluded them from "the family of faith," from "citizenship" in the celestial city of God, the solidarity of which was the central concern of the *City of God* that Augustine wrote into existence. And solidarity depended on the abilities and willingness of Christians on pilgrimage in time—"in captivity"—to remain undistracted.

> But a household of human beings whose life is not based on faith is in pursuit of an earthly peace based on the things belonging to this temporal life, and on its advantages, whereas a household of human beings whose life is based on faith looks forward to the blessings which are promised as eternal in the future, making use of earthly and temporal things like a pilgrim in a foreign land, who does not let himself be taken in by them or [be] distracted from his course towards God, but rather treats them as supports, which help him more easily to bear the burdens of the corruptible body which weighs heavy on the soul; they must on no account be allowed to increase the load.... [T]he earthly city whose life is not based on faith, aims at an earthly peace, and it limits the harmonious agreement of citizens concerning the giving and obeying of orders to the establishment of a kind of compromise between human wills about the things relevant to mortal life. In contrast, the Heavenly City—or rather that part of it which is on pilgrimage in this condition of mortality, and which lives on the basis of faith—must needs make use of this peace also, until this mortal state for which this kind of peace is essential passes away. And therefore it leads what we may call a life of captivity in this earthly city as in a foreign land.[13]

It is not hard to find here another relevant lesson pilgrims were meant to learn from their martyrs, namely, that "invisible sacrifice" required a degree of detachment from "earthly and temporal things" and from compromises in the earthly city identified with a life "not based on faith."

The same passage in the *City* suggests, in effect, that Christians transcend rather than transform the social and political order. The old order was passing. Its acceptance of Christianity early in the fourth century was understood by enthusiasts to have been a new beginning for both the church and the government. One hundred years later, it could just as well, or better, have been taken as the beginning of the end for both Rome and its new religion. Augustine was not so fatalistic; nonetheless, he was resigned to lasting turmoil. He was no optimist or agitator. He saw no reason to defy what was so obviously passing, disintegrating as every empire in history had or eventually would. His *City* takes up the issue of political disintegration and reconciles it with God's generally benevolent will. The book's comments on compromise and captivity—on "households" of politicians "in pursuit of earthly peace" and "households" of pilgrims—did not paper over the conflicts between the terrestrial and celestial cities; instead, Augustine advised Christians to take advantage of what remained of peace on earth. He counseled them to obey local magistrates and imperial officials yet to rise above their political obligations—as citizens and, occasionally, as officeholders. But there was a catch. The transcendence that he commended compassed deference to authority only as long as political authorities were no obstacles—and permitted no obstacles—to the practice of the Christians' religion.[14]

The faithful, that is, ought to obey and defer, yet without compromising their faith. Augustine was edgy when he contemplated what is known today as institutional charisma, the reach and seductiveness of political authority. Still, he was confident that Christians, once they compared the imperfect peaces of earth with the perfect peace of their celestial city, would neither confuse deference with devotion to the powers of this world nor collaborate enthusiastically with them. The faithful were in dangerous waters; their felicity and fellowship with God, which were partially given with faith and enacted in righteousness, would not survive compromises of faith and righteousness.[15] Thus they were to live as sojourners, pilgrims, as what we might now call "resident aliens." Augustine's term, *peregrinus,* is tricky to translate. Given connotations that the English equivalents acquired over the centuries, none just noted infallibly conveys its meaning. "Sojourner," "pilgrim," and "resident alien," however, come close; they denote "passing through" and do not imply complete contempt for the territory through which one passes. But any word that works denotes the martyrs' detachment from what they leave behind, their disinterest in naturalization—as well as their anticipation for all that they expect to find "on the other side."[16] Augustine ruled out one alternative in a sermon of uncertain date, submitting that there was something wrong with saying that citizens of the celestial city were expatriates or exiles on earth. The *City* intimates that the celestial city in time was as Israel had been in Egypt, yet as the sermon says most emphatically, being "in Christ," the pilgrims could never be outcasts and were nowhere abandoned. But being *in carne,* they were nowhere at home and everywhere *peregrini.*[17]

"Love Not the World"

Nowhere at home, the faithful on pilgrimage were nowhere content, because, as Augustine conceded, the injunction that they obey and defer to regimes in the terrestrial cities subjected them to persons and standards far inferior to those they otherwise might have elected and improvised, respectively. Certain cultivated Christian slaves had an analogous predicament. They were enjoined by their bishops to serve cloddish, coarse pagan masters.[18] They and other citizens of the celestial city were *superiores,* ruled by candidates compromised by rule, by persons whom the faithful knew to be less capable, less compassionate, and more corruptible, *quos novimus peiores.*[19] But Augustine let it be known that there were very few justifications for insurrection; *en politique* he was "a legitimist," as Serge Lancel argues. Unless regimes obstructed evangelization, they were to be tolerated. The wicked and worse (*peiores*) were to be endured and obeyed as if, for a time, they were better.[20]

Augustine was under no illusion. To be governed by municipal magistrates, regional officials, and emperors—by persons "who love the world"— was, even in the best of times, to invite persecutions that were more subtle than those during the church's early history. But to be so governed was obviously a condition of the Christian's pilgrimage. In sermons Augustine preached while composing his *City,* he admitted that the temporal order was passing and was persecuting those reconciled to its passing because they were also reconciled as well with its creator and savior.[21] Passages in the *City* illustrate as much and explain what it meant for Christians to adapt, as pilgrims, a martyr's mentality. Above all, they must arm themselves against temptation. They must decathect—drastically, if not completely, cut their emotional investment in political developments. They must beware and despise the Sirens' songs or charms (*blandimenta*) that kept so many from concentrating on celestial rewards. And pilgrims ought to comprehend as well that an exclusively material interpretation of those charms or allurements missed the point. Wealth and position were to be shunned, in spirit and in theory, if not also in reality, but the *peregrini* must forsake certain passions as they "despise" their possessions, notably the desires for fame and influence. *In extremis,* they should be prepared, Augustine implied, to surrender cherished liberties, much as the martyrs divested themselves of all, save the freedom to bear witness and worship their God.[22]

The boundary between despising (*contemnere*) and disdaining this world must have been hard to draw and, in the *City* and related sermons, it is very hard to discern. Augustine explicitly commended the first while refraining from the second. Yet the two seem one, especially in the *City*'s most scalding rationale for detachment. There, Augustine supplies an extended account of the wickedness and hardships that had transformed this world into a hell on earth. Governments initiated repairs, here and there replacing one plank with another, but rulers and ruled alike had neither the will nor imagination—and certainly not the power—to rebuild human relations from scratch. Augustine's conclusion was grim: "this life was a calamity to be bewailed." Wailing seemed to him more adequate and accurate than words, which, he deduced, could never give a comprehensive, once-and-for-all description of the wickedness and wretchedness. No inventory could compass all that was wrong: "harmful satisfactions," sad accidents, bad climates, depleted resources, cures that turn cruel rather than heal, the shameful conduct of many contemporaries, and so on. Augustine was sure no discourse could lay it all out and no critic or cynic could pronounce the last word on the world's misery.[23]

But Eugene TeSelle is correct: "calamity" was not Augustine's last word. Readers run the risk of becoming conspicuously "unAugustinian," therefore, when they shore up a "scoffing refusal to participate in the political debates of the time," of their time, with the *City*'s inventory of evil and misfortune. True, Augustine accepted that no terrestrial order could be other than inhospitable to what was best. He was, however, aware of the degrees of difference in what was worse than perfect peace and justice on earth. Christian pilgrims, who were less obsessed with possessions and power that rule those who rule "the city of men," nonetheless had roles to play in the hard-luck story called history.[24]

But what roles? Talk of distancing and divestiture might not be the *City*'s final words on political (non)involvement, but it could be misleading to refer to the pilgrims' alienation as a "first step," as a "clarification of [their] primary values and commitments."[25] That characterization seems to me to minimize what Augustine considered their enduring obligation. As early as 404, he was preaching about intermingled and antagonistic cities. Antagonism was unavoidable, he said, because the love for glory that constituted the terrestrial city was supplanted in the celestial by the pilgrims' love for God. To survive in time as a pilgrim was to decathect, grow distant, and despise passions and possessions associated with power in "the cities of men."[26] And if the pilgrims were unable to remain powerless, their "distancing" should go undercover as detachment, Augustine urged, as they let themselves be drawn into public administration to keep the peace on earth that profited their churches.

From Augustine's inventories of evil and his descriptions of life as "a calamity," one reasonably infers that finding peace on earth in the early fifth century was a needle-in-hay assignment. But the *City* also holds that peacekeeping this side of eternity should not be terribly complicated. Notwithstanding all that went wrong with the world, everyone and everything in time treasured peace. Persons suspended upside-down—or "perverted," as the *City* says, and evidently in distress—could count on a truce between the spirit and flesh, ordinarily antagonists. That armistice enabled the upended to bear up. With survival at stake, enemies composed their disagreements and temporarily turned into allies. And when the spirit departed, the body decomposing—dust to dust—showed that creation inclined to peace, to an equilibrium of sorts, a cosmic quiescence. Augustine, passing from physiology to psychology, more specifically reviews challenges facing peacekeepers in public administration. When confronted with ruffians, keepers would be wise to appeal to the best, irenic instincts of the unruly. Even thieves, says the *City*, valued restraint and tranquility in their dens. And remarkably, peace was prized as well by confederates conspiring against the peace, for there could be no trust and thus no conspiracy without it. Onlookers would be wrong to think that belligerents were enemies of peace. They were merely fighting to make "a peace more to their liking."[27]

Augustine once conceded that the chances for terrestrial peace improved with Christians as magistrates, yet he had nothing more to say about the technical or bureaucratic improvements that Christians should make as public officials. Aside from taking dim views of capital punishment and some forms of slavery, he was more concerned to improve magistrates' dispositions than to change the policies and structures over which they presided.[28] They should not permit themselves the civic pride that animated pagan public servants, he counseled; they must not assume that selfless devotion to the reputation of their cities counted for anything in the celestial city. Political virtues were of no importance there; so here, in their terrestrial cities, the Christian magistrates ought to keep their distance (emotionally) from the pageants celebrating provincial security or municipal solidarity.[29]

Augustine must have gathered that peacekeeping and pageants were not what readers of Cicero would have expected from pilgrims. Cicero, after all, told them not to meddle with politics but to attend narrowly to their affairs.[30] Yet Augustine concluded that it was appropriate for beneficiaries of peace and public order to become benefactors as well. God gave them incentives and opportunities when and after Constantine invited Christians to court and welcomed their counsel. Yes, the emperor put off his baptism. Was he worried that a full, public commitment to Christianity would have kept him from ruling ruthlessly and therefore effectively? Was he suggesting that his new religion was irreconcilable with conquest? Did he think governing imperiled the souls of baptized officials? Augustine may have heard excuses of that sort nearly a century later when he asked the praetorian prefect of Italy and Illyricum, Caecilian, why he was forever stalling. If only he agreed to proceed from or beyond the catechumenate to baptism, ruler and ruled alike might prosper, Augustine predicted, but he never mentioned getting a reply.[31] We know, though, that he directly confronted at least once the perceived incompatibility between the requirements of the government's new faith and those of public service. A pagan colleague of Augustine's friend Marcellinus, Volusianus—curious, yet perhaps also contemplating conversion—raised the issue, and Marcellinus relayed it to the bishop as a question. Did Christian public officials fare far worse than others who were commissioned to repel invaders, protect property, keep order, or judge and punish offenders because the faithful were urged to return no evil for evil (Romans 12:17) and under obligation to acquiesce to assailants' demands (Matthew 5:39–41)?[32]

Augustine anticipated parts of that question years before when he weighed the pros and cons of punishment. He said then that he had no objection to requiring restitution but questioned whether assigning other penalties would be appropriate. Volusianus, for his part, it seems, would have had judges—returning evil for evil, avenging villainy, and deterring would-be villains—first look to what was best for the commonwealth. Augustine, though, preferred to have them look to what was best for the criminals. How might they be brought to both repentance and rehabilitation? He was quick to acknowledge that punishment, as therapy, involved guesswork. There were no guarantees. A penalty that led one criminal to rehabilitation prompted another's resentment and recidivism. Clemency that resulted in one criminal's correction could encourage another to offend again. Given the uncertainties, Augustine advised authorities to attend not just to the best available information about the allegations at hand but also, and principally, to their own state of mind. Unable to read offenders' motives or futures, they must learn to read and to rule themselves. To be unselfconsciously punitive (or vengeful) was inexcusable; to return evil for evil with goodwill, with every good intention, was permissible.[33] Augustine adapted that conclusion in his answer to Volusianus, which implies that the Christian magistrates were not altogether unlike their martyred ancestors who had believed that the suffering of some eventually diminished the evil of others and who finally persuaded a persecuting society that their faith was in its future. When Rome did take up Christianity, the pilgrim citizens of the celestial city were thrust into the business of governing parts of the terrestrial city. They were both the legatees and executors of the empire's acquiescence. They should remain martyrs at heart and, in their hearts, treasure what their faith imparted as "precepts of patience," while they undertook what would be necessary to keep peace on earth.[34]

Estimable King David served as something of a model. Augustine regularly put David's virtues before parishioners, preaching on the psalms from the 390s and well into the fifth century, so he had David's mystique in mind when he replied to Volusianus and started to write the *City*. By then he had already split history into two kinds (*genera*) of people passing through: one set thinking, above all, about what can be had on earth; the other, content to contemplate what would be given in heaven. David ruled both yet belonged to the second. Others came after him with more or less the king's dignity or supremacy and the psalmist's humility. One could "wear the purple," be a magistrate, proconsul, or military commander, Augustine said, yet "keep one's heart on high" (*cor sursum habet*), stay above the fray, so to speak. Discharging political obligations, "the pious and faithful Christian" "despises what is and hopes for what is not yet." Several were skeptical. They tended to put politics and mischief at one pole and Christianity at the other. Augustine told them that they could find Christian politicians lifting their hearts to heaven as often as they found persons who preached about heavenly things letting their minds roll in the dirt. Hence, one should not revile citizens of the pilgrim city, of Jerusalem, simply because they conduct "the business of Babylon."[35]

Babylon suggested several things to Augustine. He used the term to refer to the materialism and *amor saeculi* he deplored. He recalled the town's legendary tower and occasionally made Babylon synonymous with confusion. He also described Babylon as the *civitas diaboli*, a global village of the reprehensible and reprobate ruled by Satan. Yet Gaetano Lettieri is probably right: when Augustine referred to "the business of Babylon," he usually historicized that city as "the state."[36] Its "business" was to administer relative justice and to maintain temporal peace. Yet Babylon in this narrow application became a time and place for compromises, a time and place of captivity. Oliver O'Donovan speculates that Augustine might have been more enthusiastic about the "business," time, and place, had he experienced "the revolutionary traditions of the Enlightenment." Had he seen political history as something other than the consolidation, and then disintegration, of empires, he might have emphasized opportunities for public service rather than servitude or captivity. But his was "a demonic history, which expresses the divine purpose only as providence, following its own hidden course, uses it to higher ends."[37] The ends would become clear in the celestial city and—although slightly less so—to readers of the final books of the *City* Augustine dedicated to defining it. The means, "the business of Babylon," would remain part of that demonic history—confused, materialistic, down-to-earth, and dragging down hearts lifted to heaven while weighted with regrettable compromises.

Augustine's *City* memorably illustrates the predicament or tension. It assumes that justices were committed to avoiding the execution of the innocent but that it was often difficult to determine guilt and innocence. Magistrates could not trust everything accusers, accused, and witnesses told them. Torture, though sometimes condemned, was widely used in late antiquity. And Christians who knew the history of their church would also have known that torture often extorted the "truths" that persecutors wanted to hear. But it was one way to probe.[38] Without others, what could Christian justices do? *Necessitate,* by necessity, they must assign blame, despite the fact that conflicting accounts of crimes frequently kept them in the dark (*necessitate nesciendi*). Torture they must, the *City* concedes; Christians, as magistrates, may do what is necessary to judge wisely. The results were not infallible. The innocent under duress might speak falsely and be wrongly executed. Sometimes the torture killed them. A culpable person, however, might learn to resist pain and successfully deny guilt, thereby leading courts to condemn truthful accusers as liars. That much and more went wrong with the process; nonetheless, "in the shadowy realm in which we live," Augustine conceded, torture was a necessary evil. But repetition of the word "necessary" was small consolation, and he knew it. So he offered more: justices committed no sin, he added, because they ordered torture without wishing to injure the innocent. Christians summoned to sit as judges must surely do so (*plane*), displeased though they may be with what had been asked of them. The displeasure, though, was their deliverance, so to speak. They prayed and pleaded that God release them, thus they hoist their hearts above "the business of Babylon," which it would have been wrong to forsake.[39]

Yet it was wrong for Christian magistrates not *to want* to forsake public service. Torture repelled them, yet something should tug the Christians drawn into administration back out (or above), namely, their obligations to call colleagues from their attachments to the terrestrial city (*evocare*). That was a pilgrim's higher calling. It was more important than the summons that made some of them magistrates, but, Augustine understood, there could be no scurrying from civic duty. Should Christians serve if asked? Clearly, *plane*. And they must learn to live with the tension between the magistrates' responsibilities for manorial justice, municipal efficiencies, or provincial peace and the pilgrims' responsibilities to embody and convey values and virtues different from those of government. To stress that imperative's importance, Augustine specified the international scope of the pilgrims' portfolio. Their higher calling was not hedged about by administrative jurisdictions; for they were to call and collect fellow pilgrims from peoples with various customs, laws, and languages. They had global—indeed, celestial or transcendental—as well as local responsibilities.[40]

They must size up each case or job accordingly. The slick certitudes of public administration ought not to apply. Public service was not a path to heaven, Augustine often wrote, and Christian magistrate Macedonius seemed to get the message when he read the *City*'s first three books. He explained that he had been convinced that political pleasures and successes often led from, and never led to, true felicity.[41] But Augustine was not completely satisfied with the magistrate's conviction and sent him a long letter, which supplied a synopsis of the theme he was working into subsequent books of his *City*. He told Macedonius that Christian public officials could very well keep the peace, preside over prosperity, inspire trust in their management of the economy, public safety, and emerging political consensus—they could do all that and still do a great disservice to constituents, who trusted them and thus trusted in human enterprise and effort. The lesson of the Bible and the *City* was not to be so trusting. Consistent with the martyrs' messages and the pilgrims' plans to forego security in this world for peace in the next, Augustine's counsel was to concentrate on apolitical answers to the difficulties the faithful faced, to concentrate on calling them, to trust God and to "love not the world."[42]

Libido Dominandi

But suppose that political successes came easy, that officials' courage and tact made friends of former enemies, that there were no more factions, and that all magistrates worked at full throttle for neighbors' gratitude rather than for personal gain. Suppose that those neighbors therefore trusted government, all the while conceding God's sovereignty. And, Augustine further adjusted his reverie, suppose that the commonwealth was spared hardship as a result of all the previous suppositions. What was wrong with that? Plenty. Neither citizens nor successful municipal or imperial authorities satisfied with that level of satisfaction could know true happiness. Trust in terrestrial administration necessarily warped one's celestial conversation, a condition for which was one's conviction that no personal initiative and no social policy could ever make a resident alien feel at home on pilgrimage. Only a Christian magistrate's exemplary religious devotion, drawing constituents to worship, could be truly advantageous.[43]

I should have been more precise and written "soterially advantageous," for Augustine did not propose that positive political results were meaningless. Public policy, after all, made North Africa safer for catholic Christians in the early fifth century. And, as we learned in the last chapter, Emperor Honorius permitted the use of coercion to achieve religious conformity—according to Augustine, an unfortunate means, much as torture, to a highly desirable end. If he had his way, Christian magistrates would enforce the rules with regret, displeasure, and a degree of detachment, aware of how grossly inappropriate it was for Christians to intimidate, confiscate, incarcerate, torment, and, kill— *necessitate.* There was no denying that their Christianity was compromised and that the world's corrupting ways had seeped into the church and soiled it.[44] But, Augustine averred, contamination was negligible, particularly during the reign of Theodosius I. The *City* reported his virtues, which were more like those of apostles and martyrs than those of magistrates: the emperor was generous, selfless, compassionate, penitent, caring more about piety than about power.[45] But even an emperor could not turn back time. There was no returning to an age in which the powerlessness of the faithful left their leading figures with fewer alternatives. Apostles then had no chance politically to leverage their good news. The martyrs then were witnesses against the government. Augustine appreciated that times had changed. Christian magistrates might imitate apostles and martyrs in disposition, but not in fact. They were too closely connected with their government's "frightening but advantageous laws."[46]

They would have had to strain to explain if they chose not to enforce them, specifically, the laws against schism. Their duty, as Christians and magistrates, was to protect their churches, and Augustine warned that there would be hell to pay if they did not.[47] Administrative positions gave them power to do what it was incumbent on every ordinary Christian to try—namely, to stop sin. All the faithful served by living faithfully; Christian magistrates, by living faithfully *and* extraordinarily influentially. They could make government a better barrier against moral and religious confusion. Citizen Theodosius would clearly have impressed neighbors with his compassion, contrition, and reverence for the church. The piety of Emperor Theodosius impressed the world; he and his sons suppressed idolatry.[48]

Might another Theodosius deliver empire and church? The *City* does not ponder that possibility. But one of its first allusions to *mala praesentia*, evils of the present day, alludes also to another remedy, with which we have become familiar. Augustine was at the time preoccupied pulling evidence from Sallust for an autopsy of the Roman republic that blamed the brutality of old Rome on its old religions. The same section, though, also previews what the *City* would later and repeatedly present as the pilgrims' way out of the empire's difficulties, an exit offered with its new religion. Augustine began with the question for pagan critics of Christianity that echoes through the *City*'s early passages: "Why do you blame your present problems on Christ who merely prohibited worship of your doubly false gods?" They were *falsi et fallaces*, fictions, deceptions that authorized deceit. "Christ detests and condemns, on divine say-so, the disgraceful, harmful human desires" that the cults had their gods perfidiously endorse. And Christ "draws his family out and away from this wobbly and wasted world (*tabescenti ac labenti*), building an eternal glorious city that richly deserves every superlative we use to describe it."[49]

History was in trouble. Christians must look to be drawn (*subtrahere*) or called (*evocare*) out and away—they must learn to cope with adversity and to concentrate on eternity. Martyrs did so; pilgrims should. Detachment was fundamental, dispositional, but until death, incomplete. For Christians in public administration, it was extremely difficult as well. Augustine could not depend on their instinctive recoil from all that was seductive in civil service. "I know how hard it will be to persuade proud people of the power of humility," he stated at the very start of his *City*. That was why he spent so much time demonstrating the obvious, that magistrates were—and would always be—dominated and driven by their lust for domination (*libido dominandi*).[50] Admittedly, Romans were well served by their rulers' obsessions. They were frequently free and relatively secure. Prodigious effort resulted in their unparalleled domination of the Mediterranean world and beyond for generations. The glory that once was Rome was indisputable, yet, Augustine added, the virtues that generated and sustained it were not, which was to say that they were not "true virtues." The way out of the problems caused by the empire's unraveling and, centuries before, by the republic's successes, supremacy, and self-glorification was to be drawn out, to rise above the pride and peril that afflicted nearly everyone who wielded power.[51]

Nonetheless, Augustine's respect for Rome's achievements shows in his *City*. His admiration is what Robert Markus now describes as "a reverse side to [his] real feelings," "reverse," yet by no means unreal. For Augustine was trying his hand at history in the *City*'s early books, and no history could pretend to erudition and omit the excellences, the times of peace and prosperity. His history, however, dwells on "the evils arising from prosperity" and from the lust for domination "that first took hold of the political leaders and then enslaved the Roman people who were more intoxicated by that obsession than by any other vice."[52]

Augustine's indictment along this line more than offset his respectful remarks, for he meant to draft something different from a historical judgment on the sad, last days of the republic. His *City* growls at public officials who schemed then and in his day to keep citizens docile rather than to make them moral. It grieves him that government seemed still, as always, subject to grasping interests. True, the *City*'s anti-Roman polemic takes aim at nostalgia for the probity and prosperity of bygone years. It echoes the laments of pagan moralists to assure fifth-century readers that they would find the past confected by the church's enemies hard to swallow. Augustine claimed that it made him ill to repeat tales of great conquests, narratives composed to cover what insolence, ambition, avarice, and envy moved the Romans to take unlawfully as their own.[53] But repeating those stories served the *City*'s purpose, which, as Catherine Conybeare now says, was to "destabilize by insistent interrogation and revision" the cultural values of "educated pagan readers." If she is right, Augustine "manage[d] to catch traditionalists unawares, to deliver a swift reprimand to complacent Christians in his audience, and at the same time to legitimate his own lingering admiration for the idealized notion of Rome," which can pass, it appears, as that "reverse side" to his "true feelings." But, Robert Dodaro notes, the reprimand was central. Augustine staged his assault on the terrestrial city in his *City* to include the attitudes of the ruling caste that held sway to his day. They made it impossible to achieve a lasting, meaningful peace and genuine justice in this world. The elites financed lavish spectacles and pretended to be concerned about fairness to deflect attention from their desire to dominate—and from excesses that followed from it. With a nod to Cicero, Augustine argued that Roman government in the public interest existed in statement and statute, although never in substance and practice. That was so when Rome was ruled tolerably well, he remarked, and more recently, when it was not.[54]

What good, then, might Christian magistrates do? And what harm? Would they practice dissimulation, as did their pagan peers? Would they, too, lust for domination? Would they despise "what is and hope for what is not yet" or grow accustomed to influence—to buying and selling it—and addicted to acquisition? Augustine did not know exactly what to expect from pilgrims in public office. From what he was saying to Pelagians, however, we may infer that he was prepared for disappointments. For public officials were no better than other citizens; all were sinners, because human nature had been corrupted. That Pelagians questioned the pervasiveness of the corruption was their cardinal sin. Their pride proved to Augustine how bad things had gotten. At best, the Christian magistrates, enabled by divine grace, might raise their hearts above the ruins—or so he hoped. In part, to assist them, his *City* repeatedly underscored its central conceits: that selfless love for God characterized pilgrims' alternatives to those who were passionate for power, and that any pilgrims who worked among the latter ought to exercise extreme caution and preserve some distance from them and from their passions.[55]

Augustine often repeated both injunctions. When he referred to the *libido dominandi,* he warned that the cutthroat competition for honor and influence was contagious. He also alleged that the political cultures shaped by it were far less consequential and far more unstable than they at first appeared. The game of government was "violently competitive," but just a game. A single slip could take a player from the top of the heap to the bottom of the barrel. A regime might hold all the aces one year and fold the next. The winners suddenly became losers, and empires expanded and contracted, as God willed, despite players' resources and ambitions.[56] To the players, however, politics seemed a suspenseful story, the outcomes of which were momentous and hinged on their clever manipulation of honor, shame, pride, and possessions. "Government did not imagine itself as government in our sense, with pallid, impersonal, machine-like images," J. E. Lendon remarks. "Its members imagined something more akin to a football league, a realm of glory, profit, and competition—and some administration."[57]

I think Augustine might have liked Lendon's analogy. It suggests the greed, glamour, ruthlessness, and superficiality that the *City* associates with "the business of Babylon," the ballyhoo of government, and the drive to dominate. But Augustine was good at trawling for comparisons in the literature of antiquity, and came up with some equally effective ones. In what would become the *City*'s most famous, he parked politics alongside organized crime. He borrowed the story of Alexander the Great's conversation with a pirate he had recently apprehended. When asked by the emperor why he troubled the seas, the pirate replied that he only did as Alexander. It was called trouble and piracy when done with a single ship but empire when done with fleets and nearly inexhaustible forces. The point was made even before the pirate's punchline: *remota justitia,* "justice having been removed, what is rule but larceny on a large scale?"[58]

The statement behind Augustine's question seems straightforward. Granted, he can sometimes be equivocal, evasive. His counsel that Christians in government think like martyrs and act as magistrates is anything but transparent and easily translated into rules for court conduct. But his observation that rulers were rogues—offered, no doubt, to urge martyr/magistrates to decathect—evidently reflects his disaffection. Or does it? Was *remota justitia,* the ablative absolute, conditional? "If justice is removed" concedes that politicians were not, *ipso facto,* pirates. They only became so when something unseemly happened to their system. To take the phrase as causal is to imply an ineradicable defect, however; politicians are pirates or thieves, because the *libido dominandi* invariably robs the government of any real justice, *vera justitia.* This choice between the conditional and causal character of Augustine's "straightforward" remark is symptomatic of the interpretive problem that has been hanging around this small corner of the *City* for generations; as readers ponder its persistence—and the problem itself—they ought to resolve not to be too trusting when they approach interpretations of themes central to the entire, massive text, including the one on offer here.

For the *City* is almost infinitely interpretable. Start canvassing the expositions, clarifications, and applications that have made it say so many things in just the last two centuries, and you will soon discover that your curtain line must fall far short of closure. The literature is vast. For nearly every analysis there is a demurral. One could, of course, confine historiographical study to scholars' most conspicuous squabbles. Interpreters of interpretation reportedly love a good fight, and the truculence of many who stake out the *City* and defend distinctive evaluations of its precincts too often demonstrates a passion to dominate while they are discussing the evils of domination. Few readers of the whole, though, would deny that Augustine invited all the attention and controversy. He set "an intellectual feast," as historian Peter Brown has said. One is well advised to dine in the company of knowledgeable guides, given the amazing range of philosophical views reheated, refuted, and tossed with biblical exegesis and historical information, then garnished with wild speculation, satire, and more than a dash of melancholy. Serge Lancel, though, rightly suggests that guidance cannot give up some of Augustine's secrets. The

City's architect "attached himself to a gigantic enterprise" but did not include clues that lead to lasting consensus about his aim and its meaning.[59]

To review the many historical inquiries and scholarly quarrels—all promising consensus at the outset, most proving inconclusive—would likely obscure rather than usefully contextualize and clarify the two claims made here: (1) that Augustine crowded lusts, loves, martyrs, and magistrates into his *City* to explain why government was to be used but not improved, and (2) that the *City* was the culmination of Augustine's progressive disenchantment with "the business of Babylon." What follows, then, is a sketch of the two interpretive developments that make this chapter's claims and arguments more plausible and most timely.

"Mark the Contrasts"

The first development built momentum during the 1950s after several influential scholars disavowed the conventional view of Augustine's political theology. Until then, historians had drawn principally on the bishop's gratitude for government cooperation against Donatists and idolaters. They heard him enthusiastically predicting the end of idolatry, and they imagined he was also proclaiming that both the positive impact of Christianity on public administration and the positive impact of administration on society were not just possible but inevitable.[60] They also heard Augustine's optimism echoing from the *City,* which, they said, looked forward to the Christian "renovation" or "regeneration" of empire, in time. *Remota justitia,* "when justice was lost," Christianity would recover it and then demand that decision-makers' decisions conformed to what genuine justice and compassion required of them. Augustine was said to have been expecting, even after 410, "a renovation that extends naturally, politically, from the conversion of the individual" to the reconstruction of government.[61]

A very different Augustine started making the rounds in the 1950s. Devastation from the recent war in Europe along with difficulties in its aftermath prompted a despair that stirred some historians to see what their predecessors arguably had not in early fifth-century social and political thinking. The historical theologians, in particular, turned the soil of the *City* and came up with statements that genuine or "true" justice could not be had in time. They inflected Augustine's comparisons between the fragile, partial peaces on earth and the comprehensive, everlasting peace of the celestial city. The church, as a portion of the celestial city on pilgrimage in time, could only experience the latter, true peace by anticipation, "in an eschatological form of self-understanding."[62] For churches and pilgrims were implicated in the influence peddling that ordinarily passed as politics. Augustine learned that much in Milan. And later, in Africa he learned that the churches' courts often were no better than the government's tribunals where bribery and extortion were appallingly common.[63] There was no denying that the church had come a long way. According to Augustine, astute readers of the Old Testament prophets would understand that Christianity's prosperity had been foretold. They would also know that the influential, who once looked to animal entrails for help in making policy, peace, and war, were coming to church authorities for counsel. "What name is more celebrated than Christ's, which everywhere is fragrant?"[64] Yes, heretics continued to disturb the church's peace, but they and their disturbances gave orthodox officials the chance to discuss, elaborate, illustrate, and drive home doctrine. That notwithstanding, Augustine conceded that the Christians who came to church to find peace, justice, and invariably insightful sermons were bound to be disappointed. "True justice" and peace were elusive in the terrestrial city, in time, in this "calamity to be bewailed," even in the best churches. Earnest and erudite preachers misconstrue the mystery of Christ's passion and "do not understand what they preach. But the righteous hold that mystery within, taking to heart that the weakness and foolishness of God are stronger and wiser than the strengths and intelligence of humanity."[65]

Augustine's pilgrims took their faith to heart, held their hopes within, and—on revisionist readings of the *City* that concentrate on interiority and eschatology—showed their disappointment in the church because it was a community of the sacraments open to Christians of great and little faith alike. It was different from the church Augustine called *ecclesia*. That church existed in time *intus in corde*, only in the pilgrims' anticipation of time's fulfillment.[66] For the revisionists of the 1950s, this was Augustine's crucial, long overlooked and outstanding contribution. His references to the city in the *City* did not denote empirical realities or abstract qualities (belief versus unbelief); they constituted "an eschatological summons," which could not be answered by public service. Diligent leadership in the churches and civic virtue were largely unrelated to the "eschatological form of self-understanding" that composed—along with selfless love for God—the city of God. Had they read Augustine as the revisionists later did, medieval theorists might have quit prospecting for any-and-everything in Christian antiquity that related *evangelium* to *imperium*. Unquestionably, Jesus' incarnation was fortuitously timed. Emperor Augustus had pacified the terrestrial city just enough for the new religion's good news or gospel to get out expeditiously. But that synchronicity—Augustus and Christ; *pax Romana* and apostolic preaching—pulled Christianity no closer to political culture in the first century, an age of Christians' martyrs, not of Christian magistrates. Similarly, in the fifth century, "no positive relation between political societies and the heavenly city" should be inferred from their respective histories.[67] No religious renovation of public life was contemplated in the *City*. Rome was a second Babylon. Augustine said so twice in the text—not to propose reformist initiatives, rather to dash hopes for a Christian empire in time.[68]

But he was misunderstood. Proponents of papal supremacy during the Middle Ages put Augustine on the payroll, so to speak, drawing from the *City* and other texts passages that seemed to support the church's right and duty to take over the terrestrial city, *ratione peccati*, because it was mired in sin, "a calamity to be bewailed."[69] Yet the revisionists of the 1950s cried foul. They argued that neither the attempted seizure nor the "political Augustinianism" that appeared to justify it was consistent with the *City*'s eschatological-transcendental orientation. Some said Augustine's political theory had been misappropriated; others, that he had no political theory.[70]

To be sure, Augustine lodged something relevant to political thinking in every precinct of the *City*, but he refrained from presenting a systematic *Staatslehre*. He composed seventeen of the tome's twenty-two books and then paused to recall his aims. He revealed that he had started writing to discredit the gods and the nostalgia of pagans who reviled Christians in the wake of 410 for having deserted the old deities for a new, less effective, less protective one. After exposing the old gods' failures and the old cults' absurdities and inadequacies, he wrote of the origins and development of the *City*'s two cities, emphasizing scriptural allusions to, and "prophecies" about, the pilgrim, celestial city.[71] "The other city," the terrestrial city, was but a backdrop; Augustine gave little attention to the distribution of power therein. He only superficially investigated who ruled when and how well. Finally, in the eighteenth book, he announced a change; he promised only, though, that he would be "outlining the progress" of that "other" and terrestrial city so readers might "mark the contrast" with the celestial.[72] Presumably, then, he would not have been surprised or terribly distressed that assorted revisionists found no political theory in the *City*. He occasionally let on how a Christian magistrate could be politically and religiously responsible, but his multiple takes on characteristic court conduct and entertainments generally stressed the unconscionable luxury, leisure, debauchery, and intolerance. He was saddened that critics of excess had been branded "public enemies" and silenced. Temporality and temptation, secularity and sin seemed "indissoluble." Augustine learned to divide the world into two cities from the psalms, from Tyconius, and from the Manichees. More than any of them, though, he featured "the absolute antithesis between" the terrestrial and celestial polities, urging readers to "mark the contrast."[73]

Because contrasts clarified; the celestial city was disclosed *sub contrario,* and to those ends—disclosure and clarification—images were better than arguments.[74] The Old Testament contained plenty of the former. Noah and the Ark, for example, were said to symbolize the celestial city in time, *in hoc saeculo,* which made the flood the *saeculum,* where passion for power or lust for domination roiled the waters long after storms blew over. That fish-eat-fish world was also prefigured by Cain, whose name meant "possession," according to Augustine, and who built the terrestrial city in which citizens hoped mostly for what they could possess or perceive as desirable and procurable in time. By contrast, citizens of the celestial city hoped less for what they might have in time and more for what they would enjoy eternally. Indictments of Cain's kind conveyed the contrast better than theories. Revisionists of the 1950s were right: Augustine often preferred indictments and images to arguments and political theory.[75]

The revisionists anticipated Robert Markus who was largely responsible for the second interpretive development directly relevant to the claims registered here. By the early 1970s, he was recognized as *the* historian of Augustine's political disenchantment. He suggested that "euphoria" connected with "the Theodosian age of achievement" and the "triumphant progress of Christianity" "had some fascination" for Augustine but that the thrill was gone by the time he began drafting his *City*. The revisionists had already dismantled the conventional paradigm that had Augustine assimilating the profane and the political into the sacred. Markus has him devising "a fresh approach to man's social condition"—which admits its "precariousness"—and authorizing Christians to commit to something less than "triumphant progress," the Christianization of a political culture or the renovation of an empire, but to something more than a celebration by anticipation, which distances them from "the business of Babylon." If Markus has his man, Augustine favored the faithful cultivating a reformist commitment to political practice and "securing a living space against chaos."[76]

Indeed, "for the citizen of the heavenly city," on Markus' watch, "concern for the *saeculum* is the temporal dimension of . . . concern for the eternal city." *Saeculum*, here, is "the historical, empirical, and interwoven life of the two eschatological cities." Public service in that "interwoven life" was, for Markus' Augustine, an expression of religious faith, of "concern for the eternal city." The field of play was "religiously neutral," and Markus adapted the revisionists' eschatological perspective to keep it so. The rules for Christians were not. Markus knew Augustine made them pilgrims. He believed, though, that Augustine approved of their "positive identification with the society in which [they] live[d] . . . belong[ing] to it in an essential way: its values [their] values." This statement from Raymond Williams' meditation on what "a sense of membership" means may seem surprising in this setting, however, Markus infers from the *City* an only slightly qualified endorsement: "within the sphere of purposes which fall short of the most ultimate," he says, "Augustine would have accepted this." And for three decades, many historians, political scientists, and ethicists, reading Markus, have accepted that alleged acceptance.[77]

Jean Bethke Elshtain, for one, imagines Augustine excited by the prospect of Christians in their households and municipalities replacing cupidity with charity and "achiev[ing] some good," "avoid[ing] greater evil." John von Heyking, for another, thinks that Augustine "affirmed political life as a positive good . . . whereby citizens reach a kind of perfection." Elshtain, von Heyking, and Markus acknowledge limits, conceding that Augustine and his *City* censured the imperious "politics of perfection" that Eusebius of Caesarea and Nectarius of Calama, from their different perspectives, found exhilarating. The *City*, say the scholars, demythologized the *saeculum*. Its "interwoven life" was not ready to be redeemed, but neither was it transparently and irredeemably wicked. Markus was congratulated by Peter Brown, in this connection, for helping us appreciate the *City*'s take on "the merciful opacity of human affairs," helping us see the *saeculum* as something of a muddle, though not a hopelessly and calamitously perverted one. Markus and "merciful," in Brown's curious characterization, appear to license a reading of Augustine's optimism in which "politics, in rare cases at its best, provides a foreshadow or intimation of the city of God."[78]

But, on the whole, the *City* matches up well with Augustine's anti-Pelagian work, which was pessimistic about what humanity might accomplish in time. By the early fifth century, then, he doubted that personal effort and social control could yield harmonious, healthy communities.[79] Might the *saeculum* somehow produce a politics of near perfection, nonetheless—an "intimation" of celestial circumstance? Unlikely; when Augustine pressed readers to "mark the contrast" between the terrestrial and celestial cities, he also appears to have precluded any significant, religiously neutral or uncommitted political practice from which anything truly just might come. He seems, that is, to have let his *City* exhibit "the strong cultural tendency of his society to analyze phenomena, and verbalize that analysis, in terms of opposites," as Gerard O'Daly says.[80] Neutrality? Opacity? *In hoc saeculo,* "in this world, in these evil days, the church on pilgrimage proceeds until the end of time with the world's persecutions," but also with "God's consolations."[81] *In hoc saeculo maligno,* "in this wicked world, in these evil days, the church prepares for a celestial future through its humiliations and humility in the present. Its preparation includes being afflicted with fear, tormented by grief, burdened with work imperiled by temptation. The church rejoices only in hope. Hope is the only wholesome joy when so many reprobate swim . . . with the good in the church—in the gospel's net—or at sea, in this world . . . until all reach shore and are separated."[82] The good and wicked swim together, but it is hard to forget that the lust for domination created turbulent, treacherous currents, *in saeculo,* when we read Augustine's comments to the contrary, *saeculo maligno.* Selfish interests at sea quite simply pollute all there is. That is a condition of what Rowan Williams calls "our fallen finitude," a condition and pollution from which few can—but the faithful should—decathect.[83]

The "fallenness" frustrated every effort to enshrine genuine justice in laws or institutions. There is no more pointed illustration of precisely that—and of the ultimate futility of playing politics in the purportedly neutral zone mapped by Markus—than the *City*'s last extended exposition of injustice. There, what Otfried Höffe now describes as Augustine's "eschatological relativization of earthly justice" curdles whatever optimism his other remarks might have inspired.[84] The first readers of the *City* may have thought its comparisons of governments, *remota justitia,* to gangs of thugs a bit excessive. After all, unlike thugs, thieves, and pirates, the magistrates generally respected and protected property. Three considerations, however, conditioned the *City's* appreciation for their work and were included, one suspects, to influence readers. Augustine conceded that, now and then, courts and municipal councils issued rulings with relatively just results. But the *City's* second consideration or calculation stalled any momentum for a positive assessment of political authority that might have been building from the first, for, more often than not, the text says, public officials devised laws and defined justice to serve special interests, to be useful to the powerful.[85] Finally, and critically, Augustine pronounced that never, shy of the eschatological divide, could governments formulate a genuinely and invincibly just proposal or protocol. Governments relied on rank and domination. Their officials, glorifying the former and lusting for the latter, crippled every regime, yet what totally disabled political cultures was an insensitivity to the requirement that all be assured their due—including God—the requirement of "true transcendental justice." Those roaming the corridors of power might see to it that persons not be wrongfully evicted from their proper places, but they hardly gave a thought to securing God's place in his creatures' affections, which was regularly surrendered to diabolical spirits—to ruthless ambitions and terrible lusts. The enormity of *that* injustice—at best, substituting moral relevance for reverence—made governing *in hoc saeculo* seem like a negligibly important way of biding time. Augustine, for his part, refused to equate what was relatively relevant, relatively just, thus ultimately irrelevant and unjust with what was good for the governed. He cared little for concepts of justice that defined "the state" as something other and better than thuggery. He cared, instead, about genuine justice (*vera justitia*), religious devotion, God's due, and God's love.[86]

For Augustine, then, genuine justice was inextricably linked to love. Creatures' love was God's due—their love for his, for he so loved the world that he sent and sacrificed his son to redeem it. And, as we know, their love for God constituted the pilgrim city. Love of self and love for the things of this world—honor, property, glory, domination—constituted the terrestrial city.[87] In "the interwoven life" that the two cities shared, *in hoc saeculo,* that first kind of love, love for God, might have prevailed sufficiently to make genuine justice politically possible, were it not for the swagger and striking power of that second sort of love. Precisely because the second was so pervasive and powerful, Augustine insisted that citizens of the celestial city were sojourners or pilgrims in the "interwoven life." Genuine justice was foreign there as well, pretty much for the same reason. Christian magistrates could be expected to do some good. People were better for having them rule.[88] As Christians, public officials accepted that genuine justice was a gift from God and not a quality of their laws. Affection for such justice and the delight it brings were also divine gifts. Laws were something different, the work of prudence, not of sublime affection and delight. And laws, despite the prudence of their makers, sometimes were imprudent and often imprudently enforced. Occasionally they incited crime, the prohibitions tempting or goading offenders to transgress. A love for genuine justice and the selfless love for God at its source, however, ought to inspire obedience and, as much as possible, the suppression of wicked impulses.[89] The love for justice and God could hardly be politicized, although the initiatives against idolatry and schism came close. But the Christian magistrates' opposition to injustice, in Augustine's view, ought to be expressed in contrasts and, principally, *in spe*, in the magistrates' hopes for what was not yet and in their prayers for deliverance from what was.[90]

In their hopes, prayers, and patience. Augustine understood that pilgrims in time would always be "amidst the crooked and perverse." As direct products of the perversity, governments could not be expected to go straight. Yet they could and should fight crime, require reparations, and protect property—especially that of the African catholic churches. Although "crooked" themselves, governments frequently restricted the effects of sin, punishing and thereby deterring bad behavior. There was no denying that.[91]

But we now know that if Augustine had his way, Christian magistrates would punish differently. Whatever they might do to deter crime or determine truth in this life would be shaped by a religious commitment that reaped rewards in the next. Rewards in time, of course, might be socially and politically beneficial, for if love underlay punitive practices, magistrates and governments would rehabilitate rather than remove troublemakers. "Pray against," punish, and purge an enemy's ill will, Augustine advised, yet with a love that shields your soul from hatred, and the souls of those you punish will be transformed. Better to lose an enemy *and* make a friend than just lose an enemy—caught and confined or executed. Augustine preached to that effect while he was composing the first books of his *City*.[92] His counsel stands to reason, but he told magistrates to depend on faith and the grace it imparted. Only God's grace overcomes one's righteous indignation against offenders. Only souls "reverently subjected to God" exercise authority as a service, to correct affectionately, parentally, rather than to avenge, dominate, and rule.[93]

In hoc saeculo, there was ample room for correction. But from what the *City* says, the most important corrections were personal first and then, if at all, political. Augustine was uninterested in regime change. Regimes—reformed or transformed or exchanged for something totally new—to the extent they were political, were fragments of the terrestrial city and not creations capable of trifling perfections in some neutral zone. That Augustine did not strenuously oppose Christians' public administration or political leadership warns us against overstating his emphasis on detachment and distance, but we must not think he expected this wretched world would tellingly improve.[94]

"If his faith allowed, he would have become a world-denier," Johannes Spörl said fifty years ago. What Augustine's faith did allow him to deny, though, he repudiated: the hopes that others squandered on significant political improvement.[95] "We are beset by evils that we must patiently endure." Patience, not politics, was the proper response to misery in time.[96] For citizens of the celestial city on pilgrimage in time, salvation was expectation (and a degree of separation or detachment). They were made sound (*curantur*) by sighing for their heavenly *patria*.[97] Augustine, on their behalf and for their benefit, put politics beyond the pale. Maybe Plato's disgust with the savagery and greed (*pleonexia*) riddling "the business of Babylon" flashed before him while he was composing the *City*'s recapitulations of Rome's woes, the terrestrial city's injustices, and contrasts with the celestial city.[98] Perhaps, quite deliberately, he took aim at other classical philosophy that saw political communities as solutions rather than problems. Personal and political redemption, for Aristotle and others—even for Plato when he put pessimism aside—was made possible by moral choices persons made as citizens. For Augustine, their choices only increased the misery of their lives in time. Perhaps they led to some semblance of peace or to the victory of one cause, faction, or legislation that looked more just than another. Fresh misfortune materialized, regardless, whenever temporal goods—quiet, order, political harmony, civic solidarity, and the like—obscured the importance of the perfect peace and genuine justice found in love for the Christians' God.[99] The pilgrim citizens of the celestial city introduced in the *City* know salvation as expectation. They also know it as some degree of separation from the choices political leaders make, for "they are not 'citizens' in a way that would have made sense to Aristotle."[100]

Because they were pilgrims, resident aliens. As such, they enjoyed certain rights or protections. They—and others who had not asked—were "saved" from schism, idolatry, and heresy. Late in his career, Augustine also prized the regime's assistance against the Vandals at the gates and discouraged a provincial military commander who contemplated entering a monastery instead of manning the empire's unpromising defenses.[101] "Sighing for the celestial city" seemed compatible with the armed services. And the *City* continued to celebrate the spread of Christianity "from sea to sea," which, arguably even then, was unthinkable apart from Rome's territorial ambitions. But as the empire's flabbiness and vulnerability became more evident, he grew less enthusiastic. He rejected the argument that the safety of the church or the spread of Christianity depended on emperors, edicts, and arms. Christianity might expand while the empire contracted. Augustine surely did not intend observations of that sort to suggest that political culture is not part of God's saving work in this world, but he doubted Christians had major roles to play in saving political culture from itself.[102]

Other "Beginnings" with Different Ends

Empires were nearly all he had known. He exhumed from historical literature a succession of them punctuated by the occasional republic, a few notable yet evanescent regional powers, and the rare confederation. But politics seemed to be about swallowing local autonomies. The lust for domination made empires inexorable, and size made them susceptible to various destructive forces. The *City* sums it up: long before 410, Rome had been "crushed by its own magnitude." It annexed Africa, Asia, Greece. It became bloated and, as we just noted, flabby. It underrated internal divisions that grew into civil wars.[103] But Augustine was not terribly distressed. Christian magistrates, in effect, were engaged in propping up a bad bet. Provincial courts and municipal councils were caught in cycles that led from greed to size and serious difficulties, only to have greed generate size once again from the debris of a previous debacle.

Ernest Fortin probably considers the claims about the *City* on offer here eminently resistible, nonetheless he appreciates Augustine's "brooding pessimism" and acknowledges that the *City* refuses to relinquish the central tenet of his prophetic view of history, that "Christianity [is] a universal religion and the political order, great or small as it may be, is always particular." One suspects, though, that Gaetano Lettieri might have aptly altered that last word. For Lettieri believes that Augustine was fully aware that the politics of size sinisterly presented itself as a "remedy for the fragility of existence." So, "great or small," a political order was not just "particular" but pernicious.[104]

For Augustine believed there was no "remedy" for fragility or for the "abiding fear of death," which he set as "the cornerstone of all political ideology and . . . empire maintenance."[105] He let on that it was incumbent on the faithful to confront the consequences of original sin rather than to cover them up with civic pride. Pilgrims would offer perfect obedience to God in their celestial city. Until then, "the habits of sin" bound them to the Ninevehs of this world, which would be "overthrown" once pilgrims "died to those habits" and excesses that made the world's cities what they were: lies, bribes, insatiable appetites for gain or glory, usurious commerce, and other corruptions. This observation was not an order to sever social ties. It was no call to rebellion, but a summons to mourn, pray, and repent.[106] To increase the chances of obedience, Augustine painted unflattering pictures of the regimes from which he expected pilgrims to decathect as they developed a desire for that "true" peace and justice that "overthrew" Nineveh. As we have learned, the *City* sometimes turns into a symposium on "the calamity to be bewailed" *in hoc saeculo*. It speaks unsympathetically about "the business of Babylon," warning that public service be undertaken with detachment, that Christians rise above, even when they are drawn into, municipal administration and "empire maintenance." But the *City* is less explicit about the places into which pilgrims ought to "rise" to find refuge. Catholic churches would seem the obvious choices. If heaven were to bend to earth, was there any likelier place for the two to touch than the communities assembling for thanksgiving or Eucharist? In all that Augustine wrote about those communities in the *City*, Robert Markus perceives "a continuity with God's eschatological community into which [they] are always growing."[107]

Augustine suspected that some persons might push their way in for the wrong reasons. Clerical status was quite a draw. Ambition sometimes encouraged conversion.[108] Yet the forgiveness of sins and the mutual affection among those within were the attractions Augustine thought most meaningful and compelling. He called them fruits of the first resurrection. Pilgrims in time could enjoy them. They would still find wars in their churches, yet those wars were waged against vices and not villains. ("The habits of sin" died hard.) Belligerence of any sort, even in the service of virtue, signaled that perfect peace was not yet available in time, although Augustine was known to call the church "the kingdom of heaven."[109]

That was premature. "The peace of the heavenly city is a perfectly ordered and perfectly harmonious fellowship." The peace of the churches was patchwork. Augustine was unsurprised to find slabs of the terrestrial city there. He had learned from the gospel of Matthew that there were scribes and Pharisees "in Moses' place." That told Augustine also to expect that the wicked would possess power in their churches. The faithful had to be on their guard. Some of the best preachers did not always practice what they preached. Bishops blundered, some criminally. The clergy who lacked character would doubtlessly hear God tell them to depart from him at judgment.[110] But for all that, the church was still "another beginning" in Augustine's judgment, as John Milbank now claims, although the bishop knew enough not to count on the "self-forgetting conviviality" that Milbank now describes.[111] Exemplary Christians therein passed into the celestial city, yet many others who received and administered the sacraments would not be among them. Self-serving rather than "self-forget[ful]," they were of Nineveh or Babylon, but, in time, they were still in and of the church.[112] As were the faithful, clergy and laity alike, those bound for the celestial city because their devotion and spiritual interests had mastered their material concerns. Faith "created them anew." They "died to the habits of this world" and "overthrew" Nineveh. They were of Jerusalem, but they worshipped and associated with less fortunate Christians in the church. To say that its politics differed from that of other communities *in hoc saeculo* is to insist on the obvious, but every church's "interwoven life" resembled that of the world, not the "perfectly ordered" fellowship of the celestial city. Augustine probably had the church in mind when he directed Christians to find refuge in this world, but perhaps something else occurred to him as well.[113]

If not the church, that is, perhaps that part of it where a longing for genuine justice and true peace was, in theory, most intense; perhaps the cloister. To the strange combination of stealth and swagger, which was the posture of choice among politicians Augustine met in Milan, the candor and humility in the cloister seemed an inviting contrast. On his return to Africa and for years thereafter, Augustine lived as a member of ascetic communities in Thagaste and Hippo. On becoming bishop, he took up private residence to offer episcopal hospitality, as expected, yet he apparently set up his "monastery of clergy" on the grounds. Select clergy with pastoral duties in the diocese, casting a cold eye on this wicked world, might find there a community of like-minded colleagues to sustain their collective passion for the celestial city.[114] But what began brightly ran into trouble and was very nearly wrecked. Probate proceedings revealed some monks owned property and held title to estates, despite their vows to divest. Augustine quickly saw that selfishness was at issue, selfishness that selfless love within should have kept outside. To preserve the integrity of the community, he promised to conduct a thorough inquiry into, and a complete report on, donations made to the community (and illicitly to individual members) and special dispensations allowed to, or assumed by, the monks. Those with property would be put out. Anyone guilty of lying about property would lose clerical standing. "Self-forgetting conviviality," the sociability of the unfallen angels, was the ideal, yet Augustine learned that the chances of maintaining a beatific sodality in this fallen world were slim to none.[115]

He once had confidence that the existence of some cinders of self-love was compatible with a consuming love for God, but that assurance eroded by the time he wrote the last books of his *City*. By then, he had discovered that *amor sui* and *amor dei,* the constitutive loves of each of the two cities, were mutually exclusive. In the end, the two loves and the two cities would be distinct. In time, even in convents, they were not. Incontestably, the cloister was "a snug harbor." Those within had some security, but the strains of common life severely tested the best intentions to rise above this wicked world. Under the pressure, many monks in harbor were known to crack (*crepuerunt*), Augustine said in a sermon that looks to have been unrelated to the protests against the propertied monks in Hippo. In this second address, his desperation seems to have obscured and perhaps replaced his determination to resolve cloister controversies. "Where then, is security? Here, nowhere," he mourned; "no place in this life, save in our hopes" for salvation "buoyed by God's promises."[116]

The "peace" God gives *in hoc saeculo* is more like a cold war or an uneasy armistice. Possibilities exist for mutual love and selfless conviviality but also for the dissension and incivility that inevitably curtail what there is, in time, of love. But the peace God promises is of a different order. *Hic nusquam*; there is no place for it here.[117]

That declaration and Augustine's straightforwardly critical remarks on church and cloister warn us not to plot the social coordinates of an Augustinian alternative. But what if, much as one of the *City*'s more celebrated readers, to whom we soon turn, Augustine had dreamed up a "no place," a *Nusquama* or utopia? What might it look like? He would likely have put it safely away from the ways that other polities conducted business—on an island, perhaps, seldom, if ever, visited. Augustine's utopians would have cared far more about changing lives than about making or changing laws. They would have no territorial ambitions. They would look to grow in hope rather than heft, and they would aspire to acquire patience, and not power. One of Augustine's sermons does, in fact, enjoin the faithful to change, grow, and aspire in that fashion, and it concludes with an exhortation consistent with the *City*'s explanations that salvation comes by expectation: *spera quod promisit*, "hope in what God promises."[118]

But the *City*, as we now know, leads scholars to claim that Augustine hoped also for meaningful political reform. He wrote there and elsewhere that to shirk public service was reprehensible. Christian magistrates were to rise above "the necessities" of office but not run from them, to interrogate, torture, punish, even execute, as "instruments" of laws they might otherwise abhor.[119] Only once in the *City* did he mention changing the laws, and the agents of change were not magistrates but martyrs.

> When our martyrs were charged with the crime of Christianity, which, they knew, would save them and give them great glory in eternity, they chose not to deny their faith to escape punishment. Instead, they confessed, professed, and preached their Christianity. They suffered faithfully and with fortitude. By dying with such impressive composure and piety, they shamed and forced a change in the laws that prohibited their religion.[120]

Laws were changed. Courts and municipal councils came to be staffed by Christians. But this world was still dangerously, sometimes disastrously, seductive. Given the choice between devotion to God's justice and dedication to establishing their own norms or standards, Augustine noticed, officials often became "enemies of grace."[121] To avoid that and them, Christian magistrates should cultivate the martyrs' mentality. They ought to be charitable and merciful, in disposition—and disengaged. Admittedly, the martyrs' disengagement, their principled and ostensibly apolitical stands, did change laws. Less was expected of Christian magistrates. It was easy for Augustine to imagine and advise them to temper enforcement with kindness. It was something altogether different, distressing, and past bearing to have them commit their religion and adjust their hopes to a reformist political practice or, for that matter, to any political strategy or practice. They thereby risked developing passions for power which would soon overwhelm them, have them dominating others, and implicate them in the very deceits that drove Augustine from politics in the 380s. He and his *City* surmised that, however well-intentioned, politically engaged protagonists were incorrectly political. It was incumbent on the Christian official to devise measures to resist evil but to avoid politicizing the good, because the pull of politics in this vexed existence, in time, was always a pull toward *amor sui*.

That seemed so to some of Augustine's readers, if not to others. Thomas More took special interest in the bishop's *City* while he was in London preparing for a career in public service. He studied law but lectured on Augustine at the church of St. Lawrence Jewry. For the next thirty years, More was preoccupied with challenges comparable to those his celebrated predecessor faced. We shall see whether he was one of the above "some" or one of the "others."

Chapter Five

Thomas More,
At Work in the World

Becoming Useful

Thomas More's Utopia was a remarkable place. Raphael Hythloday stumbled on the island society while exploring, and his so-obvious eagerness to explain its superiority to sixteenth-century Europe still captivates readers. According to More's conceit, he had observed legislators in England and on the continent *semper ordinantes,* always passing ordinances without formulating or enforcing a single one that satisfactorily maintained order. The Utopians, by contrast, ordered their island with very few laws and, it seems, without lawyers. Was lawyer More playfully, professionally disloyal for having Hythloday say so? Perhaps, but, then as now, lawyers hardly required a gaggle of laws to make a lawsuit and a living. Where two or three were gathered, there, too, contention! But Utopia was very different on that count as well: disputes were few and swiftly settled, Hythloday reported, defying English litigants and More's colleagues at court to measure themselves against the imaginary island's irenic citizens.[1] And lest his point appear too subtle, More scripted a Dickensian encounter between Hythloday and an English common lawyer who dared at dinner to defend capital punishment for petty thieves. Hythloday had gone on at length about larceny, poverty, prices, pastures, enclosures, and unemployment, indicting late medieval social policy. When the lawyer launched what promised to be a longer-winded rebuttal, he was suddenly silenced by their host. The prologue was all he managed to get out, yet it was enough to make him a buffoon.[2]

From what looks to have been More's low opinion of lawyers, one would never suspect that he was one of the profession's illustrious practitioners, an effective advocate for some of London's leading commercial interests and for the prevailing system of rules and writs. He believed the system yielded absolute certainty and order. And from reading More's remarks on law and lawyers in *Utopia,* one would never guess his reverence for his father, a lawyer for nearly four decades when news of his son's fantasy island broke. But on both counts—never suspecting and never guessing—we would be mistaken.

John More began his study of law at Lincoln's Inn, one of the prestigious Inns of the Court, three years before his son Thomas was born in 1478. By the time the younger More enrolled at Lincoln's, in 1495, his father had a thriving practice, though his promotion to the bench followed his son's success in the city and at court. His son, that is, had served in parliament, on various local commissions, as undersheriff in London, and on several cross-Channel embassies before he was named one of Henry VIII's councilors, and only then celebrated his father's appointment as a judge in the Courts of Common Pleas in 1518 and, two years later, in the Court of King's Bench. The law was good to both Mores, and, if we may trust the son's admirer, Erasmus of Rotterdam, the senior would have had the satisfaction of telling Thomas he had told him so. For, according to Erasmus, father had turned son from the study of classical literature to the study of law.[3] We are, I think, entitled to our suspicions. At the time he reported the paternal pressure, Erasmus was mourning his friend's loss to literature and could well have invented (or exaggerated) the story about the insistent father to excuse the son's apparent apostasy. Indeed, elsewhere Erasmus acknowledged that the law was an understandable career choice in late medieval London. Public service in the courts or at court beckoned the best.[4] Precocious young men naturally gravitated toward what the general population as well as grateful clients rewarded with esteem and influence. England's grammar schools would have prepared them, developing skills in argument. Thomas Stapleton, in the sixteenth century, suggested that, even when his More picked up Plato, he was looking for what was "useful in the government of the state and the preservation of civic order."[5]

One imagines that More attended to what was useful very soon after he started serving in the household of John Morton, who was then archbishop of

Canterbury and chancellor of the realm and, later, cardinal as well. Years before, Morton, while bishop of Ely, fled England for Flanders to escape the conspirators who put the Duke of Gloucester on the throne as King Richard III. When word nonetheless reached him that Richard had persuaded influential friends in Brittany to arrest his rival, Henry Tudor, Morton warned the target of the Bretons' treachery and probably saved his life. Shortly after becoming king, Henry saw to it that his savior and new chancellor was appointed to Canterbury. Morton, in turn, helped make Henry VII wealthy. He forbade cathedral chapters from meddling with the Crown's episcopal appointments, enabling the king to translate his bishops from see to see and gain financial advantages from frequent vacancies. Morton reputedly enjoined tax gatherers to be thorough or, as some subjects grumbled, ruthless. And he scrupulously (or ruthlessly) looked after his interests and Canterbury's ecclesiastical prerogatives. He was already filing petitions in Rome to have requests for immunities from his archiepiscopal jurisdiction denied, railing against the delinquency or laxity of colleagues who made those requests, consolidating his power in the church, and, as noted, proving his usefulness to the crown when Thomas More came to serve in 1490. William Roper, More's son-in-law and first biographer, suggested that Morton soon perceived his page's great promise and within a year sent him on to Oxford.[6]

We have better, direct evidence for what Thomas More thought of Morton. The chancellor's guile fascinated him. He featured it in one of the stories he collected for his history of Richard III's short reign, composed decades later but almost certainly seasoned with what he had heard in Morton's household. For Morton saw it all, for a time, from the best seats. He moved freely among Richard's intimates, feigning friendship, but he hoped to have Henry Tudor topple the regime. So, when crafty Morton ascertained that another Henry, duke of Buckingham, who helped choreograph Richard's rise to power, was unhappy with his reward, he did what he could to hasten the duke's defection. As More told it, Morton "fed [Buckingham] faire wordes and many pleasant praises" to stoke his sense of injury and envy of the new king. Indeed, that strategy and much else in More's tale were scripted to dramatize the dissembling at the center of political life. The story, though, is kind to Morton, as if dissimulation for a good cause—a Tudor triumph—was commendable. Morton knew the rules of the crooked game. He had "gotten by great experience . . . a depe insighte in politike worldlie driftes." He slyly shifted or "drifted" from the camp of Richard's early opposition into that of Richard, appeasing him at first while playing Buckingham, "so keeping himself . . . that he rather semed to follow [the duke] than to lead him."[7] After a failed rebellion, Morton fled—as noted—saved Henry Tudor, and then served him. That was how More found him, Henry VII's chancellor and archbishop of Canterbury. Even then, he must have been intrigued by Morton's survival for so long and in such a rough game. Every page at the chancellor's table would have known that Morton, all his adult life, was close to power and influential, *maximis in negotiis*.[8]

More put Morton at the head of the table when Hythloday confronted that loquacious lawyer in *Utopia*'s first book. The chancellor exhibited the good sense to listen to Hythloday's ideas about property, poverty, and punishment, which made his adversary squirm. More depicted his former employer and patron with affection. Morton could be gruff, he admitted, but the chancellor only wanted to see how many of the many petitioners parading before him had the presence of mind and courage of their convictions to withstand his glare and bluster. Causes built on sand eventually lay in ruins; Morton's masquerade only quickened the erosion. His pretend irritability, that is, seemed altogether serviceable to More. When Gloucester or Buckingham dissembled, the results were different, dangerous, and regrettable. Lawyers likewise could not be trusted to act a part honorably. Crouching over litigation, they generated more contention than they resolved. More's Morton, though, proved that an upright public servant, a man of character seasoned by experience and "skilled in law," might mislead usefully and be admired.[9]

More's take on dissimulation and indirection may have developed soon after he left grammar school for the chancellor's "court." We might be able to say with greater certainty, though, if we knew how he got there. Roper mentioned that More's father was responsible, but John More's career was inching along during the 1480s. He was not yet the man of modest influence he was to become. Like Patricius, Augustine's father, he was landed, locally dutiful, yet not terribly conspicuous. "Promotion eluded him," as John Guy notices, so his son's good fortune would have seemed all the more striking.[10] Somehow, and suddenly, the youngster was lifted from obscurity and surrounded by celebrity, cunning, and competition at one of the busiest households in the realm. He came into contact with prospective patrons whose readiness to assist him would have increased into the 1490s, as Londoners started recognizing and rewarding his father's services. Nonetheless, the senior More was only a local lawyer when his son managed to get close to Morton and then, briefly, to Oxford to study literature.

At the age of sixteen, he was at New Inn for basic instruction in jurisprudence and legal etiquette. Two years later, he entered Lincoln's Inn, where his father had completed legal studies. And five years on, Thomas More was called to the bar as a junior barrister. While still studying law, though, he retained his interests in literature and in its devotees, including Erasmus of Rotterdam, whose correspondence is one of the few contemporary sources we have for the aspiring lawyer's life at the time. In 1499, Erasmus was visiting England at the invitation of Baron Mountjoy, one of his students in Paris. More came to call on the host and hosted and, probably at the former's bidding, walked Erasmus to Eltham where three of the king's four children resided. Mountjoy apparently wanted to impress Erasmus—and perhaps to introduce him to prospective royal patrons. Erasmus told the story to explain why he later composed a poem for the king's second son and eventual heir (Henry VIII). He also noted, though, how distressed he became, discovering himself at a court of sorts without a scripted greeting or gift. "I expected nothing and so had prepared nothing," he let on; "I was rather peeved with More for having failed to warn me." At dinner, Prince Henry asked Erasmus for some verses, which he later composed and sent, but that did not cover his embarrassment. He remembered it three decades later, still resenting that he was caught off guard. Historians of the early Tudor court are fond of the episode and embarrassment, as are biographers of the two guests at Eltham, yet More's ease of access to the prince is never remarked. Still a student of law, he appears to have been welcomed in the households of the realm's rich and famous, and that, much as his earlier stay at Morton's, attests a career trajectory that kept him among the prosperous and powerful, led him into parliament and public service, and landed him, finally, as the king's chancellor.[11]

But, to repeat, he relished conversation and correspondence with the *eruditi* of his time. He enjoyed having his allusions to the texts and ideas of classical antiquity ricochet from one colleague to another, but he regretted that he had less and less leisure for study as his law practice prospered. More confided that he was out of place in the courts and at court, often declared he would rather have been reading, and told Erasmus he was grateful their scholarly friends were praying for his release from public life, from "the pettiness of politics."[12] We will occasionally return to those friends, for their solicitude elicited not only More's complaints about government service but also his criticisms of their idealism. But at the moment certain of his other "pursuits" hold our interest—his piety and plan to be a priest—because he seemed to some to be "more zealous to become a saint than a scholar." Stapleton said so, claiming young More was then known for his various austerities, looked to be ordained, and hoped to join an order of friars. Of course, those ambitions would not have precluded a useful career in civil administration. Morton was both priest and public official. Mendicants were bishops. But, Stapleton continued, More came to realize he would be unable to conquer the temptations that stood between him and celibacy, temptations that were God's way of forcing him to "face the difficulties of public life" as a layman.[13]

Is there any truth to this? More resided at or near the London Charterhouse, worshiping, if not also living with, the Carthusians, while studying law and availing himself of their spiritual counsel. And the semi-seclusion of the Charterhouse was a perfect place to contemplate a career far from what More called "the city's deceits."

> For in the city what is there to move one to live well? But rather, when a man is straining in his own power to climb the steep path of virtue, it turns him back by a thousand devices and sucks him back by its thousand enticements. Wherever you betake yourself, on one side, nothing but feigned love and the honeyed poisons of smooth flatterers resound; on the other, fierce hatreds, quarrels, the din of the forum murmur against you. Wherever you turn your eyes, what else will you see but confectioners, fishmongers, butchers, cooks, poulterers, fishermen, fowlers, who supply the materials for gluttony and the world and the world's lord, the devil?[14]

A *contemptus mundi* of this sort is not what one would expect from a young man preparing to be useful. Or is it? For More was chronicling corruption, deceit, and excess to congratulate his friend John Colet—rumored to be the next dean of St. Paul's Cathedral in London, if not already named—for having retreated to a rural refuge. And, against that grain, although in the same letter, he implored Colet to return. Other London priests, he said, were not taken seriously. They were ineffective, perceived to be infected with the very worldliness they were preaching against. Later, to a convocation of clergy from all Canterbury's dioceses, Dean Colet cited conformity with the world as the chief cause of the clergy's corruption, echoing More's criticism. Nonetheless, it is still unclear whether the wickedness of the world and the shortage of competent clerical reformers tempted More either into seclusion or into the priesthood.[15]

Stapleton was certain, as was Nicholas Harpsfield before him, but both owed their certainty to Erasmus, who had a habit of embroidering to make his English friends—Colet as well as More—attractive and Luther repulsive to his continental correspondents.[16] And some biographers—embroidering on the embroidery—think the horns of More's dilemma, priest or lust, narratively irresistible. Richard Marius remembered More was lecturing at the time on Augustine's *City of God*. "We have no idea what More said," Marius admits, yet he is startlingly confident that, "absorbed as he was in Augustine's work, More would have been saturated with the teaching that those who fall to sensuality will continue their plummeting into hell itself." Marius has More imagine that marriage would license yet diminish his lust, whereas holy orders would leave his "sensuality half tamed at best" and make him a horrid priest. Assuming that Erasmus' two parts gave us More whole, Marius propped up his subject's supposed flirtation with ordination with two flimsy supports: his admiration for John Colet and his lectures on Augustine, both of which "indicate" (to Marius) that More "was seriously contemplating entry into the priesthood." Marius is quite correct about one thing: Erasmus' reminiscence does require corroboration, but coupling admiration with imitation or inferring More's vocation from lectures lost to us cannot supply it. And there is good reason to doubt whether lawyer More took the case of *priest v. lust* seriously: his son-in-law, his most knowledgeable biographer, did not. Roper mentioned More's fondness for the Charterhouse but said nothing about his brooding on ordination or claustration.[17]

But Marius is not alone. Alistair Fox also supposes that "rival impulses" dogged More long after he overcame "his first reaction" "to withdraw from the world altogether," after, Geoffrey Elton says, he "gave up his youthful ambition to enter the cloister." The sketchiness of the evidence prohibits us from saying so for certain, yet More's time with Morton, access to royalty, legal studies in London, and esteem for his father suggest that we would be as close or closer to the mark if we remember how little is left of that "first reaction" or "youthful ambition" and date earlier than the others have what Elton calls the "emergence" of More "as one who values possessions . . . likes being important and likes deprecating such pleasure even more."[18]

The deprecating goes some distance toward explaining how More could have given the impression of having been dragged into legal practice, into London's "boardrooms," into the courts, and eventually to Henry VIII's court, while, as John Guy shows, with liberal reference, More "pursued his legal career in earnest."[19] The Carthusians and Augustine's *City* may have tempted him to rise above politics, yet, by then, he had taken other bait and was hooked. He daily left the precincts of the Charterhouse to complete his studies at Lincoln's Inn. He lectured on Augustine near the Guildhall in London, a center of the city's commercial life and now the banking district. More was intensely, restlessly interested in the world into which he said he had allegedly been "dragged."[20] And, to an extent, his scholarly friends, including Erasmus, were as well. They were known to set aside their contempt for public officials when patronage or pensions were on offer. But they were different from More. He trained as a lawyer. They had not. At a surprisingly early age and stage in his career, he was closely connected with the Tudor court. True, More shared his friends' passions for literature and their dedication to eloquence. He acknowledged the wisdom of their conventional and, as Elton adds, "conventionally sincere talk of the intellectual involved in the absurdities of a public existence."[21] But More braved the city's and government's diabolical "devices," the very "enticements" that he warned Colet to avoid. There are grounds for proposing that he was less than enthusiastic about "the promise of the secular order," and more than suspicious of its "feigned love" and "fierce hatreds." Yet he launched himself at the courts and at the court in the service of that order. Perhaps he thought it not impossible to be different from feigning and ferocious courtiers, if not possible to make a significant difference among them.[22]

Ambitions and Illusions

It is not always easy to sort out More's enthusiasms, suspicions, and sneers. His ode on the occasion of Henry VIII's coronation in 1509, an apparent attempt to ingratiate himself, proves the point. Its excitement seems genuine enough. More's friend Mountjoy was equally, effusively optimistic, writing to have their friend Erasmus return to England, find patrons, be coddled, and grow prosperous and influential.[23] More's poem promised prosperity to the people and seems to have looked vaguely for position and influence for himself. He wrote, though, as if the people needed no persuading, as if they instinctively preferred what lay ahead to the "secrets," "sadness," "tears," and taxes that had preceded.

> Men and women of all ages and social castes see no reason to stay at home and not take part as their new king auspiciously marks the start of his rule. Wherever he goes his eager subjects crowd around leaving him hardly room to pass. Homes enroute are filled with well-wishers. Rooftops barely support the weight of admirers. Everywhere, applause. . . . [T]o see the king once is not satisfactory. People move about to get another glimpse. It thrills them to see him again and even a third time, and why should it not be a thrill? Nature has fashioned nothing more worthy of affection. He stands out [excelsior] amidst his thousand companions. . . . And if nature had not forbidden it, we would be able to see that the excellence of his mind matched the impressiveness of his physical appearance.

More believed he could see—and his clients could count on—something just as important to them as their new king's intelligence and *gravitas*, namely, his benevolent disposition toward the realm's commercial interests. The new regime was sure to protect property and profits fairly earned (*nullo dolo*). Taxes then inhibiting trade were to be repealed. More's poem and special pleading, in effect, lobbied for and cheerfully anticipated the economic recovery of those who employed him.[24]

And, as suggested, More may have been thinking of his prospects as well. A line nearly buried in the coronation ode congratulated Henry VIII for having selected virtuous and learned men to receive the responsibilities and rewards of public office that, at the end of his father's reign, had gone to the crooked and ignorant. More hardly appeared overeager. Still, he could not have drafted that observation without conjuring appointments yet to be made. And retracing the royal procession and chronicling the realm's adulation was, in this instance, work for an ambitious man.[25]

Ambitious, but not naïvely so and imperceptive. Several of More's other poems, probably composed a few years after the coronation ode—yet conceivably before—show him well aware of a sinister side of public service. Sovereigns, he tells us, are unsteady characters. Officials usually derive great satisfaction from being close to the center of power, from having their king's ear, but those close get kicked first when rage replaces receptivity to good counsel.[26] Monarchs may seem mild for a time after their accession, More remarked in another poem; the honeymoon over, however, they tend to turn predatory and become insatiable. "A well-fed fly" always wants more and, he went on, is as much a nuisance, sponge, and grifter as a hungry one.[27]

More seems to have been writing from experience. Son-in-law Roper offered an anecdote that has the young lawyer and sometimes poet publicly expressing disapproval of the government's greed during the parliament of 1504 and makes him responsible for its refusal to collect funds to cover the costs of, *inter alia*, Margaret Tudor's marriage to the king of Scotland. Roper sketched a complicated plot that King Henry VII allegedly coordinated to get even, but there are reasons to doubt many details. For one, Henry was not altogether denied his reward for suturing England and Scotland; his "demands" were not "clean overthrown," as Roper supposed. For another, the plot to penalize father and son for the latter's part in parliamentary discussions is nowhere independently discussed. It sounds far-fetched, yet there is nothing that prohibited young More from then sitting in the Commons, and his opposition to the king's taxes seems subsequently to have earned him honorary membership in London's most influential livery company.[28] Add to that a coronation poem in which More indelicately harped on the dead king's depredations, associating fear, danger, loss, and grief with the old regime, gaiety and gain with the new, and one could infer a grudge against the government of Henry VII. To be sure, there is something conventional about More's ode—regime change may tempt a poet excitedly to ring out the old—but there is something rather daring as well. More warned Henry VIII, with a thinly veiled reference to his father's regime, that exercising power to collect what one can is just the kind of misrule that enfeebles the best brains and ruins the most robust character.[29] He was not shy about exposing the perils of political celebrity as well as the public's fascination with it. True, his ode chronicled the citizens' exuberance without criticizing it and added to the glamour of the occasion. Another poem, however, mocked precisely that. Its verses put a coarse peasant from the countryside on the route of a royal procession. Everyone else hailed the king as he passed, while More's peasant thought their exaggerated enthusiasm strange. For all that he saw was a normal man in a colorful outfit (*picta veste*) astride a big horse. Thomas More hailed Henry VIII, hoping for advantage for his clients and, likely, for himself. He was the crowd and something of a sycophant describing its passions, but he was also that unawed and iconoclastic peasant. As the century's second decade and the new reign got started, he had ambitions but no illusions.[30]

More, Pico, and Erasmus

Did he have regrets? The argument that he did seems substantiated by his decision to translate Gianfrancesco Pico's biography of his uncle, Giovanni Pico Della Mirandola. More readied it as a gift for a family friend, along with versifications of some of the elder Pico's aphoristic instructions and with translations of three of his letters. We are unsure whether he prepared the package months or years before its publication in 1510, but we do learn that its recipient was about to become a nun and that, unsurprisingly, More selected materials to encourage her. She would have known that she faced "losse" and "adversitie," living as a recluse, so she likely appreciated the reminder that "thou ne shalt susteyne (be not adred) halfe the dolour, griefe, and adversitie that [Christ] al redy soffred hath for the."[31] Pico mentioned death's unpredictability only briefly. He left his readers to conclude that they were wise to set aside frivolous pursuits. But his short *de contemptu*, in More's version, exfoliates: "deth stelith on ful slily" while humanity "besily provide and care for its disport, revel, myrth, and play."[32] Conceivably, More warned himself as he consoled his first reader. Yet to guess that his gift was also "a critical analysis of his own personal dilemma" looks to be stretching the conceivable toward the unthinkable. If, as Alistair Fox says, two "sides" of a "perturbed" Thomas More did find expression in what he selected, translated, and extended—"worldly ambition together with a proclivity toward 'wantonness' and an otherworldly recoil from it"—then perhaps he was trying to decide how to respond to compromises his chosen career and marriage forced on him. He might have embarked on a different course among the Carthusians, but, oddly, that would have been to try what Pico never did.[33]

Nor did Pico marry. His life, in fact, was quite unlike More's. After study-ing in Padua and traveling for several years, Pico ran afoul of church authori-ties by presenting nine hundred propositions in Rome in 1486. His thinking ranged from physics to philosophy and into theology. Many of his remarks were controversial, and Pico had not bothered to hedge them about or trivial-ize them with qualifications. Some were condemned, and the condemnation changed his life.[34]

More learned of the confrontation from Pico's nephew who acknowl-edged his uncle's impudence. Translating, More referred to it as "hye minde and proud purpose" and criticized Pico's appetites for admiration and im-mortality: he was too eager to be "perpetually prayse[d]." Gianfrancesco cheerfully reported what happened next: rejection in Rome turned his uncle into a better man. And More agreed: God was choreographing both the oppo-sition and the aftermath to have the elder Pico apply himself to pious pur-poses.[35] He pondered joining the Dominican friars but decided against it, retiring nonetheless to dedicate himself to his studies. He was peculiarly fond of the occult, of the intellectual gadgetry that discomforted others, yet he had an answer for those "others." Enlightened authorities, Pico declared, never pounced on unfamiliar opinions—even if erroneous—merely because of their unfamiliarity. Errors begged correction and did no lasting harm. Wick-edness made heretics; mistakes did not.[36]

More might have concurred, at least until he encountered the evangelical anticlericals during the 1520s, after which he viewed persistent disagreement as wickedly heretical. As we shall soon see, his position came to resemble Au-gustine's against the Donatists. But, years before, Pico's plea for tolerance may have seemed as attractive as his piety. Still, if More thought that his own time at—then away from—the Carthusians was at all reminiscent of Pico's brush with—and pass on—the Dominicans, it is unlikely that Pico would have landed in purgatory in More's translation (as in Gianfrancesco's original) for having made that choice.[37] No doubt, More admired "th'gret plenteouse habundance" of Pico's virtues as well as Pico's intellectual virtuosity, and he added a section to the biography to underscore the late medieval and renais-sance commonplace that nobility deriving from character was more worthy of praise than nobility inherited at birth. Pico's nephew celebrated his uncle's sterling character as well yet emphasized the range of his reading, capacity of his memory, and impressive intelligence that resulted.[38] That also struck More who echoed the observation that Pico, though widely knowledgeable, so impressed acquaintances with the extent and profundity of what he knew about any one subject, they believed it to be his only study. His memory, curiosity, character, and ordeal thus composed a lesson for Christians tempted to arrogance. He resolved to enjoin his friends to virtue rather than to avenge his humiliation in Rome. He talked at every opportunity about morality. His goodwill, courtesy, and convictions were said to have converted many with a message More repeated: the grief of this life pales before what Christ suffered "for the love of us."[39]

Pico's was an exemplary life, at least in his nephew's presentation and in More's translation, which starred virtues that applied to the active as well as contemplative lives of Christians. When he read, then rewrote, Pico's exclamation, "how grete is the felicite of a juste man," More elected not to associate felicity—greater than "all praise of people and all earthli glory"—with the convent. The biography was not narrowly devotional, as John Guy has noted: it "functioned as a guide to virtuous living . . . not validating any particular standpoint as to the merits of the" monastic or the mundane. Or, as Gianfrancesco intimated and More made explicit, "glory folowith virtue as an inseparable servant" whichever course or calling the Christian chose.[40]

One finds much the same sentiment in Erasmus' manual for moral theology, the *Enchiridion militis christiani*, written years before More's Pico translations. Erasmus had been approached by a pious woman whose husband's busy life apparently kept him from studying scripture and becoming as virtuous as his wife would have liked. Her husband, the "Christian soldier" of Erasmus' title, was neither monk nor crusader, the callings to which that term was often applied, because those who answered such "calls" vowed to endure ordeals of self-denial "as good soldiers of Christ," that is, to follow the apostle Paul's instructions (2 Timothy 2:3). Erasmus' "soldiers" were to live ordinary lives, to complete their business outside the convents. He wrote to supply them with a weapon, with an *Enchiridion* or "handy dagger" for the wars they would encounter there. It was intended, he said, to take the place of those books on virtue written by Thomas Aquinas which were too bulky for men on the move to carry and consult. "Who can haul around his *Secunda secundae*," his *sententiae* on the virtues, Erasmus asked, allowing nevertheless that "living well is everyone's affair; Christ wants everyone to have easy access" to principles that develop Christian character. Reclusive scholars have time to leaf through the pages of massive tomes on morality. But Christian soldiers with proprietors' obligations and commercial interests could rely on Erasmus' *Enchiridion* for a short course in applied theology to identify "a sure path to felicity." They would have his pocket guide with rules and rationale with which they might "set [their] sights on Christ as the sole objective" and "direct all their desires, efforts, leisure, and business towards him."[41]

Special vows were unnecessary. Complicated regulations, wearying routines, and high cloister walls might help some Christians be humble, patient, chaste, and charitable, yet Erasmus valued as highly what could be achieved "in the world." There, a Christian might feel exposed, uncertain. It was a messier place than the convent. In the terrestrial city, people were tempted to act only for personal advantage. But if Christian soldiers recalled what Christ's death conferred on them and comprehended what his life might mean for theirs—if they "set their sights" rightly—they would not "calculate whether a neighbor's advantage was also theirs [or] how well they knew their neighbor. Perish the thought" (*nihil horum*)! Christians would instinctively treat others as brothers, without vows to that effect.[42] Erasmus distinguished that prospect from the immorality reported of many monasteries at the time. He had an explanation for what happened among nuns and monks: conduct was unimpeachable when convents were just finding their feet, he said, yet as wealth increased, discipline deteriorated.[43] With property came privilege; with privilege, envy; with envy, came insolence and pretence (*lubricam fidem*). That seemed obvious to Erasmus, and, he accused, it was obvious as well to the convents' superiors who let those they supervised go through the motions, repeating penitential psalms, though uncontrite. Fasting and praying, monks and nuns withheld what God wanted most: their humility and charity. They were known for professed abstinence, known by their diet and dress. But Christians were known by their character and that character could be cultivated by "soldiers" immersed in ordinary affairs.[44]

But Erasmus counseled his "soldiers" not to expect their ordinary affairs to settle in place and satisfy their desires for friends, fortune, and honor. Reputation and revenue were always at risk; "a thousand perils" threatened every venture. Merchants engaged in overseas trade understood the uncertainty, and the *Enchiridion* made their anxieties stand for those of others "in the world," not yet "striv[ing] with determination" to serve "under Christ's banners." They should learn that "fortune often follows those who flee from it and flees those who follow it [and that] whatever occurs to those who love God cannot but be favorable."[45]

"Glory folowith virtue as an inseparable servant": that claim is not identical with those in the *Enchiridion*, but the sentiment behind it is quite similar to Erasmus'. Hence, it is hard to imagine that Thomas More, translating Gianfrancesco, gave no thought to his friend's design for Christian soldiering. More and Erasmus had known each other for ten years when the Pico translation was published. Pico's "twelve rules, partly exciting [and] partly directing a man in spiritual batail," looks to have inspired Erasmus' manual for Christian soldiering. More translated those rules with the rest of his Pico, turning them, along with a list of "twelve weapons," into a series of brief ballads.[46]

> When thou in flame of the temptation fryest
> Think on the very lamentable payne
> Think on the piteouse crosse of wofull Christ
> Think on his blode let out at every vayne.[47]

If Pico did not put Erasmus and More onto spiritual warfare, at the very least, he assured them that a "byttir, sharpe, and sowre" belligerence led to the overthrow of "the enemy," variously, the devil, temptation, and complacence. More's objective: "glorious victorie, tryumphe, and conquest" leading to a Christian soldier's "peace" which was pleasing to God. The battle imagery also punctuated the three letters that More chose to translate, two from Pico to Gianfrancesco, the third to Andreus Corneus, a public official in Urbino. In all three, Pico commented on courtiers' "battles," struggles that his two correspondents knew only too well.

> Be glad said [the apostle James] my brethren when ye fall in diverse temptations . . . for what hope is ther of glory if ther be none hope of victory, or what place is ther for victory wher ther is no bataill. He is called to the crowne and triumphe which ys provocked to the conflict. . . . [Yet] of the court and service of this world ether is nothing that I need to write unto the, the wretchedness whereof the experience hit selfe hath taught the and daily teachith. In obtaining the favour of the princes, in purchasing the friendship of the company, in

ambitiouse laboure for offices and honowres, what an hepe of hevines
ther is, how gret anguish, how much besynes and trouble I may
rather lerne of the then teche ye.[48]

Pico took a similar tack in another of the letters. He described courtiers
as swimmers caught in swift currents, "born forth with the violence of evel
custom, as hit were with the boystious course of the streme." They thrashed
about and lost all sense of decency. They would surely libel his nephew ("back-
bite thy vertue"), as they would any honorable rival. No wonder, Gianfrancesco's biography reported his uncle's distaste for "palaces of the proud and
powerful." Pico stayed away and, according to his nephew's sketch, once jok-
ingly protested (*pauxillum subridens*) that if ever compelled to choose, doubtlessly he would consent to a conventional marriage and to a dreaded domes-
ticity before being drawn into a public office. But to the "servitude" of either,
Gianfrancesco and More knew, Pico preferred his study and his freedom.[49]
      Corneus rebuked him for precisely that preference. Cautious to a fault
and far too reclusive, Pico "spent tyme inough" with books, he said, and
should get on with "actuall besines."[50] Pico disagreed and, mixing self-
disclosure with counter-complaint, he must sometimes have seemed utterly
incorrigible. "Abiding fermely in this opinion," he

> set more bi my little house, my study, the pleasure of my bokes, the
> reste and peace of my mynde then by all your kingis palaces, all your
> commune besines, all your glory, all the advauntage that ye hawke
> aftir, and all the favour of the court. Nor I loke not for this frute of
> my study that I may thereby herafter be tossed in the flode and rom-
> beling of your worldly besynesse, but that I may ones bring forth the
> children that I travaile on, that I may give owt some bokes of myn
> owne to the commune profit which may sumwhat savour, if not of
> cunnyng yet at the lest wyse of wit and diligence.[51]

Pico thought philosophers who sought "the commune profit" amid the
"rombeling of . . . worldly besynesse" were mercenaries who sold out their
studies, as some might say today. Yet he relented in a section of his reply to
Corneus that More left untranslated. He styled himself a loyal subject and
hinted that, in a pinch, he could be "turned."[52] We can only guess why he

relented—or what moved him to "give owt" political counsel in the books he wrote for "commune profit"—but perhaps we have been shuttling between Italy and England too long already. Besides, the line that More added to Corneus' appeal, as imagined or repeated by Pico, is of much greater interest for our purpose. It occurred to More to elaborate or amplify Corneus' advice. Pico's correspondent dared not deny the contentment that would come to those who devoted "wit and diligence" to improving their minds. "I wolde have you outwardly occupied also," More has him urge. "Love them both and use them both, aswell study as worldly occupation."[53]

More's elaboration suggests that the Pico translations were not part of his own supposed recoil from "worldly occupation" and public life. What has been described as More's "well known feeling against holding public office" was, in this text and context, Pico's sentiment.[54] Indeed, if, as is likely, the translations were finished shortly before publication in 1510, More worked on them "in the flode and rombeling of [his] worldly besynesse." Four children distracted him, as did a thriving legal practice. He had served once in parliament and would soon serve again, soon to lose a wife and then remarry, all the while acquiring a reputation for reconciling London's rival commercial interests.[55] He was, as it happens, closer to Corneus and to Pico's nephew than to Pico. Whereas Pico typically cared neither to "hawke aftir" nor dwell on "commune besines" and political advantage, Gianfrancesco strained to keep peace among partisans of Girolamo Savonarola, a Dominican who agitated for political change and moral regeneration in Florence into the 1490s. Long after their leader's excommunication (1497) and execution (1498), they found refuge at Gianfrancesco's court in Mirandola, a font of Savonarolan literature into the 1520s. For his part, their host continued to walk a fine line, exposing corruption and indolence in high places without incriminating the highest political and religious authorities. Sly, self-deprecating on occasion, he managed to avoid incurring official censure.[56]

But we are ahead of our story. Earlier, as Gianfrancesco labored to repossess his family's estates in Mirandola, More was reaching for new responsibilities in London. In 1510, he was appointed as undersheriff, a position that required him, every Thursday, to listen to creditors' concerns and small claims of all sorts in the Guildhall. On request, he offered legal counsel to the city's various commissions, serving on one to repair London Bridge and on others tackling public health issues. From 1514, he was supervisor of the sewers. And he assisted the city's chief legal officer, its Recorder, representing London in the courts at Westminster. Apparently indefatigable, More also drafted his history of the reign of Richard III, a narrative that, as Peter Ackroyd notices, fondly lingers in the London streets and knowingly remarks on municipal government. Doubtlessly, More's contempt for King Richard reflected that of Morton and borrowed from Tacitus, Sallust, and Suetonius to achieve dramatic effect, but what More took from the others ought not to obscure his improvisations. The protagonists of his piece were late fifteenth-century Londoners, the honorable citizens of the city, whose descendants he and his father were serving. They had resisted Richard's public relations initiatives in a sensational display of what looked to More to have been incomparably good sense. Lawyer More's clients thus acquired a peculiar pedigree. At least in his history, their ancestors shared More's frustrations with the games government played, while they, as he, were spliced into the government's pageants and protocols. Participation was inescapable; so fishmongers, bakers, and other tradesmen hired Thomas More to protect their interests.[57]

"I am constantly engaged in legal business, either pleading or hearing," he wrote Peter Giles, explaining (and complaining) that his work as advocate and arbiter left him no time for literature. That same letter, however, accompanied a copy of More's finest fiction, his *Utopia,* which contained a description of an imaginary island republic, conceived and composed while he was in or around Bruges on business in 1515.[58]

He had been to Bruges before. London clients had sent him there to negotiate favorable conditions for their overseas trade. They had been acting "with thavise of Thomas More, gentilman" for nearly a decade when problems with the Flemish arrangements to buy and sell English wool and cloth drew him back. In those years, he refereed squabbles among members of— and between—the leading London trade fellowships that shared Mercers' Hall. In 1509, he served as the principal negotiator when an emissary from Antwerp came to the Hall with concessions. The following year, the Mercers put More in parliament, in part, to safeguard the prerogatives of entrepreneurs ambitious for the Anglo-Netherlands commodity trade, Londoners with whom he frequently conferred and whom, it seems, he represented readily and well.[59]

Ambition, politics, and commercial competition: the prevailing view is that More wrote his *Utopia* to question all three. It is often suggested that

Raphael Hythloday, who explains in the text why Utopians live harmoniously, speaks for More when he disdains place-seekers, shuns public service, and conjures a commonwealth in which property is held equally by all. Hythloday, however, wants to live as he lists and, in that, resembles the Pico of More's translations.[60] Yet we see at once that Thomas More was different: "constantly engaged in legal business." "Hearing," he was guided by custom and law. "Pleading," he was ruled by his clients' crises and interests. More went where he was told to go, on "short warnyng."[61] Quite possibly he envied the freedom he created for Hythloday when he took time off from talk of tolls and taxes to draft his *Utopia*. Yet Hythloday was not an emblem of More's regret that he had entered public service. He was, and is, however, a signal that More was less hopeful than many of his scholarly colleagues about the prospects for meaningful political reform in 1516. He was the gadfly; his creator, the pragmatist. Their conversations in *Utopia* about work in this world, "designedly enigmatic," George Logan says, deserve a separate chapter.[62]

Chapter Six

Utopia?

Hythloday on Power and Integrity

Utopia gives us Thomas More's doubts about what the best courtiers and consultants could do to improve public administration. To defend that statement we must look at both parts of More's text, the discourse he wrote in Bruges in 1515 while negotiating favorable trade arrangements for London commercial interests and the dialogue he composed in 1516, on his return to England.

The discourse was a relatively straightforward report of Raphael Hythloday's discovery of an exemplary, harmonious island society. More's fictional explorer and narrator, in effect, put the island's customs on a catwalk, parading them in Latin before his creator's scholarly friends, the text's intended and first readers, to whom many of that society's traits must have seemed attractive—and a few of them, perhaps, seductive. Still, Hythloday's discourse, More's first *Utopia*, was not a typical modeling job. Readers can be assumed to have recognized, and almost certainly to have appreciated, those pieces of Plato's *Republic* on exhibit along with some Seneca—specifically, his efforts to reconcile Epicureanism with Stoicism. And scholarly readers should have been delighted with the way Utopians honored their scholars. More's morally scrupulous friends were no doubt pleased with Utopians' modesty, industry, and decency. Yet, as we shall see, everything in Utopia was not to everyone's liking. Hythloday's enthusiasm for the distribution of resources in Utopia, *omnia omnium,* was controversial. More expressed reservations in the text, but he was not about to have his narrator back down. On the contrary, when he revised the discourse, he had Hythloday eulogize the Utopians' renunciation of private property. "Though no one owns anything, everyone is rich." When citizens stop pursuing selfish interests, they possess peace of mind. They know their progeny are provided for, as are society's less fortunate. Security and social justice![1]

More scripted a nod to Augustine at this point in the narrative. Hythloday invites readers to compare Utopians' policies and practices with "the justice that prevails among other nations, among whom I'll be damned if I can discover the slightest trace of justice and fairness." He all but endorses Augustine's observation that political cultures in time, "among other nations," were always more or less *un*just. Yet whereas the fifth-century bishop presumed that "genuine justice" could be experienced later and elsewhere—in the celestial city—More's narrator found it nowhere, nusquam—in Utopia.[2]

He described his nowhere in the discourse, but when More revised and expanded its concluding remarks, he also extended the preamble, turning it into a dialogue between Hythloday and himself. More entered his script a pragmatist. He agreed with Hythloday, his idealist, that politics in England and on the continent discredited everyone who came to counsel at court. He agreed that significant, wholesome change was unlikely. Still, he could not sanction Hythloday's refusal to advise princes. He defended in the dialogue a public servant's readiness to play the game of politics by the terrible rules of the times, if only to do damage control. Then, in the discourse that follows the dialogue in the printed text, Hythloday introduces a civilization in which the rules were radically different. But my précis misleads if it suggests More's message is self-evident. For one thing, Hythloday seems to undermine his insistence on staying removed from politics in the dialogue, that is, he offers political counsel there and with his discourse. On other counts as well, *Utopia*'s two books are subtle and slippery. It is hard to make out what More was trying to tell his friends and hard to see what he and Hythloday are trying to tell us. Ascertaining both is necessary, however, if we are to appreciate what More thought was politically incorrect.

We might start with what we learned in the last chapter, specifically, that More was actively engaged in, although rather ambivalent about, the public affairs of his day. Whether in London entertaining emissaries from abroad or being entertained in Bruges or Antwerp, he apparently understood how important it was in the run-up to deliberations to impress diplomats with power materialized in brilliantly decorated halls, fine clothes, and striking jewelry. Nevertheless, his king, clients, and hosts, sparing no expense to impress, seemed rather ludicrous to him.

So he dreamed up Utopians who scorned extravagance. His Hythloday illustrates how little costly fabrics and precious metals meant to them by reporting what happened when ambassadors came expecting their great coats, gold chains, and gemmed fingers would awe the island's statesmen and give them some advantage in negotiations. But instead, all the fur and glitter embarrassed Utopia's elders and amused their children.[3] More and his close political and commercial associates accepted that political exhibitionism was *de rigueur*. But he and his scholarly friends—whom history textbooks now call humanists, and who occasionally referred to themselves as Erasmians, *Erasmici*—hoped for something different, for a culture that invested less in apparel and appearances. Erasmus and More, as we learned, were particularly close. Writing as More was contemplating his *Utopia,* Erasmus submitted that wise and virtuous rulers did not share the common folks' fascination with ornament. As for the commoners, they ought to be taught to look less for excess or extravagance from their leaders, he said, and look to them more for economy, prudence, and integrity.[4]

But as long as the crowd's loyalty could be acquired by a good show, majesty would materialize power in pageant, plate, or wardrobe—or, more likely, all three. For early modern monarchs required loyalty at home if they were to feed their extraordinary appetites for conquest abroad. King Henry VIII of England had to keep subjects in awe and in line, if he were to annex more of the continent than just Calais and Tournai. The Valois kings of France must discourage discontent at home if they were to take more of Italy. The Habsburgs were hungry for territory. Scotland longed to expand south. The *Erasmici* were known to urge would-be aggressors to be consoled with what God (and heredity) left them to rule, because nothing exhausted subjects' goodwill and wrecked regimes more efficiently than foreign wars that hijacked sovereigns' attention. How could princes not know that cruelty and conquest did nothing to solve their dynastic or domestic problems? Thomas More knew the answer: princes were reared to be soldiers. No wonder they were obsessed with arms and with the land and glory that might be acquired by arms. To counsel princes to make or to keep peace was senseless, his Hythloday said. Why set oneself so impossible a task?[5]

Current court wisdom was against anyone who counselled peace. The most influential courtiers, that is, reasoned that security depended on a standing, seasoned army. To have soldiers obtain experience, their "seasoning," kings must manufacture causes for war. From the pacifist's point of view, the excuses were transparently fluff and flimsy. To Hythloday and, presumably, to More as well, wars begot wars and undermined security. Yet Hythloday was created to say that there was little chance such an opinion or objection could counter peers' ostensibly provident belligerence.[6]

Those peers were entirely wrongheaded (*morosophi*), but at least they used their heads. *Utopia* has greater contempt for counselors devoid of reason and opinion, for yes men who wagered that flattery was the surest route to promotion. According to Hythloday, they put the court beyond meaningful reform. Rulers, raised for war and addicted to adoration, were unlikely to reprove them and far likelier to reprimand their critics. Hence, the conditions of court life, in effect, "immunized" every prince against the protests and political wisdom purveyed by the likes of Erasmus. More apparently deplored that effect, and he acknowledged that the court's impenetrability and increasing militarism had been costlier at the start of the sixteenth century than it had ever been before. In 1415, Henry V crossed to Agincourt with nine thousand soldiers; in 1513, Henry VIII crossed with thirty thousand. Money followed soldiers out of the kingdom. Taxation was a terrible burden. Veterans returning to England and unemployment stole still more of other subjects' revenues. The crime rate soared when comrades came marching home. Meanwhile, "parasites" at court looked to please rather than advise. They stroked their sovereigns' self-importance, creating a culture in which it was impossible for virtuous counselors to make a difference. More let on as much, when he scripted Hythloday's encounter with the toadies at Morton's table and, much later, when he described sycophants who had surrounded Thomas Wolsey—like Morton, a cardinal, papal legate, and chancellor.[7]

Was it realistic to expect improvement? Hythloday thought not; More, his dialogue partner, disagreed, but the disagreement was so staged that the position of More, the stage manager, is difficult to determine. We will find here that the message of his *Utopia,* on the whole, was that significant improvement was impossible. Everyone at court, save the king, compromised. The wisest, most honorable courtiers had to accommodate their fellows' foolishness if they wished to be heard. So, if Hythloday was right, aspiring advisers were well-advised to relinquish whatever yearning they might have to inspire their governments to implement comprehensive, philosophically grounded, religiously motivated plans to reform character and social conduct. To get ahead, they must trade idealism for influence. More wrote himself into his fiction to excuse that exchange.

But neither as author nor as Hythloday's savvy interlocutor in the dialogue did More underestimate its cost or consequence. As Dermot Fenlon now proposes, he was almost certainly "exploring the possibility that Christianity and public life" were worlds apart and "might have become mutually exclusive." Or did he want *Utopia* to illustrate the predicament—and not just "explore the possibility"—that the persistently self-absorbed political regimes of the sixteenth century were insurmountable obstacles to a refashioning of society?[8] For was it not utterly preposterous to speak of alleviating the poverty of the deserving poor when everyone at court jockeyed for position and for undeserved wealth? Was it not absurd to speak of honor and dignity when courtiers and counselors delighted in dignities they could purchase?[9] And what hope for meaningful reform could there be without talk of honor, dignity, charity, and equity? To expect meaningful change, therefore, was unrealistic. But what then should one do? Pico withdrew. More knew it and translated three letters Pico wrote to defend his decision and excoriate colleagues who feverishly pursued celebrity and riches, colleagues "in ambitiouse laboure for offices and honowres." Hythloday, for his part, declined to serve in government. But Thomas More was already committed to public service.[10]

More answered Hythloday in the dialogue as Cicero answered Plato: subjects should serve what cities they had rather than conjure commonwealths more worthy of their service. They might dream of more perfect worlds and grumble some at imperfections, yet to thrust one's opinions on those governing (*ingerere*), "to vent," one might say today, though personally gratifying perhaps, was politically inexpedient. Scholars' colloquies were appropriate venues for passionate advocacy. At court, *in consilio principum,* during times of crisis as well as those of relative calm, counselors who counted sailed with the prevailing breezes.[11]

More understood, of course, that influence, on those terms, was limited, that counselors who counted could be critical only to a point. But he argued that self-pity, self-righteous indignation, and self-imposed isolation were unpleasant as well as unproductive alternatives. Obliquely, stealthily perhaps, well-intentioned advisers might occasionally be allowed to formulate policy that was, if not conspicuously better, at least no worse than that of their less astute and selfishly motivated colleagues. Virtuous administrators and advisers ought to play the hands dealt them, More urged, and let circumstance dictate compromise. They should negotiate with those of opposite conviction—or with no conviction at all—*commode*, "tactfully," to see what concessions might be made on all sides.[12]

Hythloday's groans are nearly audible; to him, tactful politicians were time-servers. Peter Ackroyd calls him "a blusterer." George Logan, however, suggests that More made his Hythloday that way to convince readers that the narrative's next revelations were "dramatically plausible." If Hythloday were controlled and circumspect, he would never have volunteered controversial views about government to the text's two government agents, Peter Giles and More, whom he had just met. And only a terribly indiscreet idealist would have gotten to the main argument of *Utopia*'s second half so quickly, the argument that private property precluded social justice.[13] There may be something to Logan's suggestion, though in the dialogue More also becomes agitated, "urgent," and "assertive" just as he and "blustery" Hythloday start talking about public service. More admits idealists were unwelcome at court and visionaries unable to keep both their visions and their places or influence there. Nonetheless, as Dominic Baker-Smith notices, More also echoes Cicero who was optimistic about counselors or politicians being principled, honest, and still somewhat useful. Poor More: drafting the script, he no doubt anticipated his Hythloday would catch that contradiction and impertinently call it to readers' attention.[14] For at court one must be seen to approve "the bad advice offered by influential others. One must subscribe to pestilential policies. Anyone whose approval seems tepid is judged to be unpatriotic. You can do no good among colleagues who prefer to corrupt the best of men than [to] be corrected by them. . . . You can improve nothing with an indirect approach." Accommodation and tact all too obviously implicated idealists in the dissembling that they resented most, according to Hythloday, who advised that a courtier's "integrity and innocence," should it be rather miraculously preserved for a time, would be exploited to cover "the wickedness and folly" of one's compromised colleagues.[15]

Seduction, corruption, manipulation, or irrelevance: a courtier's choices were uninviting, to say the least. It might have been different had princes' upbringing been the only obstacle to good government. Or, if the impenetrability of court culture were all that stopped wise counsel from becoming wise policy, the most resourceful counselors would have found ways to pitch their ideas and ideals directly to their princes and people. And if ordinary people's prejudices were the only problem, a virtuous counselor could play for a hearing higher up. But in combination—princes' training, counsellors' selective awareness and self-congratulation, and the crowds' preferences for show over substance—they all stacked the deck against idealists in politics. Hythloday implies that the same was true in the past; for More learned from Augustine how inextricably all Romans—emperors, elites, and proles—were trapped by their lust for domination and their pursuits of glory and power.[16]

Theodosius, we know, was Augustine's exception to the rule that power corrupts. Hythloday also found an exception, a man with both power and integrity, when he visited England. He had an occasion to offer a few recommendations for tidying up Tudor social programs to chancellor Morton and his guests at dinner. More staged the episode to have those guests prove Hythloday's point about courtiers' hypocrisy and insensitivity. In the telling, they were ready to reject good advice without weighing it. They demonstrated splendidly how courts thwart candid criticism and reform. But Morton listened, eager to hear what Hythloday had to say (*libenter audierim*).[17] And, later Hythloday, for his part, praised his host while skewering the obsequious others who dined with them. Possibly, had the chancellor not been at the head of the table and in the tale, those guests would have made the case that there was no place at court for good advice. Yet he was there, clearly in a league of his own, a notable exception. And his hospitality to Hythloday, particularly, his receptivity to that guest's good counsel undermined the very observation that moored his refusal to get politically involved. Morton was thoughtful, irreproachable, cunning. And Hythloday, insisting that he could not honorably counsel courtiers or kings on matters of moment—and would not try to—proceeded to do exactly that. At Morton's table, he gave advice. He told Giles and More about that and other politically relevant encounters, and he rehearsed it all for readers of *Utopia*.[18]

A good guess is that More composed the rehearsal to recycle the same part of himself that translated Pico's criticisms of court life. Stephen Greenblatt, though, has a slightly different take on what More meant readers to hear from Hythloday. *Utopia*'s idealist represents to Greenblatt "all that More excluded from the personality he created and played" in life. More "was a man with a well-defined, widely acknowledged public identity," of which he was somewhat secretly ashamed, because maintaining it required him to edit out his idealism. On this reading of his self-fashioning, what was "excluded" got deposited with Hythloday.[19] But, in this context, the word "exclude" might suggest something less severe or surgical. Conceivably, it can be reconciled with "recycled," if we concede More was interested in maintaining tension between political involvement and political skepticism, pretty much as Augustine often appeared to be. After all, Hythloday was part of More's "public identity." More was eager to have him published. Erasmus handled the arrangements, yet More hovered over the project and sent instructions across the Channel. Controlling the script, he saw to it that Hythloday's politically incorrect counsel was cogent, that his complaints about current policies were pithy, and that his no-nonsense analysis of economic inequities was penetrating. And, as we shall soon see, he has Hythloday expose the irrationality of Renaissance humanists' hopes to make public virtue more pervasive without provoking radical political adjustments.

So Hythloday was too important to be a repository for suppressed or "excluded" sentiments, though he was a safe place to put More's criticism of his clients. Hythloday blamed them for difficulties that their realm's rural commoners were experiencing. More could not have censured them so and stayed in business. In fact, he was then deliberating in London, Bruges, and Antwerp to increase their profit margin, to enrich fellow Mercers who either produced cloth or exported wool. The awful truth may have been that, as one result of his representations, raising sheep became ever more lucrative. And as land was enclosed for pasture, cottagers had less of it to cultivate. They were left idle, made poor, set adrift. Landlords evicted tenants with insufficient yield to pay their debts. Families were sent packing before they were able to make arrangements to be received elsewhere. "Sheep," Hythloday said, "devoured men." Wool transformed England into a wilderness. In effect, More's narrator was denouncing what More's advocacy was making possible. Cities suffered as well, he explained; their streets were crowded with the indigent and desperate. *Utopia*'s readers probably followed the line of argument from rural greed to municipal crime. After all, More introduced the conversation as a reflection on crime and punishment. He could easily have glossed the causes of crime, for he was concerned, it seems, chiefly to comment on the inappropriate severity of punishment. But instead he had his surrogate turn on his clients and suggest that their exploitation and depopulation of rural England created the criminals the government was so cruelly punishing.[20]

For More to declare as much directly would have been to bite the very generous hands feeding his growing household. Hythloday had no dependents. He was unencumbered and, of greatest advantage, unreal. Equally to the point, within the confines of *Utopia*'s conceit, Hythloday was no threat. His repeatedly stated reluctance to enter government service—and struggle to right the wrongs he described—demonstrated the difficulty of reaching equitable resolutions. His analysis and sympathies, More might have argued, were playfully put into play. One could say Hythloday was neutralized, declawed by his conviction—and More's—that meaningful remedies were unlikely to come by degree or by decree. The courts turned a deaf ear to good advice. People were preoccupied with profits. "Well and wisely trained citizens" were nowhere to be found. But Hythloday came across them when he made landfall in More's narrative nowhere.[21]

Wordplay

There, "nowhere," he stumbled upon an England of sorts. The trench separating the island commonwealth of Utopia from the mainland could have passed as the English Channel. The number of Utopian *civitates,* confederations of towns and surrounds, quite nicely matches the number of counties in England and Wales. And the seat of the island's senate looked like London relocated alongside a Utopian Thames.[22] More may only have meant to arch some eyebrows. Or did he post similarities to prompt his English readers to contemplate contrasts, to ponder how topography so like theirs yielded a society so much more equitable, educable, and charitable? Was that the point? Was More trying to shame his countrymen? Was *Utopia* a manifesto for change and a model, to boot? Similarities and differences can be shuffled into an affirmative response to such questions, yet More resisted doing so. He led readers on a merry chase, and authorial intent remains beyond reach. The sturdy door that keeps us from it refuses to give, in part, because More made it hard to get traction for a determined shove. He deposited in the text an assortment of ironies and incongruities that signal Utopia's fictionality and subvert its possibility.

The Greek names are telling. Utopia's commercially crucial river was the Anyder, "without water." Its capital, a city of handsome homes, lush gardens, and broad thoroughfares, was Amaurot, "dreary and dark." Hythloday, the island society's great admirer and publicist was "a piffle peddler." Utopia itself was "nowhere." Of course, one ought not to say that every serious search for social reform and possible political remedy starts on the near side of unreality. That would eliminate Swift and most satire. Still, what More brought forth from his word-hoard suggests his commonwealth "belongs to language," Alan Nagel now says; *Utopia* was "pure fantasy." Yet to infer its political irrelevance would be a mistake, although one could reasonably conclude that More expected the readers of his text to be "thrown back from the nowhere of . . . near perfection to the somewhere and sometime of [their] own imperfection," clutching something other than plausible solutions to their reality's problems.[23]

Granted, the arrangements in More's imaginary civilizations can seem tantalizingly practical. Take, for instance, the "near perfection" of the Polylerites, a people "of much nonsense," whom Hythloday said he had also visited. At Morton's table, he introduced their penal system as an alternative to Europeans' frequent recourse to capital punishment. He let the Polylerites, in effect, protest putting felons to death. Even before readers of *Utopia* met the Utopians in the discourse, therefore, they got a glimpse, in the dialogue, of how wonderfully well another of More's mythical civilizations managed its affairs.[24]

It put convicts to work, not to death. After making restitution to their victims—or while doing so—criminals completed projects that improved the population's well-being. In addition, Polylerites requiring special services might hire them, "at a set rate, a little less than that for free men." The term "prisoner" should not be applied without qualification, for, at labor or leisure, convicts wore no chains. "Unless their crimes were compounded by atrocities," they were identified only by badges, by the cut of their clothes and hair, and by the clipped tip of an ear. The death penalty was reserved for those who tried to flee. It apparently worked as a disincentive; Hythloday was told that the noose was seldom used. Convicts understood that submissive behavior earned them pardons. *Utopia's* praise was glowing: "How mild and practical" the Polylerites were, "for the aim of punishment is to destroy vices and save men" who "are treated so that they *necessarily* become good and have the rest of their lives to make up for the damage they had done."[25] Commendable and sensible, perhaps, for "a people of much nonsense," but was the system practical? And were the conditions that made it so, desirable?

Sensible and commendable, some might say today. All the more unfortunate, then, that More and Hythloday neglected to enclose instructions how to build it. From what they do say, though, social planners would have to agree that piecing it together would be no small task. Isolation appears to have been the chief, enabling condition. Hythloday put the Polylerites and their convicts in Persia, surrounded by mountains. They raised or produced everything they needed and had no reason to travel abroad. Rugged terrain and Persian garrisons kept others at a distance. Reclusive Polylerites, however, were not about to complain that their pocket in Persia was very nearly sewn shut. The quarantine was critical to the success of their system. More had set up their Shangri-La to incubate their quaintly casual way with felons and to make everything work.[26]

Hythloday emphasized the isolation, though not as an obstacle to adaptation. He was, after all, insinuating that the Polylerites' penal practices were readily assimilable to English society. But More—on behalf of his clients, exporters all—had been arguing against protectionism for nearly a decade. Moreover, he and Erasmus prized free trade in ideas and texts. The humanists' preferences for Latin, in which *Utopia* was written and first published, importantly signaled their commitments to the early modern equivalent of globalization. The *Erasmici* knew no frontiers. So, admire as More might the Polylerites' achievement, he would never have welcomed their kind of quarantine (or claustration) as the cost of "near perfection."[27]

Yet Utopia was isolated as well, although Hythloday seems to have learned enough while there to identify the origins of its admirable practices. Residents had lurched into social planning, he said, because they were pushed. There had been no elaborate courtships: kings with courtiers, moral philosophers with kings, rulers and ruled. There were no backroom negotiations. Utopus conquered the Utopians, "gained a victory at his very first landing" over "the rude and rustic" natives, "decreed" insularity by digging a channel that turned their peninsula into an island, and imposed their "near perfection" on them.[28]

Tyranny, then! And, however much the *Erasmici* decried "the conspiracy of the rich" to rob the poor—however much they griped about the petulance of the old aristocracy, noble by birth, not by virtue—they were well aware of the perils of political absolutism. They agreed with Hythloday that the principal social problem of their time was the desire to acquire that lay at the root of ambition and envy, but they also agreed with More that ambition and envy fueled political pretensions and unsettled societies.[29] He and they recognized that there was often a close connection between display and diplomacy; therefore, he and they assumed that the problem of settling the unsettled would forever be a prickly one. More explicitly conceded to Hythloday—as conversations in *Utopia* came to an end—that, although he was tempted to wish for many things (*penultima;* not for everything) in the imaginary, ideal republic, he never expected to have a wish of that sort fulfilled. He was hardly hopeful.[30] But to recall this remark is not to deny that More wanted his dialogue and discourse together to be a fruitful exercise in "comparative political study" nor to deny that he meant Hythloday's presentations of "successful solutions in other polities" to be "highly instructive."[31] Quite the contrary; nonetheless, we must continue to ask what can be made of "solutions" that seemed "successful" to a narrator whom More named nonsense and what can be learned from "other polities" that were nowhere, save in narrative. For the moment, though, we need only point out that he was disinclined to look for a monarch-messiah. By 1516, he was disappointed with his king's military adventurism: English armies crossed the Channel, yet Henry VIII of England no more belonged in France than the French nobility belonged in Italy. And courtiers close to Prince Charles, soon to be the Habsburg Emperor Charles V, made his duties in Bruges an ordeal. They stalled negotiations, the speedy conclusion to which would have returned More to England and his family. Benevolent despots were not on the early modern menu, and it is not at all certain that Thomas More would have ordered one if they had been.

But Erasmus was ready to cook one up. He wrote his *Education of the Christian Prince* for young Charles shortly before visiting More in Bruges, where the two almost certainly spoke about participation in politics. We can reconstruct with some certainty what they said from what Erasmus wrote and from what More was soon to write. More, that is, would have Hythloday calculate the overwhelming odds against getting through to the conscience of a king. But Erasmus was more optimistic; he imagined that sovereigns very quickly learned what sailors always knew, that the wise seek advice in storms. And rulers, he went on, had only to look around to discover that political practice was tempestuous and that rule was, in essence, weathering one storm after another.[32] The trick was to distinguish between advisers prone to flattery and fraud—about whom Hythloday complained—and those who reflected selflessly on circumstance and government strategy, who charted courses for the ship of state competently and honorably. Erasmus trusted that the trick—discrimination—could be taught. Instructed by scholars familiar with the lessons of classical antiquity and Christian morality, sovereigns would learn the differences between flattery and friendship. And the scholars' lessons in history would compellingly explain how flattery and tyranny wrecked commonwealths. Erasmus confidently presumed that Europe's princes could be trained to be prudent and benevolent.[33]

They definitely should learn Plutarch's distinctions between flattery and "frankness." Plutarch, Erasmus said, wonderfully (*mire*) depicted how subtle and sly a corrupt courtier could be. And the depiction was worth a new translation into Latin, he figured, dedicating it to Henry VIII. One need not quarrel with the obvious—that the translation and Erasmus' *Education* were exercises in flattery—to suggest they were also attempts to instruct patrons. Erasmus thought he could teach Henry and Charles to recognize greedy, groveling "friends" at court before counselors of that kind did their kings and countries great disservice. And if the wordplay of scholarly advisers could make princes pious as well as discerning, all the better. To be sure, sovereigns might forever be partial to hearing subjects refer to them as "Majesty," "most noble," "invincible," and "most serene." Affectation bordering on arrogance seemed irrepressibly as well as incorrectly political. Yet Erasmus trusted that *Erasmici* might prompt princes, if not to relinquish those titles profoundly in tension with the realities of their rule, at least to strive to earn them: to vanquish their anger, restrain their ambition, bridle their lust, rule according to "the precepts of wisdom," and care for their subjects' happiness as if it were their own.[34]

More does not appear to have shared Erasmus' confidence that kings could be coached to virtue. Yet he could only have approved efforts to alert subjects and sovereigns alike to what ought to make them genuinely happy. The goal was to make Christian moral theology both comprehensible and compelling. The major obstacle was the typical theologian's contempt for applied theology. Universities usually gave it a pass. Students were directed to dispute *quaestiuncula*—propositions that Erasmus called petty, obscure, and irrelevant to ordinary lives. His *Enchiridion*, as we saw, offered an alternative. His *Praise of Folly* ridiculed theologians who preferred questions and quodlibets to practical applications.[35] In turn and indignant, the theologians denounced him, inciting *Erasmici* to circle the wagons and fire back. More, while at Bruges, took aim at Maarten van Dorp, whose criticism was particularly hurtful. Dorp had befriended the *Erasmici* and, studying theology at Louvain, satirized "uncultured professors." But shortly after he was awarded his doctorate in 1515, Dorp closed ranks with theologians who accused Erasmus of being unscholarly and irreverent.[36]

Dorp defected. He had been part of a network the *Erasmici* tremendously valued. Manuscripts were exchanged, patrons shared, books promoted, and egos inflated. Indeed, only months before his apostasy, Dorp published an encomiastic preface to several satires by Gerard Geldenhouwer, a friend of another of More's correspondents.[37] Praise, prefaces, dedications, and promotions were fashionable, of course, yet they were also parts of a strategy to maintain solidarity among humanists. Erasmus urged friends and devotees to write him and to write each other—to encourage, applaud, and commend initiates. He drafted letters and dedications to cultivate a siege mentality, to create the illusion that "barbarous" dialecticians surrounded earnest *eruditi*, wordsmiths, whose high praise of each other's work kept "barbarians" at bay, but who, as itinerants, seldom assembled in any place long enough to be surrounded. Correspondence, therefore, was critical to the illusion of a siege and to the *Erasmici*'s defenses against it, which depended on the maintenance of a broad consensus. Disagreements among the *Erasmici* seldom greatly alarmed any of them. They bickered, as friends do, about personal slights, favorite authors, and other minor matters. But on some fronts—the reorientation of formal theological study, the importance of moral theology in the revival of popular piety, contributions to both Christian studies and Christian piety that literature associated with classical antiquity must make, the need to correct errors in Latin translations of venerable texts, and the value of satire to entertain as well as complain—on any and all of that, dissent such as Dorp's upset them. Comrades-turned-critics discredited their "new learning." More's reply to Dorp persuaded him to stay his criticism and, provisionally, to reaffirm his humanistic interests. Dorp's later lectures and letters were once again network documents, as was More's reply, which circulated among the *Erasmici* with his *Utopia*.[38]

The wordplay gives it away, strongly suggesting that More pitched *Utopia* to the *Erasmici*. As Logan notices, he "aim[ed] so far above the heads of most Europeans and their rulers" that only accomplished linguists could have caught it. Erasmus asked several of those humanists for help, for prefatory tributes. Idle hands, he implied, could do worse than compose "puff pieces" to assist a friend. More was grateful to those who obliged.[39] They apparently warmed to the feisty Hythloday and found much in his discourse to endorse. Their confreres in Utopia were enviably positioned. Unsupervised, they supervised public instruction. Citizen-students so enjoyed the Utopian scholars' lessons that they came in droves to predawn lectures. They participated in discussions of moral philosophy during common meals after hearing texts the scholars selected.[40] Everyone wrestled with issues that had preoccupied the philosophers of classical antiquity. Debates were civil, and faction was avoided because irenic scholars were not only the impresarios of educational exercises; they ruled Utopia. More's commonwealth was a literocracy. Its officials—every municipality's block or precinct captains, higher magistrates, religious authorities, ambassadors, and governors themselves—were chosen by and from an *ordo literatorum. Erasmici,* powerless in Europe and besieged by "barbarians," read how their counterparts managed Utopian government, bowled out barbarity, and brought ordinary people around to respect and labor for learning and virtue.[41]

Social Control

Erasmus looked to be rallying those ordinary people in his *Enchiridion.* We have called it a pocket guide to piety, a self-help manual of sorts, instructing the laity what to do, what not to do, and why. "Free yourself from the errors of this world," Erasmus encouraged the laity; "find your way into the light and lead a spiritual life." More's Utopians, though, had not emancipated themselves. Utopus, their conqueror and king, herded them into their greener pastures, where ordinary citizens were less free to find than "free" to follow the way "into the light." Regeneration depended less on pocket guides, trainers' exhortations, and personal exertion than on social pressure.[42]

Many of the results in Utopia, as noted, appealed to More's friends. How could they not? Scholars ruled. All Utopians were even tempered and quick-witted. Their diligence and discipline overcame whatever problems with soil or climate they encountered. They were robust. Exercise and diet kept them fit. Excess was off limits. Utopia looks like a late medieval Lake Woebegone, with extras to charm the *Erasmici*. The Utopians, for example, had long stretches of the day to indulge their love for literature. On More's watch, they reconciled Stoicism with Epicureanism, making it both a pleasure and a virtue to conform to the dictates of a benevolent nature.[43]

The *Erasmici* could not have asked for more, according to historian Jack Hexter, whose introduction to the Yale edition of More's text famously draws parallels between what "northern [European] humanists" were trying (yet failing) to do and what *Utopia*, narratively, did. Hexter, however, admitted an important difference. To their frustration, the humanists—of whom the *Erasmici* were a significant subset—tried to educate the old "power elite." More got rid of it. By hiring mercenaries to do the lion's share of their fighting, Utopians saw to it that an indigenous military aristocracy never developed. Wisdom and virtue, rather than valor, qualified candidates for public administration, precisely, Hexter says, as the *Erasmici* wanted. He allows that "the virtues of Utopia's rulers begin to seem a bit bourgeois," because early modern middle classes, after John Calvin, became known for austerities—especially for modest consumption—that rivaled what was prescribed and practiced in More's "nowhere" commonwealth. Hexter, though, thinks that the resemblance is misleading. More did not anticipate Calvin; the "Utopian magistrates with their sobriety and appetite for hard work are modeled on the scholar," and "the end of their way of life is not to maximize gain or profit or wealth, but to maximize leisure, *otium*, in the good sense of time free for study and contemplation." Hexter's humanists would have arranged it just so, had they not been less adventurously committed to counseling and convincing intransigent elites. *Utopia* exhibited, as did More's letter to Martin Dorp, "the common purpose and common sentiment [that] bound More and Erasmus together in 1515." Yet, for all that was "common" between those two, More's fictional island society was the product of more radical changes than Erasmus and the *Erasmici* were ready to sanction. Hexter's observations, to this point— and on this point—hold, yet his conclusion that Utopian values were as "liberal" and More's outlook as hopeful as the values and views of the humanists requires considerable qualification.[44]

Quentin Skinner, the premier historian of early modern English political thought, would likely disagree; he pronounced Hexter's commentary "entirely convincing" soon after it appeared, hailing it as "the best work on *Utopia* that anyone has done." Skinner seems overly fond here of eye-catching claims that relegate centuries of interpretation to second-class status, but before putting Hexter's assessments among the incontestables of historical scholarship, we should see whether his approach to common sentiment, intent, and outlook weathers informed speculation about how More's fantasy island might have irritated the *Erasmici*.[45]

Those first readers would have understood, of course, that More set for himself and his Utopians a formidable task. He and they would have to impose dispositions that Plato's *Republic* associated with the governing "classes"— rationality, contempt for opulence and indolence, selflessness—on all commoners in his ideal commonwealth. The *Erasmici*, as citizens everywhere, were accustomed to some degree of regulation and surveillance, yet were they ready for the regimentation that More invented to achieve uniformity? What did they make, for instance, of the Utopians' common meals, the suppers served in Utopia's cities to every block of thirty families?

The seating is always by groups of four. If there is a church in the the district, the priest and his wife sit with the syphogrant [a local magistrate] so as to preside. On both sides of them sit younger people, next to them, older people again, and so through the hall. . . . The reason for this, as they explain it, is that the dignity of the aged, and the respect due to them, may restrain the younger people from improper freedom of words or gestures, since nothing said or done at table can pass unnoticed by the old who are present on every side. . . . They begin every lunch and supper with some reading on a moral topic but keep it brief, lest it become a bore. Taking their cue from this, the elders introduce proper topics of conversation, though not gloomy or dull ones. They never monopolize the conversation with monologues, but are eager to hear what young people say. In fact, they deliberately draw them out in order to discover the natural temper and quality of each one's mind as revealed in the freedom of mealtime talk.[46]

One cannot miss what Baker-Smith calls "the dominant concern with social control": Utopian elders, "on every side," channel conversations. Arguably, More turned each block party into an "ideal humanistic symposium," though fear of "improper freedom" dictated a "constant pressure to right doing" that "remove[d], as far as is possible, the moral challenge of individualism."[47]

Seating, reading, and speaking: nearly everything was planned, and everything was watched carefully. Texts and topics were chosen, as in the refectories of medieval monasteries, where routines were similar to those of the Utopians. We should admit the possibility that More's meal plan combined "the virtues of the cloister" with "the hopes of contemporary humanists," as Alistair Fox claims, but ought we also to presume that the *Erasmici* appreciated the result?[48] For one thing, the Utopians' mealtime decorum would have prohibited Hythloday from holding forth on their virtues as he had done at Morton's table. For he was extraordinarily long-winded; nothing in *Utopia* suggests he could "keep it brief," whatever the "it" might be. And, clearly, "the freedom" of Utopians' mealtime talk did not allow for loquacious guests, because elders and scholars reserved dinnertime to test their youth. "They deliberately drew them out," as Hythloday reports, and one wonders whether the young, drawn-out examinees eagerly anticipated or dreaded the colloquies on their prandial proving ground.[49] Erasmus might not have liked the premeditation and orchestration of conversations. Conceivably, he would have fled the cities' suppers, much as he left the priory at Steyn, suffocated there, he later said, by his superiors' choice of topics and tests. He was partial to travel and compared himself with such celebrated itinerants as Pythagoras, Plato, the apostle Paul—luminaries, to whom, he might have argued, conversation was too precious to restrict.[50]

But Erasmus could not have left the cities and traveled at will in Utopia. He would have had to obtain a government pass to visit other municipalities. Officials punished unauthorized travel by enslaving offenders.[51] Utopians' "freedoms" were hedged about on all sides with rules. Rules dictated fashion: how clothes were cut and from what material as well as how often they were replaced by new garments just like the old. A rule told Utopians when to work; another, when and how to play each day. Rules told them where to reside and when to move (every ten years) to a residence identical in all but location to the one they vacated. Everything seems patterned, except their gardens. They cultivated those prescribed spaces more or less as they wished, while otherwise Utopia's regulations prohibited them from remodeling their homes, determined their diets, framed their courtships, bridled their lusts, preserved their marriages, and raised their children. The few Utopian officials with special exemptions usually forfeited them for the sake, it seems, of solidarity.[52] Hythloday spoke of the Utopians' freedoms—"the freedom of mealtime talk," as we saw—yet the descriptions More scripted document the "steady constriction of freedoms," as Stephen Greenblatt says. Hexter imagines Erasmus and the *Erasmici* could have been content with that, and one could argue that many more centuries had to pass before readers knew enough to inquire whether the word "freedom" was grossly misapplied to what More's *Utopia* presents. But it is arguable as well that the *Erasmici* would have joined Greenblatt and, I believe, More to complain that the Utopian emphasis on social control and conformity indicates "a failure to appreciate the opacity of social existence, to grasp that men thrive on particularity and variety, to understand that endless sameness destroys the individual."[53]

That Utopia is not liberal by twenty-first-century standards—appreciative of complexity or "opacity," tolerant of or excited by diversity—is very much beside the point here, which is that Thomas More and other *Erasmici* would have found certain features of it illiberal, undesirable, and unrealistic. To be sure, along with their regulations, Utopians counted on public orations to "spur" or "stimulate" virtue. Humanists would doubtlessly have welcomed such opportunities. They were fond of displaying their rhetorical skills. They preferred persuasion to regulation. And, from their impatience with patterned or formulaic expression, from their criticisms of convention and imitation, and, notably, from Erasmus' enthusiasm for epistolographic ingenuity and the encouragement he lodged in his *Enchiridion* ("free yourself"; "find your way")—from all their wordplay, that is—we may infer their likely opposition to the "endless sameness" that Hythloday recounted in the discourse.[54]

But the "sameness" was sometimes punctuated by wars. The Utopians thought them awful, but apparently necessary. A favorable balance of trade made it possible to hire others to do their fighting. They had produced a surplus of nearly everything they needed, so even after they generously extended credit to trading partners and saw to it that some portion of their exports or profits went to the neediest abroad, the Utopians' treasury was bulging with silver and gold. As we heard, they neither desired nor used it domestically, so they could afford to pay for soldiering. They were known to boast that it was sound policy to risk others' lives to further their foreign interests.[55] Zapoletans often got the nod. They were an utterly unpleasant lot, opportunistic, entre- preneurial, *ad solum nati bellum,* "born for war." They changed loyalties on a dime for a dollar added to their original fees. Unaffected by family and friend- ship, they fought each other when retained by rivals. Their Utopian retainers, in Hythloday's account, come off as rather glib; "they do not care in the least how many Zapoletans they lose, thinking they would be the greatest benefac- tors to the human race if they could relieve the world of all the dregs of this abominable and impious people."[56]

Erasmus was no kinder to mercenaries. Those who fight for pay, he said, were "more degraded and damnable" than any other caste of characters. Yet he also warned that wages for war corrupted those who gave them as well as those who received them. The latter were the worst of criminals; the former, corrupted by contact. They compromised the most righteous causes, he said, by summoning and salarying the most unrighteous soldiers.[57]

Less than a year after Thomas More formulated Utopian foreign policy and, in a sense, sanctioned his fictional island's way with wars, Erasmus ad- vised "truly Christian princes" to avoid soldiering altogether. He pulled no punches. War was savage. No beast could compete with a human-turned- warrior, whose brutalities—impulsive or deliberate—undercut God's plan to have humans cooperate with each other.[58] It may be too much to say that Erasmus repudiated war unconditionally in 1516, as the Turks were marching through central Europe, yet he came very close to scolding soldiers who rose to defend the Christian religion violently—and "thus quite differently from the ways it got started and spread."[59] More's Utopians had fewer scruples about combat. To protect their interests abroad—but even when they had no hound in the hunt—they got involved in others' armed struggles. At home, they regularly drilled and devised intricate rules of engagement (rules again), notwithstanding the mercenaries.[60] Instinctively, *Erasmici* would have shied from fighting in person or by proxy. True, *Utopia*'s second book had conjured up many of the great changes they were unable to effect as educators, yet More, on war and on other fronts as well, seems also to have been asking whether those changes justified the cost. He made his friends and first readers confront "an inescapable trade-off between the requirements of securing the commonwealth and the attainment of freedom for its inhabitants and full justice in dealings with its neighbors."[61]

Omnia Omnium

Those friends and readers were accustomed to the prevailing insecurities and injustices of their time. Erasmus catalogued them in his *Praise of Folly* and would not have quarreled with the summation More scripted for his narrator: "All the best things flow into the hands of the worst citizens" who make everybody else wretched without making themselves less miserable.[62] To begin with, they were hostage to their "insatiable greed"; they darted to taverns, frequented brothels, hovered around gambling tables; they sneered at virtue and were never at peace. They set terrible examples for fellow citizens with far fewer means. They were socially irresponsible as well as awesomely unhappy.[63] Those problems (and More's solution) were already familiar to the *Erasmici*. Plato put everything in his *Republic*. He understood that opulence led to indolence; poverty, to jealousy and social unrest. He knew that, to have the ruling elite remedy social ills, its members—"Guardians"—would have to pool their resources. They owned no property, ate together, and relished the constitutional assurances that their families were forever provided for. The elite, therefore, was beyond bribery and flattery. The republic was governed well. Plato supplied posterity—in this instance, the *Erasmici*—with a plan.[64]

More modified it. His Hythloday remembered Plato as that "supremely judicious philosopher who, to achieve general well-being, proposed an even distribution of all there was."[65] But the *Republic* was not that egalitarian. Excited by the cure-all that the Utopians demonstrated for him, Hythloday fudged a bit. More, of course, invented the demonstration and excitement: *Omnia omnium*, everything belonged to everyone! Rid of their obsessions with possessions, the citizens of More's ideal commonwealth were amiable, accommodating, and content.[66] *Omnia omnium* was the Utopians'—then Hythloday's—answer to inequity, envy, immorality, inordinate ambition, and social dysfunction, but neither Erasmus' nor More's answer. When Erasmus mentioned that friends share, he only meant that scholarly colleagues ought to circulate their most precious properties: their writing and good opinion of each other. He was surprised Christians found Plato's notions about common ownership so unlike those of Christ's apostles, yet he idled only long enough to say so before moving on, leaving no time for sentiments on sharing to congeal into a social program.[67] As for More, he packed his reservations on the redistribution of resources *omnia omnium* into the *Utopia*.

> I was left thinking that now a few of the laws and customs [Hythloday] had described as existing among the Utopians were really absurd. These include their methods of waging war . . . but my chief objection was to the basis of their whole system, that is, their communal living and moneyless economy. This one thing alone utterly subverts all the nobility, magnificence, splendor, and majesty which (in the popular view) are the true ornaments and glory of any commonwealth.[68]

Was More being mischievous? Ironical? Why would he worry at the text's end about "magnificence and splendor"? Indeed, the discourse seems to finish with a reversal of all that went before. Hythloday represented the Utopians' conduct of their wars as if nothing saner was imaginable, only to have More conclude it was lunacy (*perquam absurde*). But the second turnabout in this short passage is more mysterious, for More's chief objection to the Utopians' "communal living" reads as an apology for the way things were, for diplomacy's dependence on display.[69]

"Nobility, magnificence, splendor, and majesty": More intimated that he would lament their loss, yet the terms must have reminded his readers of the old aristocracy's excesses that he and the *Erasmici* deplored. Along with Erasmus, he derided courtiers who took magnificence and splendor too seriously. Yet Thomas More was a seasoned politician in 1515, emissary for the leading commercial interests in London and influential officer of its courts. Position, experience, and perhaps acquired taste for what might pass today as glamour led him to accept pageantry's part in politics. And what of "nobility" or "majesty"? To claim that they were irrelevant to the public good is, as Dominic Baker-Smith says, "to take a very negative view of their meaning." Hence, More's reservations and "chief objection" appear to "have their nagging validity."[70]

Historian Brendan Bradshaw thinks they signal More's recognition of the political importance of "social deference." Many of the *Erasmici* likely cheered—and all must have been amused by—the Utopians' aversion to dip-lomatic initiatives which relied on display and glitter to intimidate, impress, or appease. But, as *Utopia* concluded, More wanted his readers to consider that it was not outrageous to suggest some degree of display—"magnificence," "splendor"—was necessary to inspire obedience. A government's authority was only as grand as it seemed, or showed. Citizens followed whom or what they found worth following, and worth was measured, *ut publica est opinio,* in the popular view, by its strut or swagger, pomp and pageant. So whereas More—renaissance critic of contemporary folly—entertained the *Erasmici* by having Hythloday "burst the bubble of chivalry," More—emissary, under-sheriff, and pragmatist—questioned "the feasibility of removing the basis of social deference," Bradshaw shrewdly argues, and doubted that "removing the prop of political order" would do the realm any lasting good. Most important to More, perhaps, it was never excusable to encourage anarchy. So, until the "popular view" changed, subversion of "nobility, magnificence, splendor, and majesty" was unthinkable. I suspect that More offered his reservations in a spirit of resignation; Bradshaw holds that he was optimistic and ended his *Utopia* with an invitation. As he led Hythloday to supper, More's More con-fided that he was looking forward to further conversation. To Bradshaw, that anticipation, strategically uttered as the discourse winds down, clearly indi-cates that the author and the character that bears his name—More in and be-hind his *Utopia*—meant to declare and reconfirm for humanists—who might have forgotten—that "the possibility for constructive social and political progress resides neither in the moral idealism of the intellectual alone nor in the skeptical pragmatism of the politician." Hope for social, political reform "reside[s] in . . . a constructive and continuing dialogue between the two."[71]

Bradshaw's More was hopeful rather than resigned to politics as usual in the early sixteenth century. He believed that government could be fetched, towed, and repaired by would-be public servants prepared to participate in constructive conversations between idealists and pragmatists who were de-voted to that sort of salvage work and unafraid to entertain others' ideas and to innovate. Hythloday, after all, had given top marks to the Utopians' recep-tivity to new ideas and implied in his glowing report that such openness was the basis for their civilization's "happy flourishing." They learned much from him, as they learned from others marooned there. The island's citizens grew to appreciate and eventually adapted much of what initially seemed to them outlandish or grotesque. From their willingness to experiment and resourcefulness (and from Hythloday's admiration), Bradshaw infers that More was not just urging, but expecting, the Europeans to enter "a constructive and continuing dialogue" about Utopia's strange yet sensible arrangements. But, as it happens, Hythloday was much less optimistic. After announcing that Utopians had immediately "made themselves masters of all our useful inventions," he let slip that he "suspect[ed it might] be a long time before we adopt any institutions of theirs which are better than ours."[72]

Before pinning More's hopes to Bradshaw's inference, therefore, we ought to factor in Hythloday's suspicion, which, as we shall see, matches More's at the very end of *Utopia*. For the text does not quit where Bradshaw has More "close the conversation by remarking on the need for further reflection and discussion." In fact, right after that, More's More appears to doubt that he and Hythloday will confer again soon: "if only [a discussion] might someday occur." That riveting "if only" (*utinam aliquando*) suggests that he put that talk and topic behind him, perhaps with a sense of relief. Hythloday had been getting rather too exuberant. Did More let him get out of hand, grow incapable of taking criticism or contradiction, lose perspective?[73] The last sections of the discourse have him "singing the praises of all that is worst" on the island, Richard Sylvester says, allowing that the supper could have been an excuse to call a halt. More may have been canceling rather than postponing, because Hythloday, "blinded," Sylvester says, "by his absorption in his own vision, cut off from his auditors [, and] hypnotized with himself, can no longer find his own way back to reality."[74]

That would explain More's exasperation (*utinam aliquando*). And his last words were less optimistic about what might come of "a constructive and continuing dialogue" between idealists and pragmatists. We must neither forget nor finesse those final words with which More's More discloses that he desires, yet dares not hope, to have the best features of Utopian society established in early modern Europe.[75] He found courtiers closed to new ideas. Hythloday convincingly commented on their inhospitality. More knew, moreover, that, even when and where the best ideals were generally accepted, implementation was often an embarrassment. Cloistered communities, for instance, were in place to practice *omnia omnium*. Monks and nuns vowed to be philanthropic, discreet, discerning, and obliging. A letter More wrote to a London Carthusian a few years after he finished *Utopia*, however, scolds ascetics for having become gossipy, greedy, foolish, and stubborn. Their rules resembled those of

the Utopians, but their societies hardly exhibited the selflessness and solidarity of More's ideal commonwealth. They valued private devotions over cor-
porate worship, the solemnities of their convents over those of others in their
orders, and their orders' customs and saints over those of other religious orders. To More, the early Tudor court and convent appeared too well fortified
against humanist reformers eager to talk up progressive political theories and
tidy up religious practices.[76]

Why, then, the discourse, if not to urge some marked improvements in
public administration? Plato had an answer: to improve conversation. Idealists harbored no great hopes for government reform, once they comprehended that theory squared with truth as practice never could.[77] Yet they
could live without those hopes and live more enthusiastically in the cities they
managed in their imaginations than they ever could in the cities of this world.
More and the *Erasmici* would have known that the ninth book of Plato's
Republic closed with that distinction, which all but put political theorists in
exile. They were "exiled," so to speak, to their imaginations and conversations.
Their studies and conversations did not meaningfully change the regimes
they suffered through and sometimes served. But their discourses built character, refined intelligence, and enlivened friendships. Behind the scene, Plato
is the Prospero of More's enchanted island. He reminds knowledgeable readers of the magic the mind can work and of the exhilaration—but also of the
limits of intellectual exploration.[78]

Genuine Justice, Nowhere and Never

Nowadays, readers of *Utopia*—notably, Hexter and Bradshaw—see possibilities, not limits. They say More was trying to translate theory into practice
or, at the very least, to bring humanists' ideals to bear on the behavior of early
modern governments. There is no denying he was among the *Erasmici* in 1515.
His letters to Dorp and to the Carthusian can fairly be called critical parts of
"an impassioned defense of the Erasmian project."[79] Nonetheless, his defense
of its belletristic preferences, educational objectives, scriptural emendations,
and historical scholarship does not signal his confidence in that "project's"
politics. More, in fact, believed his friends' rationalism might never trump the
egoism that prevailed at European courts. He had to accept the probability

"that the humanist reformers [would] find their proposals stuck fast on the printed page."[80]

Can we determine whether those "humanist reformers," specifically, the *Erasmici*, came to terms with Thomas More? Did they sense his anxiety about their influence (or, to be precise, their lack of influence)? "Nowadays readers," impatient for an interpretation that resolves something, look for utopian values that political planners may take to heart. But *Utopia*'s first readers were content, it seems, to leave issues of influence unresolved and to have "the counter-argument, the case against *Utopia* . . . internalized within the narrative itself."[81] They normally saw no need to have every humanist text explicitly endorse their "Erasmian project." They would have known about Erasmus' efforts to counsel kings. He completed his textbook on leadership for Prince Charles the year before More finished his *Utopia*. But Erasmus never drilled the *Erasmici* on political elements or implications of his "project." His *Education of the Christian Prince* was published without their imprimatur. More's fiction, however, came draped with their expressions of approval. Erasmus and Peter Giles prevailed on them to compose compliments that accompanied the first editions of the *Utopia* into the world, the prefatory letters and verses—or "puff pieces"—to which we have already referred. The very first words of the contribution solicited from Cornelius Grapheus, the youngest to oblige, illustrate the *Erasmici* embrace of More's *Utopia*, with its irony, ambivalence, and ambiguity. *Vis nova monstra* directs readers to More's marvelous or monstrous improvisations.[82]

Grapheus worked for Giles in the municipal government of Antwerp. An aspiring poet, he likely jumped at the chance to have his lines alongside More's, knowing literary careers were advanced by composing promotional materials as well as by having composed what they promoted. He must have imagined that he would be joined by veterans submitting phrases that praised More's text. Giles himself, less by equivocation than by exaggeration, signaled his sportive recognition of *Utopia*'s impossible perfections. He trumpeted that Hythloday was wiser than Ulysses. "By comparison, Amerigo Vespucci," esteemed in Spain and Portugal for voyages of exploration, "seems to have seen nothing at all."[83]

Erasmus waited to supply his commendation. It appeared with the third edition in 1518, saying next to nothing about Hythloday's discourse. Had he not orchestrated publication and solicited prefatory tributes, one might assume he harbored reservations about the reach of *Utopia*'s ridicule. Perhaps, that is, "the deafening silence from the doyen of northern European humanism," notably, his letter's brevity and selective inattention, registers his regret that the text tilted at humanists' political strategies and optimism.[84]

But Guillaume Budé, nearly as well known as Erasmus, was quite enthusiastic. More respected him immensely.[85] Historian and diplomat, Budé had edited Emperor Justinian's digest of Roman civil law and appears to have been spurred to reflect once again on justice and equity by reading *Utopia*. For he tucked a rather despairing commentary into the prefatory letter he prepared in 1517 for the second edition of More's text. He concluded that there was no "genuine justice" in sixteenth-century Europe and observed that anyone who talked about that deficit, or about principles or equity—while everyone else legislated and litigated to accumulate or protect property—was treated as discourteously as self-important citizens treat their kitchen help.[86] Budé professed that the Utopian distribution of resources, *omnia omnium*, appealed to him. Property in bulk became a burden, he complained, mentioning the management of his estates and efforts to cope with tenants and hired help. But was he really ready to be rid of those responsibilities? He adroitly embedded "the case against *Utopia*" in his letter, so we gather that he was not. Yet he admired More's radical alternative to politics as then practiced. His mournful rumination on injustices masquerading as law and order echoes Hythloday's parts in the dialogue and parts of Augustine's *City* as well. His prefatory letter introduces Utopia as something of a model, recommending that Europe import certain of its customs. Still, he also stresses its implausibility here and now. Utopia was "celestial," Budé said, a city of saints or "hagnopolis." It was not just *utopia*, "a no place," but *udepotia*, "a never-to-be place."[87]

We may be wrong to infer undesirability from Budé's—and from the others'—emphasis on the unreality of Utopia's odd new social order. Conceivably, any sense of undesirability we may have derives from recent experience with totalitarian regimes, as Richard Marius maintains, pointing out that the *Erasmici* never referred to More's fantasy island as "a bad place."[88] Yet only a tin ear could fail to hear the relief they occasionally expressed that it was a "no place," utopia or *udepotia*—remote and surreal. The prefatory piece from Joannes Paludanus brims with praise for More and other *Erasmici*, and, like Budé's, it proposes that public administrators in early modern Europe could learn from the Utopians. But Paludanus' strategy for educating Europeans shows how eager he was to have that happen. He planned to send "eminent and invincible theologians" to Utopia; their clinics in Christianity would hasten the island's conversion, and their return should ensure that useful Utopian practices and institutions improved the way Europeans were governed. The plan sounds reasonable, yet when we remember that the *Erasmici* thought those theologians insufferable and unteachable, we catch Paludanus tongue-in-cheek. He was public orator and professor of poetry at Louvain and would have known of Dorp's defection and of the contempt other *Erasmici* had for the arrogance and pettiness of his university's theologians. If the humanists had the chance to send them off, they would not have wanted them back. Paludanus could hardly have been well-disposed to the place he was proposing to send them.[89]

He and the other contributors were obviously having fun. They piled unanswerable questions on More's fantasy island foundation. How could they get to Utopia when ill-timed coughs kept Giles from hearing directions? Should they locate Hythloday and consult him? Or was he back in Utopia? Had he retired to Portugal? As Peter Allen now says of the *Erasmici* submissions, "playful delight in *Utopia*'s literary form" is evident in the prefatory material, although it did not obscure the "basic seriousness about the book's meaning."[90] The challenge is to get past its "deliberate irony" and reach consensus about what serious meaning More and his friends might have had in mind, a challenge we meet at nearly every turn in the text though never finally master. Conclusions, nonetheless, are due; we are close enough to this chapter's end to take stock of the two surmises offered here to throw light on what dispraised though delighted the *Erasmici*.

First, More's *Utopia* concentrates on entrenched social practices—both those of European courtiers and those of the Utopians—to fret humanists for assuming that political clout could eventually be earned by moral exhortation. More, in effect, criticized their *modus consulendi*. Jerome Busleiden seems to have caught on; his prefatory letter alludes to the insufficiency, if not also the impossibility, of incremental change. He says that Utopia, the society, can only be useful if swallowed whole, if Europeans "organize themselves exactly on the one pattern of the Utopian commonwealth and do not depart from it, as they say, by a hair's breadth." Telling truth to power, in measured doses, to achieve some good gets one "nowhere."[91]

My second surmise is simpler: according to *Utopia,* the best virtuous, resourceful scholars could do was provide moral perspective on current political practice. Outcomes were indeterminable. Imagining a better world was
propaedeutic, not prescriptive.[92]

For nothing can dramatically, politically change until human nature
changes. And, as *Utopia* implies, humanity will not change unless there is dramatic, political change. At the narrative's end, More leaves us with that co-
nundrum. It is not meant to excuse Hythloday's withdrawal. In fact, More's
idealist discredits his position by overselling it. And More's counter was
scripted, I believe, to be more persuasive: the wise ought to advise. However
irresistible they find retirement, they can take no refuge from public service in
counterfactuals, "what ifs," utopias. *Quaecunque fabula in manu est, eam age;*
play the play at hand; participate in public service with no illusions.[93] At every
turn, the courts and court culture made it impossible to get genuine justice.
Budé's prefatory letter, as we just heard, made that point at length, arraigning
all magistrates and lawyers for making and enforcing laws to the advantage of
the affluent and powerful, who, he wrote, were "always taking something or
other away [from poor neighbors], drawing it out, scooping it out, twisting it
out, hammering it out . . . plucking it away, pouncing upon it." No better illustration of Augustine's analysis of humanity's *libido dominandi* materialized
as greed can be found in the *Utopia* ensemble than Budé's lament for law
perverted and justice lost. Remember, More's Utopia did very well without
lawyers.[94]

England did rather well with them. More practiced successfully and
would have known that Budé's description of "plucking" and "pouncing" was
close to the mark. He had Hythloday say as much. "It is scarcely possible for a
commonwealth to have justice or prosperity unless you think justice exists
where all the best things flow into the hands of the worst citizens."[95] How,
then, might virtuous English public administrators "play the play at hand"
to keep matters from turning worse still? They were unable to tell truth to
power. Power frowned on anyone thrusting (*ingerendi*) even an excellent
opinion that questioned the arrangements that deposited power where it then
lay.[96] So, for want of a better world, More countenanced damage control, political participation that, at best, as he told Hythloday in the dialogue, aimed
to make wickedness less consequential. But if something close to as comprehensive as the Utopians' equanimity and harmony were to come, it would

descend. It would come from above and not from within, as Budé's prayerful petition suggests.

> Would that the gods by their divine power could cause pillars of Utopian polity to be fixed by bolts of strong and settled conviction in the minds of all mortals! You would promptly witness the withering away of pride, greed, idiot competition. . . . The immense weight of all those legal volumes which occupy so many brilliant and solid minds for their whole lifetimes would suddenly turn to empty air, the paper food for worms, or used to wrap parcels in shops. . . . One might even assert that . . . the old poets were mistaken when they said Justice had fled the earth. . . . For, if we believe Hythloday, she must have remained on the island of Utopia and not yet have gone to heaven.[97]

In heaven, that was where Augustine put *vera justitia*, genuine justice; not here, but elsewhere. In Utopia, that was where More put "her"; not here, but "nowhere."

How to participate politically? In 1516 and into the 1520s, Thomas More was still stalking answers he could translate into specific tactics and tasks. But his *Utopia* proposes the answer he would have occasion from then on to confirm: one must participate without illusions.

Why participate politically? That's a different question altogether, and *Utopia* offers two of the three responses More likely took to his grave. "If we believe Hythloday," justice was found "nowhere"; if we believe More, it was nonetheless worthwhile to fight the tides of wickedness, to make them less destructive of what little good there was of public life. And More also scripted Peter Giles's remark that political careers enabled careerists to provide for their families and to do favors for friends. But a third response could only have occurred to More years later, when heretical books and ideas smuggled from Germany appeared to jeopardize the religious understandings that had evolved for centuries. From the early 1520s, he tried to pilot government into a position to help save his faith and rituals. Augustine appealed to government to stave off the Donatists. More continued in government to stop the Protestants and stabilize the church.

Both Augustine and More recoiled from what Michael Oakeshott has described as "the politics of faith," "harnessing government to the pursuit of perfection" and requiring "an immense and ever active concentration of power" to impose perfection on communities. That requirement alarmed Oakeshott, but More was more accustomed to absolutism. What distressed him was that governing, in Oakeshott's terms, seldom attracted "men of moderation and self-control concerned to avoid the defects of the enterprise," that power drew to it individuals "intoxicated by the chance of doing big and clever things." So the politics of faith was not for More (or Augustine), though others around them cruised quite comfortably with regimes depending on it. Those two took it upon themselves to exert "the pull of skepticism" that might just keep regimes from turning into tyrannies.[98]

Augustine's pious magistrates were to stay sober, to resist the seductions of power. They had a duty to decathect. When he wrote them with that advice, he was looking after their spindly souls rather than their "states." But More got closer to power and learned to mistrust it. A convincing case could be made that, were it not for Martin Luther and his English admirers, More might have left public service sooner. Arguably, he continued to serve and accept promotions, in part, because he believed that religious reformers' assertions about the authority of scripture and the invisibility of the faithful Christian church invited anarchy. *Det nobis regulam,* give us a rule, he begged Luther, so intelligent laity might learn what reformed exegesis might mean for the survival of some ecclesial order. Hearing no rules, however, he appealed to the ruler he was then serving as counselor and chancellor. Henry VIII, with his assistance, declared against heresy in 1521. For several years thereafter, the king remained the best barricade by far between the realm's Roman Catholic church, in need of reform (as More admitted), and a small herd of wild-eyed, evangelical reformers in need of, and with designs for, an independent English church. That was how More read the situation. At first unruffled, he began to fear that those reformers' supplications would elicit more favorable royal responses, that "the siren voices of the anticlerics" would beguile Henry and wreck the realm and its church.[99]

We shall never know when, and to what extent, More reassessed his reasons for continuing in public service. He seems to have been disillusioned in the early 1520s, as we shall see in the next chapter, but he soldiered on. His family was never more secure, yet he continued to accept promotions and acquire properties. Had More retired instead, we might be tempted to read *Utopia* very differently, to argue that the text was "steeped" and not "merely dipped" in Platonism, as Hugh Trevor-Roper says. Had he retired when his family's fortunes were settled, soon after the irrationality of political life was closely and helplessly observed, we might have said that he behaved the philosopher, bid adieu to court, and "disengage[d] from . . . the practical compromises" and "sordid trivialities" in which a Tudor administrator's spirit was "trapped and buried."[100] But More set Plato and Hythloday aside. From the 1520s into the early 1530s, he toiled to ensure the government would cooperate with church authorities to stop the spread of evangelical anticlericalism, to punish mutinous English priests who had come under Luther's spell. He granted that the Catholic church, as any terrestrial institution, was imperfect. Its critics were unwelcome only when they challenged the rituals and practices fundamental to its survival, because that church, although flawed, was indispensable. It maintained order, taught virtue, and saved souls. Martin Luther's "invincible" faith and invisible churches, by contrast, were perfect, but unreal. Severed from a righteousness that was defined by good works, faith was meaningless. And a church dispersed among the meaninglessly faithful few (*diffusa*) was cut off from Catholic Christendom, as were the churches of fourth- and early fifth-century Donatists. More stayed in government to save England from a faith that was never to be and from a church that, like Utopia, was nowhere.[101]

Chapter Seven

Crisis

Promotion and Commotion

In 1519, Erasmus told a story about Thomas More's appearance before King Henry VIII of England some time before. Stories of that kind circulated to encourage as well as to entertain the *Erasmici*. Henry had heard a theologian preach against the study of Greek language and literature, Erasmus wrote, and had connived to have him match wits with More, a relatively new member of his council at the time. It was not a fair match. More spoke first, resolutely, fluently, brilliantly. He was everything the *Erasmici* expected of their colleagues in battle against barbarism. Even the outgunned theologian knew to be impressed. He declined to answer, admitted his offense, and begged the king's pardon.[1]

Erasmus probably embellished. More may have had greater difficulty with the Graecophobe than he let on, though the king's new counselor was influential on cultural issues from the moment he left the service of the city for the king's council. His opinions mattered on commercial matters too. He was often involved in cross-channel negotiations during the 1520s, became undertreasurer of the exchequer, chancellor of the Duchy of Lancaster, and, in 1529, Henry VIII's lord chancellor. He put himself in ever-better positions to help friends like Cuthbert Tunstall, who was with him in Bruges when *Utopia* was started, and who, as bishop of London, authorized him to read and reply to heretics' polemics. As Hythloday was told, public service could justifiably be turned to such "private" advantage.[2]

The *Erasmici* were happy to have influential friends and patrons, hoping to have them disarm the humanists' enemies. In England, for instance, obscurantists at Oxford opposed the study of classical antiquity, saying they were out to disinfect the colleges, to rid them of profane, useless erudition. More responded by touting prudence. He advised Oxford students of law, literature, philosophy, and theology urgently to acquire it as part of their schooling. Nothing, he claimed, could be more useful in their careers than prudence, and, he went on, no "study contributes as richly to this practical skill as the study of poets, orators, and histories."[3] More was willing to put the power and prestige of the government behind his brief against the "barbarians." He suggested the king was not indifferent to the curricular fate of classical antiquity. Prudent university officials, knowing how prudence is acquired and how important royal patronage had been and would be for the colleges, should suppress anyone warning in public addresses or pub arguments against the *Erasmici* and literature they preferred. Silencing obscurantists would please the king.[4]

When pressed, More professed to have little influence, but petitioners thought otherwise. He was close to the king—"intimate," John Fisher said—asking for a favor in 1521 and getting it.[5] But to be Henry's friend and do well for one's friends, one had to make enemies of the king's enemies, and that might lead to the difficulties Hythloday predicted, as when Edward Stafford, the third duke of Buckingham, was arrested and executed for treason. Cardinal Wolsey's suspicions of the nobility had already landed Stafford's son-in-law and brother-in-law in trouble when a servant—or perhaps a spy planted by Wolsey—anonymously accused the duke of sedition. "In his fumes and displeasures," he seems to have been indiscreet; a few days after his trial in May 1521, Buckingham was beheaded.[6] More played only a small part in the drama. As Geoffrey Elton points out, he had yet to assume "administrative responsibilities of the first order" and possessed no significant political power, so even if we presume his "outraged sense of justice," we cannot imagine what he might have done with it. Besides, Wolsey kept him occupied. He twice sent More to aldermen in London, where Stafford was popular, to urge their compliance and assure the city's calm. More himself complied, yet regret showed when he referred to the sad fate of "a great duke ... his court al broken up" in *Four Last Things*, which More may have started as a "penitential exercise"—but left unfinished.[7]

Complicity? Guilt? Regret? Repentance? We know only that More purchased property from the duke's forfeited estates, resigning himself, it seems,
to the vagaries of court cronyism and intrigue. To suggest he had done so, of
course, is not to say that he was unfeeling or that Buckingham's reversal had
other than a sobering effect. Indeed, soon afterward, when William Roper
congratulated More for having earned the king's esteem, he cautioned his
son-in-law and first biographer with a memorable and cutting qualification:
"I have no cause to be proud thereof," he replied; "if my head could win
[Henry] a castle in France . . . it should not fail to go."[8]

But More crossed his Rubicon before Buckingham was betrayed. He came
back from Bruges in 1516, completed his *Utopia,* became a member of the
king's council, and closely watched Wolsey, whose administrative skill he admired. Only five years older than More, Wolsey had rapidly been promoted
from chaplain to chancellor from 1507 to 1515. Henry noticed how expeditiously he got things done, entrusting ever more to him. More was impressed
yet probably understood that Wolsey's "magisterial bearing" compassed a
dangerous addiction to extravagance. The arrogance and extravagance, in
fact, could be blamed for his fall. The courtiers whom he humiliated exploited
his failures in foreign policy and his inability to have the pope annul the king's
first marriage. Missteps of that magnitude, combined with the resentments of
those around him, were sufficient to get him reviled and removed by the late
1520s, proving his colleague and sometime rival, William Warham, a prophet:
"Do he never so well," the man "in most favor and most of counsel . . . shall be
maligned."[9]

But Wolsey was relatively unmaligned and still "in most favor" when
More came to court. Possibly, he reminded More of Morton, who was both
chancellor and cardinal—powerful and honorable, the London lawyer would
have said. But we cannot be sure why More stayed on after Buckingham's fate
confirmed what Hythloday argued in *Utopia* about the unpredictability and
imperfection of politics. We know only that Wolsey's trust tethered More to
court when, in 1523, the chancellor chose him to pilot the king's business
through parliament. He had More named speaker of the session called to
finance Henry's second war with France. Chancellor and speaker worked
together—although differently. Wolsey made demands, appearing twice in
the Commons, to intimidate acquiescence to a war tax many members opposed. The parade of retainers and their display of the symbols of high office

elicited only "a marvelous obstinate silence," according to Roper's report, which emphasized More's irritation. But Roper wrote long after Wolsey had died, deposed and discredited. Other chronicles make no mention of the speaker's dissatisfaction, and records of the deliberations have not survived. Only Roper mentioned that his father-in-law and the chancellor were at odds. The likelier prospect is that More, on cue or otherwise, ventured to say that nothing could be discussed or agreed in "obstinate silence," and that Wolsey's departure (and absence) might yield the desired outcome. Then, after the chancellor left, More pressured government loyalists with seats in the Lower House to urge their peers to pay a large portion of what king and court wanted. When it was "in the bank," Wolsey saw to it that the speaker got a bonus for his services.[10]

Had More veered from virtue into politics? William Tyndale later thought so. He was then trafficking in the new religious ideas that More found repulsive, so he had some reason to discredit the speaker and suggest he made a habit of "betray[ing] the truth to get promotion." Tyndale referred to *Utopia*, where he sensed an anticlerical sentiment, no less forceful for being only obliquely expressed. Hythloday, after all, censured prelates, including popes, for having goaded princes to war and, more specifically, for bleeding England to distract France and deliver Italy to the Roman church. More scripted that censure "before he was the cardinal's sworn secretary," calculating how costly clerical self-interest and independence had been to the commonwealth.[11] Yet Tyndale looks to have been scavenging in the text unfairly. *Utopia* was not quick to implicate Catholic Christianity in the sordid affairs of state, and More's history of the reign of Richard III, on which he made most progress soon after completing his dialogue with Hythloday, is ambiguous, at best, on that count. True, a speech he wrote for one of Richard's partisans argued, in effect, that the church mismanaged its most controversial immunity: fugitives granted sanctuary and thus shielded from searches and seizures were permitted to creep out and commit new crimes.[12] Yet More would have recalled that the pope proposed a remedy for recidivism. Rome let the English government appoint custodians to keep in place troublemakers who sought refuge. What More knew of the church's other efforts, monitoring mismanagement and restructuring regulations, almost certainly induced him to put a good spin on sanctuary's inviolability.[13] But Tyndale missed that and, consequently, was wrong to think More (before Wolsey) milled around with the church's implacable critics and subscribed to the drastic doctrinal alterations commended by Martin Luther. To More, they were "the worst heresyes"—unimaginable in 1516 and unacceptable thereafter, when English evangelical anticlericals echoed them—which was why he appeared eager to "biteth, sucketh, gnaweth, towseth, and mowseth Tindale."[14]

But he began by gnawing at Luther. Henry VIII later remembered that More had gotten the government to go along, "procuring and provoking" the king himself to draft a defense of sacraments and the papacy. But that story is untrustworthy. It was relayed as part of an indictment charging More with undue influence and attributing opinions that Henry held yet later repudiated to More's "subtle, sinister sleights."[15] More's memory, however, may be no less faulty. He said Henry and his team of theologians approached him and that he had not advocated a forceful English response to the German heresy. He recalled trying to dissuade the king from "set[ting] forth" the case for papal authority "to the uttermost." More's version is ordinarily preferred to the king's, but, in 1534, he was obviously interested in having the opinions ascribed to him then—to his disadvantage and discomfort—associated with his sovereign's views in 1521. More claimed that Henry was more papal in his *Assertion*—in return for which the pope named the king *defensor fidei*, a defender of the Catholic faith—than More who was advising and assisting him at the time. Nonetheless, even if we accept More's story, we cannot escape the impression that he "was a linchpin from the outset" in the government's "anti-Lutheran campaign."[16]

Wolsey probably put him up to it. As papal legate, he read the bull excommunicating Luther when it arrived in London in 1521. He ordered Luther's books burned and had John Fisher preach at the ceremony, confident the learned bishop of Rochester could bore down to the core of Luther's "pernicious doctryn" and expose Luther's lies. What Wolsey and Fisher so deeply disliked was the German reformer's insistence that their churches be judged by the Bible, that any church custom or practice or office without explicit scriptural warrant be jettisoned. Fisher complained that Luther overlooked or forgot how "many moo thinges which [the apostles] spook, unwritten, [were] of grete authoryte," equally as authoritative as—if not more authoritative than—what the apostles and evangelists wrote. Paul made just that point, harping on the importance of oral tradition (2 Thess. 2:15), of "thinges unwritten," among which Bishop Fisher numbered the prevailing ecclesiastical structures and five of the church's seven sacraments. The Bible was silent, he said, about a number of profoundly significant "wordes," "gestures," and "orders." *Tenete traditiones,* the Latin had Paul directing; "kepe those instruccions and erudicyons," Fisher translated, preaching either before—or while— Luther's books were burning. And he promised that a far better book than any of Luther's was forthcoming, one written by none other than the king, in which readers "shall se those blessed sacraments clered and delivered from the sklauderous mouthe and cruel teethe that Martyn Luther hath set upon them."[17]

The king had help preparing his *Assertion* in defense of the seven sacraments. Wolsey saw to that. He probably prevailed on More, who admitted that he was a "sorter out and placer of the principal matters" in the book, which, he said, "layed unto Luther" and "destroyeth the grounde and foundacyon of all heresyes" popular on the Continent.[18] Luther denied "the grounde and foundacyon" of his reform was "destroyed" by Henry's *Assertion,* and More was commissioned to return fire. In 1523 he printed and circulated his pseudonymous reply. It charged that Luther misrepresented the English king's statements, much as he misconstrued what the Bible had to say about faith and the churches. Echoing Fisher, More explained that Luther's exclusive scripturalism (*sola scriptura*) itself was unscriptural. The apostle's directive, *tenete traditiones,* clearly validated "thinges unwritten," and it made Luther's barking at them look ridiculous. But what made his bite so much worse than his bark was the unparalleled religious individualism he purportedly drew from scripture and defended against Henry. Simply put—and More tended to oversimplify the reformers' discourses on religious authority—Luther and his crew wanted to set aside rules and rituals "confirmed by the unbroken agreement of the whole church," merely because biblical warrant was not *prima facie* prominent. In effect, they licensed Christians to drop several of the sacraments, forget purgatory, scoff at the veneration of saints, and scorn pilgrimages. More feared that the liberties Luther inspired or condoned led to a dissolution of all laws and order, that Luther's protests imperiled the admittedly imperfect, though absolutely critical, maintenance systems that government magistrates and church authorities had cobbled together.[19]

Madness; "the raving of a rascal."[20] More scolded Luther for refusing to confront the political implications of his fideism and individualism, for blindly "trust[ing] that the law of the gospel sufficed and that human laws were of no use [*inutiles*] when faith was preached rightly and magistrates were good" and faithful. That kind of faith in faith and in the faithful seemed foolish to More. The wicked were resourceful enough to do monstrous things when magistrates enforced the laws guarding the public; in the absence of both laws and enforcement, notwithstanding reformers' sermons and the most diligent magistrates, the wicked would ruin whatever was worthwhile and rule ruthlessly. The results: corruption and chaos.[21]

Luther left statesmen with too few tools and too many worries, More concluded, insisting that the reformers' antinomianism in the early 1520s would undercut any effort to keep order, settle quarrels, punish crimes, and encourage hard work. The authorities were either armed with "definite laws" or subject to "indefinite whims," which would be no match for the problems that Luther's reform created for governments favoring it. For Luther's fideism severed connections between personal salvation and public morality. And, More argued, when "faith alone suffices [to save sinners], not only without good works but with crimes of any kind," the faithful are free to become so-cially irresponsible or criminal. So princes and magistrates were left two op-tions: lethargy or tyranny. That was Luther's political legacy.[22] Of course, there were alternatives to Luther. Augustine tested them centuries before: coopera-tion between church and government and the church's control over scriptural study and interpretation. Recalling that venerable bishop's struggles against "all the rable of the old heretyques," More averred that

> drown[ing] them selfe in those dampnable heresyes was nothyng but hyghe pryde of theyr lernynge in scrypture wherin they folowed theyr owne wyttes and lefte the common fayth of the catholyke chy-rche preferrynge theyr owne gay gloses before the ryght catholyke fayth of all Crystes chyrche whiche can never arre in any substancy-all poynt that god wolde have us bounden to byleve. And therfore to ende where we began, who so wyll not unto the study of scrypture take the poyntes of the catholyke faythe as a rule of interpretacyon, but of dyffydens and mystrust study to seke in scrypture whyther the fayth of the chyrche be trewe or not, he can not fayle to fall in worse errours.[23]

Had Luther only taken those "poyntes of the catholyke faythe as a rule of interpretacyon," More guessed, he might have meaningfully rehabilitated and not undermined the church. Certainly, he would have avoided straying far from scripture while pretending to stay so close. For More, Luther's fideism was always the obvious illustration. It treated human effort as soterially insignificant. It reduced humans to hatchets in God's hand; it drastically devalued Christians' strenuous efforts to answer "by good endevour" God's summons issued, in effect, by the patriarchs, psalms, prophets, and apostles. Had Luther forgotten that scripture was full of summonses: "Turne to me, and I wyll turne to you"? Was that something God, through the prophet Zechariah (1:3), would have said to a hatchet?[24]

As we shall soon see, More's polemics continued to undermine the biblical basis Luther laid for the fideism of the reformed churches. His first replies to the Saxon renegade, though, concentrated on defending the sacraments and papacy and on responding to Luther's unflattering comments about his king's intelligence, honesty, and piety.[25] More was not so much out to rein in a raging bull in Germany as to stroke Henry for trying. He determined that, if Luther had listened to the king explain "the right catholyke faythe" in what the scripture signified, he would not have mistakenly opposed purgatory and penance. He might not have so terribly misread the mass, notably, Jesus' declaration that the bread was totally and truly his body—and the wine, his blood—at his last supper and, thereafter, at every Eucharist. The king's *Assertion* took Luther to task for denying that the mass was a sacrifice, the "work" of Christ and of a priest, as well as a memorial (or "testament") to God's promise made at the cross. More agreed: the mass was *both* a work and a testament. The Catholic church long held that what began at the supper was completed on the cross and repeated in the mass. Biblical passages on the supper invited no other interpretation: *haec quotienscunque fecerit,* as often as priests consecrate bread and wine, they do as Christ did, *in coena et cruce,* both in the meal and on the cross. More and Henry did not think to ask "whyther the faith of the chyrche be trewe or not." They accepted that it was true and biblical. But the reformers were "follow[ing] theyr owne wyttes" and were insolently unconventional, anticlerical, and unscriptural.[26]

More stressed that he and Henry were none of the above. They were respectful. Their expositions and applications of scripture were secondhand; they drew them from learned exegetes and never considered the results "equal to the word of God." True, the king's interpretations were "trewe" and superior to what More called the "false glosynge" of the reformers, but that was no cause to boast. More claimed authority for a tradition of interpretation, not for his, or Henry's, conscience or conscientious contributions.[27] As for Luther's "glosynge," it might have been a bit easier to bear, were it not symptomatic of a religious individualism destructive of the Catholic consensus and social order. What was in store for faith, church, and commonwealth, More mused, "if every man can fynd out a new fonde fantasye upon a texte of Holy Scripture" and have "hys owne exposition byleved" by an appreciable number of Christians? More, after all, could start a sect just as easily as Luther had. He would "saye by scripture" that each Christian must sell all but one coat. Such spin on gospel commendations of selflessness might at first seem preposterous, yet near-biblical maxims were not hard to pass off as plausible and biblical: "I were able . . . to fynd out fyften newe sects in one fore noon that shulde have as much probable hold of Scripture as thys heresy hathe."[28]

In one respect, Luther was exceptional. Tongue-in-cheek, More gave him credit for ingenuity, for unabashedly and "so sodeynly" fathering on scripture something "the old, holy, wise, and well lerned doctors [of the church] in all thys longe wyle" had never anticipated: Luther proved that former friars might marry nuns. Presuming mutual affection, More saw each coupling as a double helping of "abomynable lechery." He could only imagine, though, that "the ryght catholyke fayth" would have condemned Luther even had he not tried to disguise his lust as piety. Pious Germans must have known that worse was in store in 1521, when the swaggering Saxon reformer announced at Worms that he had come upon a fideism unknown to "all the olde holy doctors" and incomprehensible to Catholic theologians and authorities of his time.[29]

What now seems certain is that More, soon thereafter and increasingly, became convinced of Luther's incomprehension and impertinence. He was distressed by Luther's indifference to dire predictions of what might politically come of the religious liberties he was heard to have preferred.[30] More looked to the king for continued support, for help in averting the worst. He formed a literary alliance of sorts, drawing passages from Henry's *Assertion* into his own response to Luther and docking them alongside Luther's misstatements of what was at issue. He did that so often and extensively that his document could be described as "a polemical anthology," "a collaborative enterprise."[31] But the purpose of its prodigality, as noted, had little to do with persuading Luther. More's aim, above all, was to preserve the king's goodwill and parade it before readers. Possibly he had not then believed what he later said of Henry—that "there was never . . . brought in thys worlde a prynce of more benygne nature nor of more mercyfull mynde"—nonetheless, he was careful to keep "hys hyghnesse['s] fervant affeccyon to ryght and justyce" as the mainspring of his—and the realm's—answer to Luther.[32] He would cultivate and count on the king's "fervant affeccyion" for the church through the 1520s. And he would often remind his sovereign during that period of the alternatives to royal protection of the sacraments, the papacy, and the English prelates who defended both. More warned, that is, of the dreadful consequences should the government fail to support Catholic consensus: Henry's subjects would busy themselves "makynge sectes" and "brekynge unite," as the Germans did, and continued to do, on hearing their local heretic. Many of them cheered when Luther made "idols of [his] owne fals opynyons . . . sowying sedycyon and dyssensyon to styrre up rebellion and insurrection against theyr neyghbours and theyr governours." And, by the mid 1520s, those seditions and dissensions were a clear and present danger in England. Scurrilous expositions and mistranslations of biblical verses had gotten across the Channel and were introducing unsuspecting commoners (*plebesculae*) to the new heresy.[33]

"The Comon Knowen Catholyke Fayth" and the Church

Books were the problem. Expositions and translations. While helping Henry see the devastating political implications of what the reformers were thinking, More helped Wolsey keep other Englishmen from reading their thoughts. Early in 1526 he led a raid on the Steelyard where foreign merchants lodged and landed their goods. The premises were searched and heretical literature confiscated. Weeks later, Wolsey staged another bonfire. Fisher preached, robustly celebrating "the continuance" of the Catholic church and defaming sectarian impulses. Who could doubt, he asked, that "the true sede of the worde of God . . . the scriptures of God have been truely taught unto the people, and the people hath truely believed and given true faith unto the same doctryne of the scriptures" for fifteen hundred years? Luther showed terrible judgment giving up all that truth and "truly" for his "sudden" revelations.[34]

On that, Fisher and More agreed. They also agreed, in principle, that the church's teaching "the true sede of the worde of God" did not preclude having that word translated and printed in language Christian commoners could understand. But heretics precipitated something of a crisis. The time was not right for an English Bible.[35] Nonetheless, before or just after More prowled the Steelyard and Fisher preached on "continuance," they received word that William Tyndale's translation was crossing to England. Perhaps when he was at university, Tyndale was already contemplating the challenge and complaining that the study of scripture was unduly postponed until scholars mastered scholastic philosophy. He said as much subsequently and may have made that observation part of his overture and argument to Bishop Tunstall when he requested a commission to English the New Testament.[36] Tunstall refused, but layman Humphrey Monmouth supplied the means to send Tyndale abroad, where he acquired a collaborator, a publisher, and a pronounced anticlerical snarl. He promised to restore "the ryght sence" of scripture "destroyed" by Catholic clerics, he said, "wyth theyr leven." But More found his unleavened version "unsavery," incorrect, "corrupted." It was so shot through with ambiguity and anger at traditional religion, he expected readers might be driven from, rather than drawn to, the religion of Jesus. As for revisions or repairs, he judged that "the fautys be . . . so many and so spred through the hole boke" that "it were as sone done to weve a newe web of cloth as to sow up every hole in a net." What was to be done besides making it illegal either to smuggle copies into England or to possess them there?[37]

Other dangerous texts were coming from the Continent. Luther sent a conciliatory letter to the king. Might it make Henry more receptive to the reformers' "fals opynyons"? John Bugenhagen, pastor of the city church in Wittenberg, where he officiated at Luther's wedding, wrote *ad Anglos* to answer More's criticisms and explain that piety and virtue followed *from* faith, though they were not required *for* it. One who believes in Christ is "a good tree that cannot but bear good fruit."[38] More bristled: the church, and not faith alone, teaches virtue. The church makes Christians. What gave Luther and Bugenhagen away as naïve was their faith in faith; what made them offensive as well as socially irresponsible was their having shamelessly libeled the church's initiatives. They called the Catholic authorities and their apologists pelagians. They charged that Catholicism had long "peddle[d] works instead of Christ." Worse still, reformers put nothing in place of the traditional religion they pilloried. Their talk of trees and fruit could not hide that, in effect, Luther and Bugenhagen created a moral void.[39] Their pairing piety and faith did not fool More who knew and rehearsed for Henry how the rhetoric of reformed religion already incited sectarian violence on the Continent: "Unbridled license rages to such an extent under the pretext of freedom of the gospel" leaving "bitter reminders of looting, rape, bloodshed, sacrilege, fire, ruin, and devastation."[40]

More prepared these remarks to respond to Bugenhagen in 1526 and to alert the king once again to the likely political repercussions of Luther's religious reform. Henry, however, needed no persuading. He saw to it that an angry letter was sent under his signature, refusing Luther's olive branch and reiterating his opposition to the new German doctrines. But Henry's disposition would soon change, as we shall see, when the pope procrastinated rather than responding promptly to his request to have his first marriage annulled. Anticlerical pamphleteers capitalized on the king's discontent and tried to put their prince in a panic: the church, they said, was stealing and often sending abroad his realm's revenue. Several years later, when Henry was closer to proclaiming parts of the reform they desired, evangelical anticlericals were depicted as moderate and doctrinally upright enemies of excess. But More was having none of it. How could they "purposely saye evyll and openly speke heresye, and for all that thynke well"? More believed their complainers' cult was bent on bringing Luther's "fals opynyons" to England. When they "speke" against pilgrimage, purgatory, and pardons, they show that they "dyspyseth trew poyntes of the comon knowen catholyke fayth." Bishops were right to denounce them to the government, which was right to punish them as public enemies.[41] More was ready to help. Bishop Tunstall of London, looking for a Demosthenes, he said, for an agile, energetic "assertor of Catholic truth," licensed More to read and reply to the forbidden books. He promptly did so, even after he was appointed chancellor the next year (1529). And he replied with "urgency," Peter Ackroyd observes, with "a clamancy which [was] not untouched by a sense of weariness and feeling of doom."[42]

But fatigue and pessimism came later. At first, More proved to be just what Tunstall wanted, a keen critic of the church's critics. He slashed at the premise that braced the anticlericals' complaints, the assumption that clerical stealth depleted the realm's wealth. He conceded, for example, that the pious and affluent often endowed chantries, but he declared that the effects of such charitable bequests on the Crown's coffers were negligible. As for larger legacies, they seldom, if ever, took money from secular circulation; the church was simply reallocating its resources when it established "abbays or such other great foundacyons." So, despite the reformers' sirens, Henry did "not nede to fere that all temprorall land in the realme shall come into the spyrytualtye."[43] Yet the anticlerical pamphlets persisted in opposing that "spyrytualtye" to sovereignty, specifically to Henry's sovereignty, and More nervously watched as the king, awaiting some resolution in Rome, warmed to the critics' case. Their literature was taking its toll on "the good mynde and devocyon of the temporaltye." Henry may not have "embraced [Simon Fish] with loving countenance," as John Foxe said, although he likely read with interest Fish's and Tyndale's sketches of the scandalous practices of Catholic prelates.[44]

Fish's *Supplication of Beggars* appeals to the king to protect his poorest subjects from clerical extortion. It describes the clergy's resourcefulness in making the laity pay for pardons. Purgatory was a prime example, a cash cow, an unscriptural, mythical hot spot devised—and described in gruesome detail—to draw funds from credulous commoners. More answered conventionally. He produced the biblical passage about the purifying fire to which church authorities referred when explaining purgatory.[45] Fish was not unfamiliar with the explanation, yet, More claimed, malice made him forgetful. Fish, Tyndale, and other English satellites of Saxony simply despised the Catholic clergy, and their contrariness, according to More, turned priests' everyday practice into petty larceny. He begged Henry not to take the worst of the church as typical. Priests normally pray for the laity—for souls on earth and in purgatory—"of theyre owne cheryte." When the laity pays them to pray, priests are "double bounden," but, more important, commoners who pay express their compassion, which grows with expression and spreads to others. Love abounds, and there is "myche more good and profyt upon all sydys." More would have the king compare that prospect—compare, that is, a realm packed with caring subjects to one populated by spiteful, tightfisted anticlericals who, "for hatred whych they owe to prested wolde make you beleve that there were no purgatory and wold rather wysh by theyr wyllys that theyr owne fathers lye here in fyre tyll the day of doome then eny shulde geve a preste one peny to pray for them."[46]

More went on to speak for those left to "lye in fyre." A supplication for souls in purgatory, after all, should have greater weight than the one Fish composed for beggars supposedly beguiled by greedy priests, for the deceased were made wiser by death. They learned that material possessions were ultimately unimportant, and they discovered what happened to all they had accumulated on earth. Indeed, if the miserly among them had not hoarded so, buying time in purgatory, as it were, with their pinching and skimping, they would have been amused watching their executors, "bysyly rifling and ransackynge [their] housys as thogh they were men of warr." What was most galling, though, was the speed with which the dead had been forgotten. They repented their own forgetfulness on earth immediately on seeing the wretchedness of those who preceded them to the grave and into purgatory. They only consoled themselves by imagining—in More's imagining—the "sorrowfull shame" of other "sely soule[s] furst commyng hyther" when faced with their forgotten friends. The melodrama was designed to counter reformers' assurances that purgatory was a fiction. By bitterly complaining about their kin's thoughtlessness, the souls More impersonated raked reformers into the heap of delinquents. If forgetful relatives could but "byhold in what hevy plight we ly," their "slouth wold sone be quickened"; their "oblivion, tourne to freshe remembraunce." If anticlericals could so "byhold," they would quit harping on churches' scandals, sparring with well-meaning clerical colleagues, and perfunctorily repeating the standard, stale prayers for the dead. "May God be merciful to all Christian souls," they often prayed, but "it cummeth out so coldely," More observed, "and wyth so dull affeccyon that yt lyeth in [their] lyppys and never cam nere the harte."[47]

More might have hoped that his impersonations and insults would rehabilitate reformers. He was probably longing to reach them with his proof of purgatory and—he would have said—with proof of Fish's malice and misrepresentations—"almost as many lyes as lynes." Yet he was again composing for the king, who should know that Fish's *Supplication* was "rethoryk wythout reason."[48] For it stands to reason, More went on, that righteous rulers punish sin, that God rules righteously, yet that punishing sins perpetually after a sinner repents and converts would be unrighteous. Penalties, therefore, ought to be limited, although many died before the limits were reached, with retribution "due and undone." Hence, "purgatory must nedes appeare." It would be irrational to issue an amnesty at the first sign of remorse. It would give "gret occasyon of lyghtnes and bold corage to synne."[49]

The strategy was to make the government suspicious of the anticlericals' intent and fearful of the unintended political consequences of their fideism. More would have Henry consider how hazardous it was to contemplate the reformers' promises of freedom from Rome and to approve their arrogant statements about the Crown's sovereignty over the spirituality. Henry, that is, gave his subjects "bold corage to synne" when he listened to the reformers' moaning about purgatory, pilgrimage, veneration of images, or prayers to saints; that was More's point. He conceded that the English anticlericals had become as seductively clever as Luther with the Bible. He figured that he could slow or perhaps stop altogether the erosion of the Catholic position, however, by making a mockery of their idiosyncratic, heretical expositions of scripture. Still, he seems to have accepted, that battles for the Bible had been costly. His interlocutor in the *Dialogue Concerning Heresies,* completed a few months before his *Supplication,* expresses the commoners' anguish that More either heard or imagined: "better it were that God had not gyven us scrypture at all than to gyve us a waye to walke wherein we were more lykely to synke than save our selfe."[50] More responded that the only way not to sink was to swim in the channels cut by the Catholic church's venerable interpreters. As evangelical anticlericals appealed to the king's self-interest, More invited readers to see how recklessly reformers probed alternatives to traditional views and practices and thrust them forward. They were sinking under the weight of their idiocy, grandstanding all the while, stirring sinners with the encouragement that their sins were wholly remitted, and daring to explain mysteries that were, More said, "farre to profounde to perce unto."[51]

To save reformers from sinking and from scuttling others' salvation, More did what Augustine had done when Donatists would not be argued back into Africa's catholic churches. He relied on government intimidation. He sensed government support slipping, but, as chancellor, he backed the bishops who pressured their critics to abjure. More, like Augustine, continued to debate the dissidents. He answered their accusations with sometimes scorching, always extended, polemics. Admirers now regret both their tone and his cruelty. (Unlike Augustine, More approved executing the incorrigible.) They refer now to More's lapse from the ostensible liberalism of *Utopia* into an apparently ultraconservative, militant clericalism. But Brendan Bradshaw is right to question their chronicle of decline and fall. He thinks More, answering fideists, advocated "an alternative reformation" consistent with Renaissance humanism's "call to perfection." Bradshaw's More is "populist" and "radical," not clericalist and conservative. He worked from the humanist premise that "self-development by rational means" could lead to a reformed polity with improved efficiencies and firewalls against corruption.[52]

Bradshaw's study concludes with the "strangely grim . . . brooding figure" of More peering at us from the family portrait painted by Hans Holbein in 1528, just as More's polemical career was about to kick into a higher gear. Many Tudor watchers, regretting that kick, see something of a scowl. The curious "brooding" betrays to them an irritability that marks More's lapse from liberalism into fanaticism. They say he was soon to abandon Christian humanism. To Bradshaw, however, the "brooding" signals More's determination to advance humanism's "alternative reformation," despite intense and increasingly influential opposition. His opposition was nothing if not resourceful during the late 1520s, when the king, for the most part, grew kinder to beckoning anticlericals whose fideism undermined the humanists' reliance on reason and "call to perfection." Henry seemed ready to abandon Catholic traditions for the reformers' biblicism, which, More argued, gave interpretation of the scripture over to unsteady, unsavory characters. If he was as "grim" as Holbein made him appear, More's ill humor was understandable, not "strange," Bradshaw says, because he perceived that his humanism and the surging anticlericalism were on a collision course in 1528. But I think More's determination to avoid a coming collision was different. He resolved to shore up the partnership between church and government yet did not expect one partner to improve the other. He was resigned to the government's staggering imperfectibility. He countenanced cooperation—specifically, the government's protection of the English Catholic church—because it secured a context in which Christians reached spiritual maturity through time-honored rites of passage that secured, in turn, some degree of social stability. More was "grim" because he was losing his faith in argument even as he argued, drafting sprawling answers to critics' relatively spare yet effective treatises. He explained, elucidated, traded insults, and gradually lost hope. Heretics' "hertes are ones fyxed upon theyr blynde affeccyons." "They nothing ponder what is reasonably spoken to them." More said sullenly that he might as well preach to a post.[53]

But the anticlericals were more menacing than a post; they were bent on doing away with the realm's Catholic church, not just on dissolving its partnership with their government. The Bible was enough for them. They refused to accept that it needed all the explaining Catholics lavished on it for centuries "to stablish their lies," Tyndale complained, maintaining that the meaning of every passage was "playne."[54] But More answered that anticlericals could or would not comprehend the more self-evident texts, notably Jesus' promise in John's gospel (16:13–14) that God would give Christians "a spirit of truth." The passage stipulated that the spirit "shall lede you into all trouth," not that "the holy gooste shall wryte unto you all thynges nor shall wryte you all trouth." To More, the "deduction" was inescapable: "the spirit of truth" revealed to the church—and through it—tenets and counsels "as good and as sure to salvacyon of oure soules, without any wrytnge at all."[55] The spirit was a guide, not a text; it was the church's to receive and relay. Without the church's guidance, Augustine would have remained a Manichee, as he said, and as More recalled: "I wolde not byleve the gospel, but yf the authoryte of the catholyke chyrche moved me thereto." The rumor More gladly passed along was that the anticlericals thought extrascriptural guidance irrelevant. Tyndale, then, was unscriptural as well as maliciously anticlerical, willfully ignorant and irreverent, when he "layeth hys myry handes upon" the church to "pulle [it] downe . . . and so leve no churche at all"?[56]

"Leve no churche at all" was an exaggeration. More's *Dialogue Concerning Heresies* acknowledged that Tyndale and the anticlericals proposed something vaguely ecclesiastical. Still, it looked like "no churche at all" to anyone accustomed to religion "amonge the grete unchaungeable crysten countrees whiche have kepte theyr faythe in one constant fassyon derived from the begynnynge." The reformers' "church," that is, was "secret," "scattered," and composed of "suche as byleve a right and lyve well where so ever they be, though the worlde knowe them not and though fewe of them knowe eche other." For all the uncertainties that "secrecy" or invisibility occasioned, More conceded, one thing was plain: the anticlericals' "chyrche of cryste is not nor [for] many dayes hath not bene the people that seemeth to be the chyrche." But that negation solved nothing of practical importance. To whom should one refer an infidel curious about the Christian faith? Who might smooth the path to Christian conversion? More's interlocutor in the *Dialogue* had a ready reply. He was "studyouse in holy scrypture, which was, he sayd, lernynge ynoughe for a crysten man." Bibles should be handed to infidels, he directed, confident they would find "so grete swetnes in the texte it selfe" that they would never want "to lese any tyme in the [church's] gloses." To More, the interlocutor was asking for trouble. He "set the matter . . . so well and [so] lustely forwarde" that it was evident he had "fallen in to Luther's sect." "Yonge scolers be somtyme prone to newe fantasyes," More observed, and ought to heed the warning he repeatedly issued to cinch his case for "the authoryte of the catholyke chyrche": reading a sacred text without special guidance exposed rifts in the ranks of the faithful, abraded faith, and destabilized society.[57]

In More's judgment, the English anticlericals' "secret," "scattered" church took Luther's religious individualism to an extreme. Tyndale and his associates fragmented the church. It existed only in holy pieces, and, More argued, the alleged perfection of each piece mocked Luther's observations about the pervasiveness of sin. Augustine, on that count, would have lined up with Luther and against the anticlericals. More was certain that the venerable fifth-century bishop would have repudiated the claim that a Christian "onys clensed and made fayre ys never after foule." Augustine's paramount concern after 410 was to save African Christianity from both the individualism of the Pelagians and from the perfectionism of the Donatists. More thought he was adopting his predecessor's mantra: "holy chyrche is not called holy because every peyce thereof is holy."[58]

Yet imagine that personal holiness were possible, More asked; imagine "every peyce" were perfect, conforming its intention to God's will. From experience, one must still conclude, he said, that the very best intentions traveled badly over time. Temptation and indecision afflict everyone, shortening the shelf life of any piece's perfection. If the church must be perfect, it dies with doubts, hesitations, and slips. Or it must exist only in spurts—in the morning, with a good Christian's resolve, More explained, only to be gone by night and, perhaps, back at dawn with the next day's repentance. So to have personal holiness as the bedrock of the church was, in More's book, absurdity, not ecclesiology.[59] Even Luther, he conceded, was not as spectacularly irrational as English anticlericals. "The sole sign by which the church is recognized with certainty," for Luther, was not each member's perfect righteousness but "the preaching of the gospel." But sermons only seemed to be sturdy props. Luther's further thoughts on the church and ministry, especially his delirious pronouncements on "the priesthood of all believers," made it impractical to put such great weight on preaching. For Luther's remarks on lay emancipation invited parishioners to interrupt pastors, "preach with fists" in their stead, or, More reported, stay at home. If preaching the gospel is the "sole sign" of an authentic church, Christians were well advised to look to Catholic priests. Luther disagreed, of course, and insisted that the gospel was only preached in the truly reformed church, a statement that undermined his seemingly sturdy prop. More pecked at the circularity, proving to his satisfaction that Luther could hardly have been less straightforward: the gospel must be preached before the church is "recognized," yet we know it as the gospel and good preaching, *propterea quod ecclesiam cognoscimus*, only because we recognize the church as *certa*, certain or dependable.[60]

More let the negatives fly: neither preaching nor personal holiness made the church *certa*. The opposition was adept at pulling passages from sacred literature to prove the contrary but only proved to More that the Catholic church was indispensable. After Luther and the English anticlericals so resourcefully draped scripture around their silly ideas, "reason may bytwene dyvers textys stande in great doute which waye to lene." For their part, the heretics seemed devoid of doubt, yet they preyed on that of others. For his part, More trusted his church's exegetes and authorities consistently to apply the Bible to Christians' predicaments. Such consistency and the consensus of the faithful that it had developed around applications—affirming the usefulness of pilgrimages, the sacrament of penance, the veneration of saints, and related rituals—demonstrated over centuries "that God with his holy spyryte ledyth his chyrche into the consent of the trouthe."[61]

"Divisions"

David Bagchi now refers to "ecclesiastical fundamentalism," saying that More "magnified" the virtue of acquiescence to the authority of the church in his *Responsio*, his first reply to Luther in 1523, and persistently thereafter. There were acceptable levels of dissent, but, unsurprisingly, as the crisis worsened, More was inclined "to keep a tight control of . . . irrationality as well as evil and folly," and, to him, that meant imprisoning and silencing some critics of the Catholic church, the "bearer, custodian, and criterion of divine truth." Criticism would detonate controversies and take the faithful from consensus to chaos.[62]

Lawyer Christopher St. German styled himself a moderate caught in the middle. More was unconvinced. He believed St. German was wrong—and deliberately so—when he characterized religious dissent in the realm as a conspicuous symptom of widespread disaffection from and resentment of the English Catholic church. To More, St. German seemed as dangerous as the church's most strident critics. He sounded tame at times, proposing that if the realm's "prelates wolde a litel meken them selfe and withdrawe suche thinges as have brought the people into this murmur and grudge, then . . . they shulde anone bringe a new light of grace into the worlde."[63] Yet he proceeded to humiliate the church, stirring "division" rather than merely assessing or reporting it, as he pretended. He went on about "confederacies, wherby spiritual men pretend to meytene the lawes of the church," although stand "sometyme ageinste the kinges lawes and the olde customes of the realme." He claimed that the confederacies or conspiracies "of pristis" aimed to avoid government regulation. As much as More mistrusted government, he appreciated that he would have to rely on it to protect the churches from heresy. He could not let St. German's ammunition pass as evidence. He could not permit his highly and perilously prejudicial observations to go unanswered. What if Henry and his council believed that these "heyghnouse confederacyes" were scheming to avoid justice in the king's courts, as St. German alleged? What if the ruling elites could be persuaded that priests plotted to avoid limits set on the legacies, mortuaries, and tithes they might receive? And what if commoners concluded that the church was all about turning a profit? St. German was dangerous indeed. More worried that few would notice his complaints about prelatical collusion named no names, that he had simply cobbled conspiracies from an angry word here and a grievance there. Of course, angry words saddened More, though they did not shock him; "a man that is on the lesynge side"—whether charged or denied a fee for sacerdotal services—may gripe, much as a loser at cards. But, "in thys matter," he averred, on the issue of inordinate charges, "I here no suche talking." Were St. German's ears sharper than his? Perhaps so, but be that as it may, More added, "hit is an olde courtesye at a cardys perdye to let the leser have hys wordes" without construing them as telltale signs of the winner having cheated.[64]

Whatever St. German might make of occasional angry words on either side of the "divide" separating clergy from the laity, he could not, to More's satisfaction, prove premeditated evasion or, worse, a clerical assault on the prerogatives of government or on the purses of commoners. Yet More could not risk having Henry misjudge the critics' abilities to deepen that "division" with "murmur and grudge." St. German minimized their stridency while incriminating the church. More, for his part, turned incriminating talk about "heyghnouse confederacyes" against the dissidents. Predictably, "amonge good Catholyke folke," the most charitable citizens and temperate monarchs will be tempted to let heretics rant "unchekked." After all, the Bible assured that true faith would never fail. Hence,

> good men in theyr owne mynde conceyve of the strength and fastnes of the catholyke faith, whyche they verily thynke so strong that here-tykes for all theyr bablynge shall never be able to vaynquyshe. And therein undoutedly theyr minde is not onely good but also very trewe. But they thynke not farre inough. For as the see shall never su-runde and overwhelme all the lande and yet hath it eaten many places in and swalowed hole cuntrees uppe and made many places nowe see that somtyme were well inhabyted landes . . . so, though the fayth of Cryste shall never be overflowen with heresyes, nor the gates of hell prevayle agaynste Crystes chyrche, yet as in some places it wynneth in new people, so maye there in some places by neglygence be lost tholde.[65]

"By neglygence be lost"? To More, that was too simple an explanation for the erosion of the Catholic position on the continent. Reformers there had made political elites their accomplices. "Gapyng after the landys of the spyry-tualtye," the temporal lords listened to the critics of the church who proposed seizing clerical properties and prerogatives. Before long, though, the religious reformers and the laity they led to protest the prevailing ecclesiastical order turned "agaynst all theyr governours."[66]

More warned the elites of England that they, too, could face commoners' protests and perhaps a peasant rebellion if, "by neglygence" or greed, they let Tyndale, Fish, and their friends speak freely against the church. The sacra-ments would soon be gone, More said; the clergy, disrespected and in despair. People would grow weary of good works and ignore vows. They would mock martyrs, monks, and the church they served. And, with the church compro-mised, squeezed, and soon stripped of its resources, "then shall the realme encreace in rychesse"—or so the reformers promised. But More urged the government to consider the contrary. Repudiating authority was an infectious disease. "Divisions" multiplied. Secession became the order of the day. Entire populations grow feverish and hysterical. "Unruly people rebelle agaynst their rulers." Tyndale, Fish, and Luther's other English disciples appeared willing to "lette all runne to ruyne."[67]

Reformers argued that God licensed disobedience. When established authorities upheld improper doctrine or let standards for behavior fall, they ought to be repudiated. Jesus denounced the Pharisees. His followers fled the synagogue. But, More countered, the English anticlericals' insolence had nothing in common with the earliest Christians' exodus. "Chryst and hys apostles and saynt Johan baptyste went out of the chyrche or synagoge of the Jewys bycause the tyme was come in whyche by godess owne ordynaunce, the Jewys chyrche or synagoge sholde have an end." Had Tyndale contemplated Christ's commission to the apostle Peter (Matthew 16:18), he would comprehend that there could be no leaving or disobeying "the catholyke chyrche of Chryst" in England and Rome. "The gates of hell shall not prevail against" that church, entrusted to Peter, "whiche whyle the worlde endureth is ordayned of God to have none end," and the same could not be said of the first-century synagogues. Renewal, therefore, starts and stays within the church without end. Undivided, it moves forward in an orderly fashion. It may experience over time a battalion of changes, but never a new beginning.[68] What looked at first to be "new bygonne" churches, on close inspection, appeared to be short-lived sects. Augustine hoped to make them disappear quickly. As chancellor, More sanctioned methods that helped English bishops and their courts follow suit. They could interrogate suspects without identifying informants, thus encouraging the latter to come forward and identify sectarians. Moderates objected. St. German said suspects ought to be permitted to prove their accusers were simply settling personal scores. But More was satisfied that robust inquiries would expose accusers' rancor masquerading as piety. He replied that "spyrytual judge[s] sholde medle with any man for heresye without an open accusor complaynyng" when the alternative was to "suffre many great harmes to grow" from sectarians' disparaging religious authority until "all runne to ruyne."[69]

More's estimates of possible damage varied from lost souls "in some places" to the realm's "ruyne." Yet he consistently proposed and defended precautions to ensure against posterity's possible complaints. He did not want descendants to say about the Catholics of his generation that they should "have waxen warmer afore and repressed those heretykes . . . at the[ir] fyrst springyng." So suspicion was sufficient, without a publicly documented accusation, to apprehend and interrogate an apparent critic of the church. Judges could proceed without juries. Other "protections" or "freedoms" were forfeit, and, in instances, the lives of evangelical anticlericals were forfeit "els many mischiefes pass."[70]

The choice between dissidents' "mischiefes" and officials' cruelties did not seem obvious to everyone at or around the court. More acknowledged that "many men thought it harde and an uncharytable waye . . . to put men convycte of heresye somtyme to shame, somtyme to dethe." But he argued that the anticlericals' cruelty left the government and church no option, save to silence their enemies. "Good pryncys . . . for preservacyon not of the fayth onely but also of the peas amonge theyr people" were especially obliged to act when critics of Catholicism stopped listening to reason. That was More's constant refrain. Anticlericals, their "hertes . . . fyxed upon theyr blynde affecyons," stole souls, slandered the church, and jeopardized public safety. Religious and political authorities would "never in dede [had] fallen so sore to force and vyolence agaynst heretykes if the vyolent cruelte fyrst used by the heretykes . . . had not dryven [them] thereto."[71] More, perceiving England was in the very early, reversible stages of disintegration, wrote his *Dialogue Concerning Heresies* and had it published in 1529. Anarchy in Germany had proved to him what "vyolent cruelte" the reformers were capable of inspiring in their partisans, and he believed Augustine, too, would have recognized that problem and approved his solution, for

> the heretykes of Affryke called the Donatystes fell to force and vyolence robbynge, betynge, tourmentynge, and kyllynge suche as they toke of the true crysten flocke, as the Lutheranes have done in Almayne. For avoydynge wherof that holy man saynt Austyn, whiche longe had with gret pacyens borne and suffered they malyce, onely wrytynge and prechyng in the reprofe of theyr errours and had not onely done theym no temporall harme but also had letted and resysted other that wolde have done it, dyd yet at the laste for the peace of good people both suffer and exhorte the counte Bonyface and other to represse them with force and fere them with bodyly punyshment.[72]

Tactics used "to represse and fere" English anticlericals got nasty ("over fervent"). "We be all men and not angellys," More said, admitting prosecution occasionally turned into persecution. But he defended the procedures: there could be no reconciliation without sincere, lasting repentance. The church must excommunicate recidivists, and, because their "conversacyon" was "peryllous" not only to the faith but also "of the peas," the church's officials must deliver or "leve" them to "the seculer hand"—finally, to the executioner.[73]

Henry VIII's Matrimonial "Matter" and God's "Greate Cause"

Some months after he published his justification for the interrogations, More was in a position to turn that "seculer hand" into a lethal fist: he was appointed chancellor in late October 1529. At that time, he was the only lay member of the king's council who was invited to depose suspected heretics and, he suggested, to help them to get to heaven by prescribing harsh punishments that prompted repentance. He saw some off at the stake but denied that he had ever beaten any. Stories to the contrary circulated widely and still sully his reputation, which suffers as well from what one learns about his fierce, sometimes frightening determination.[74]

The anticlericals' determination matched it. When their bishops could not break what they saw as addictions to error, the government executed those determined critics. More said, almost smugly, that they had gone "strayte from the short fyre to the fyre everlasting."[75] But he seems unhappy to have been harassing them. He confided to Roper that he would gladly relinquish office and influence if he believed the Catholic church might be otherwise protected from the irreverent likes of Luther, Tyndale, and Fish. A second condition for his resignation was the settlement of the king's pending suit for an annulment of his first marriage. If only he could see that "brought to a good conclusion," "a great part of Christendom" would be spared "disturbance[s]" that put Christianity's prestige and the church's privileges in jeopardy.[76] To the king, a conclusion was only good if it freed him to marry Anne Boleyn, whom he had loved since 1526. By then, he and his wife, Catherine of Aragon, likely lost hope of having a son; her last pregnancy, eight years before, was quickly followed by the infant's death. She was past her fortieth birthday. Henry was much younger, eager for a male heir, crazy for Anne. During the late 1520s, he "paced the cage of his wedlock, thrusting at every bar."[77]

Wolsey was in charge of releasing the cat. Papal legate, cardinal, and chancellor, he tidied up his king's affairs for over a decade. He hoped to resolve Henry's new matrimonial problems close to home and asked Rome to let his legatine court render the final verdict. Pope Clement VII sent him a partner, fellow legate Lorenzo Campeggio, along with authorization only to hear the arguments for and against annulment. To the king, it seemed at first that Wolsey could manage his gout-stricken colleague, who was demonstrably unenthusiastic about his English assignment, and have his commission extended. At least, that was the word (and the confidence) circulating among Wolsey's associates, including More, who left with Bishop Tunstall on a diplomatic mission to France while the legates deliberated. He insisted later that he "never medeled" while they "satt upon the matter."[78]

At issue were Queen Catherine's first marriage to Henry's brother Arthur, who died within months of its solemnization in 1502, and the questionable validity of a papal dispensation that permitted her second. Henry's partisans argued that the impediment of affinity of the first degree collateral was divinely decreed: according to Leviticus 18:16, "thou shall not uncover the nakedness of thy brother's wife." No Pope could waive that away.[79]

Long before Campeggio came, Wolsey collected evidence that the dispensation was defective. He had depositions attesting that Prince Henry never consented to it and that Arthur and Catherine lived together when they were married, two weeks in London, thereafter in Wales. The language of Leviticus 18, "not uncover nakedness," made it nearly imperative for Wolsey and other advocates of annulment to help Campeggio infer consummation from cohabitation.[80] Henry, for his part, whatever doubts remained about Catherine's first marriage bed, convinced himself that he committed incest and that God had punished him for marrying his brother's widow. The penalty was not quite what the scripture prescribed (Leviticus 20:21, "they shall be childless"); one daughter survived Catherine's problem-riddled pregnancies. But Henry was extravagantly contrite.

A penitent Henry and persistent Wolsey might have prevailed had the obstacles been less formidable. Campeggio confounded them. He seems to have been persuaded by Queen Catherine's protest that she had been a widowed virgin. And Bishop John Fisher's capable defense of the papal dispensation also impressed him.[81] Deuteronomy, declaring that a man must marry his deceased brother's wife (25:5–9), created problems, quite apart from Campeggio's conscience. The Deuteronomy directive made brisk acceptance of the Leviticus prohibition unlikely, making it appear that the latter simply forbade adultery, specifically, intercourse with sisters-in-law while their husbands still lived. Only a few canonists thought differently, and the leader of that pack, Peter Paludanus, had retracted his opinion soon after he published it.[82] But the greatest obstacle facing Wolsey and his king, oddly, was the pope's plan for Italy, the success of which depended on Catherine's nephew, Emperor Charles V. His troops overran Italy in 1527, creating an assortment of problems that Pope Clement VII could not address without his cooperation. Clement's family had been forced from Florence. Venice grabbed Ravenna. If the Medici were to be restored and Ravenna recovered for Rome, the papacy had to please Charles, to whom the annulment in England that removed his aunt and cousin, her daughter, Mary, from the royal family was obviously unacceptable. Campeggio, therefore, was instructed to delay and then to adjourn without reaching a decision. Wolsey should have been relieved to escape with a draw of sorts; Catherine and Fisher had shown better than expected. But referring the matrimonial dispute to Rome was as good as a loss to Henry who blamed and booted out his chancellor.[83]

Thomas More was then appointed. His sympathies were with the queen and her friends, but Henry trusted him to be discreet. After all, More, so far, had been quite good at ducking under the debate. Campeggio appears to have known him simply as "a man of worth and merit" and not as a partisan of either side.[84] Wolsey seems not to have pressed him on the matrimonial controversy. But if he did, More likely got some good early mileage out of the excuse he later unfolded for the king: the subtleties of Old Testament exegesis, he said, "a great way pass my learning."[85] Perhaps More figured that he would have been of no use against the evangelical anticlericals if he publicly expressed sympathy with his sovereign's opponents. But, if we trust the dispatches sent by Eustace Chapuys, Charles V's ambassador to England, the new chancellor secretly encouraged Fisher and privately coaxed the king to forget Anne and the annulment. Chapuys wrote to the emperor of More's valuable support, yet the diplomatic pouch also suggests that the drawbridge often was up and that More once urged the ambassador to stop stalking him.[86]

But, notwithstanding Chapuys' observations and overtures, More seems to have kept his distance from the advocates of annulment as well. In effect,

Thomas Cranmer took over from Wolsey on that front. Nothing suggests that More was consulted about the decision to have European universities pass on the indispensability of the Leviticus prohibition. Fisher argued that popes having sometimes set it aside sufficiently proved Rome's right to do so. But Cranmer was smart to canvass the universities' theological faculties, known to harbor critics of the papacy. The results from Orléans and Bologna were particularly satisfying; those from Paris, Padua, Toulouse, Oxford, and Cambridge were generally favorable to the king's cause. The consensus was that the first papal dispensation was invalid, that the church could not set aside what God decreed, that Henry and Catherine were not legitimately wed. More's job, then, was to see that the faculties' findings were announced to the Commons.[87]

He did so unenthusiastically. Cranmer and the king, in their "great matter," were almost certainly better served by Thomas Audley, Speaker of the Commons, and Thomas Cromwell, formerly Wolsey's chief counsel. Those two stoked parliamentary discontent with the church. While Cranmer labored to burrow under English Catholicism's *de jure* dependence on the papacy, Cromwell, especially, was decrying its independence from the government and carving out a place for the king as overseer of the English church. There was no disguising More's opposition to the latter initiatives. The Commons chronically complained about clerical profiteering before he became chancellor. Members agitated for government regulation in the parliament that met from 1529. More consistently proposed ecclesiastical self-reform. The anticlericals figured More was confusing the hare with the hounds and further resented his supremely confident vindication of the church's right and duty to interrogate their preferred preachers and pamphleteers without a nod to the safeguards afforded suspects in secular courts. Anticlericals in the Commons, that is, objected to the chancellor's endorsement of clerical intimidation as well as clerical independence. Still, he held firm during his short term in office and, as we discovered, after he resigned in May 1532, in exchanges with Christopher St. German who echoed the Commons' concerns. But earlier that year, Cromwell had gotten the upper hand and choreographed the crisis that led to More's leaving. A Supplication against the Ordinaries was filed in parliament. The bishops' response amounted to a strongly worded assertion of the church's privileges and immunities, a spirited answer that torched much of what remained of the king's religious conservatism, which

More spent so much effort cultivating. Cromwell had a flair for deploying the king's irritation; he was soon able to compel Convocation, the bicameral assembly of prelates from all Canterbury's dioceses, to subscribe to a Submission, the document that provided for a royal commission to sift through ecclesiastical legislation and strike anything considered prejudicial to the Crown's prerogative. That Submission also prohibited any session of Convocation from meeting unless summoned by the government. More promptly surrendered the Great Seal.[88]

He did not stop writing; alarmist accounts of the heretics' incursions played what Brendan Bradshaw describes as More's last card. Ten years before, Henry was honored by the pope, acknowledged as the "defender of the faith," the mainstay of the prevailing ecclesiastical order. Rome later thought him the archfiend of the English schism, all too willing to experiment with far-reaching religious changes, yet, into the 1530s, Thomas More must have believed that he was able to tap into the king's "continuing aversion to heresy."[89] If he could only show Henry that evangelical anticlericals feigned doctrinal orthodoxy while professing to expose clerical abuses and restore the regime's rights to correct them. If he could just get Henry to doubt that any anticlerical, "whyche in hys wordes openly inveyeth agaynste good and faythfull thynges [relics, reverence for saints, penances, pilgrimages, and the papacy and who] despyseth trew poyntes of the common knowen catholyke faythe, doth in hys hart secretely thynke and byleve ryghte."[90]

More's *Apology* begins with an extended justification of his previous polemics. He was, he said, attentive to the church's tradition, drawing on the works of "olde holy doctours and fathers of the faythfull doctryne" to answer "lewde Luther" and his petulant English accomplices. The former chancellor countered claims that he been unduly hostile to the heretics. Once he had "overthrowen Tyndale" by demonstrating that "all thynges" necessary for faithful Christians to comprehend their faith had not been "wryten allredy in scrypture," he could certainly not be blamed for demonstrating as well that the church reliably ascertained and conveyed all those extrascriptural "thynges."[91] Nor could he be blamed for disclosing that the reformers took liberties with what the Bible did say about salvation, specifically, about the value of "good endevoure" that makes the Christian "a worker wyth God toward atteynyng of fayth." More argued that the church was largely responsible for inspiring and channeling that "good endevoure." His *Apology* defends its record, "thys viii hundred yere," and justifies the ardor with which he had defended England's bishops. Their critics, and his, had been spiteful. They reviled any Catholic Christian who ridiculed the standard anticlerical argument, the argument that "all the corps of crystendome hath ben led out of the ryght way fro God, and have lyved al in idolatry and dyed in servyce of the devyll because they have done honour to Christ's crosse, and prayed unto the sayntes, and reverenced theyr relyques and honored theyr ymages." More admitted that his rhetoric was sometimes excessive, but he submitted that, given the arrogance, anger, and error of critics, he had been remarkably restrained. Their exegesis was sloppy; their innovations, outrageous and politically dangerous; they were offensive. His exegesis, which reiterated that of the church's "olde holy doctours," was, by contrast, cogent. The church was not paying him for it, as the anticlericals said to depict him as the bishops' "hired gun." He wrote the *Apology* to vindicate his honor and sincerity as well as to repeat his appraisals of current protest and his warning about its effects. Unbribed and undeterred by the government's growing antagonism, Thomas More was trying once again to portray the church as the Crown's best defense against disorder.[92]

He recorded how prelates distinguished themselves by trying to contain "the pestilence" of error and anarchy. Bishops might have looked the other way or regarded the anticlericals' "slaunderouse lyes" as nuisances. Yet, More declared, the church knew its duty to God "in hys great cause of repressynge of heresyes and maynteynynge of hys faythe."[93] The king had once embraced that as his duty as well. But by 1532, he appeared to reverse himself, and if the reversal was irreversible, More feared that Henry would live to see the "faythe decaye and peryshe in many other folke."[94] St. German claimed that the "evyll mynde" of "the spyrytualty," notably the cruel and unusually dogged pursuit of its critics, had already diminished, if not extinguished the faith in those "many folke." More was skeptical about the opposition's analysis, but he had to grant that, if sentiment were truly running against "the spyrytualty," the English church—after the Commons' Supplication, Convocation's Submission, and his resignation—would be unable to reclaim its laymen, including Henry, "but onely praye God to mende theym."[95]

Historians once thought the Henrician reformation was a swiftly successful, top-down movement that capitalized on the laity's disaffection. But scholars who stray from the court and line up commoners' sentiment now tend to agree with More that loyalty to the old church in the 1520s and 1530s was greater than St. German let on. The "spyrytualty" was in some trouble, to be sure, but it changed creatively and often during Henry VIII's reign (and during those of his heirs) to appease the realm's rulers. Nonetheless, one may be forgiven for thinking that things were worse; the impresarios of early Tudor reform—the evangelical anticlericals—were clever publicists. They created an impression of great momentum by relentlessly exposing absurdities and abuses. They mocked reverence for such ridiculous relics as the toes of the Trinity, for example, as well as stories of miracles that attracted pilgrims and their purses to traditional religion's outlets or shrines. More was embarrassed by some of what the critics disclosed and by the commoners who believed every tale of miraculous healing and every reported apparition. Obviously untrue stories were easily snuffed, he said, because God did not want flimflam to obscure the important role genuine miracles played in identifying the Catholic church as the place for canonical interpretation and application of scripture. "God worketh hys miracles in his trew chyrch to shew his trew chyrch"; its wonders distinguished it from its rivals. More thought that it was "inough" to "confound" Tyndale and his kind simply to point out "that among all the false chyrches of fals heretikes there be no miracles at all."[96] The anticlericals, however, were "wyly" and unstoppable. They harped on what Peter Marshall now calls "the forged miracle theme." They equated the words "miraculous" and "feigned." And their government snapped to attention on learning how many expressions of opposition to its matrimonial maneuvering and religious reforms were "authorized" by visions or voices. We cannot tell for sure whether the government encouraged the anticlericals' incredulity or the anticlericals exploited the government's fear of insurgency. Probably a bit of both. Thomas More soon became aware he was powerless to prevent either. "So semeth it now," he mourned while still the realm's chancellor, that "the chyldren of darkenes be more polytyke . . . then are the chyldren of lyght."[97]

Discomfort

After he resigned, they came for him, the denizens of that "darkenes," Cromwell in the lead. Henry was unhappy with his former chancellor's unwillingness to subscribe by oath to the Act of Succession confirming the annulment of his first marriage and the legitimacy of the son expected from his second. And More soon became notorious for prudently concealed, yet readily and widely inferred, suspicions that "the Reformation parliament" overstepped in early 1534, when it declared the king supreme head of the English church. The government looked to discredit its new critic. It searched for any sign of corruption that might taint his term as chancellor but turned up nothing of consequence. Cromwell's scheme to implicate him in others' seditions failed. But More failed as well. He unsuccessfully argued that what he might casually have said while confined—and what he declined to say under oath—about succession and supremacy did not support prosecutors' presumptions of malice. Imprisoned from April 1534, he was tried for treason and executed in early July 1535.[98]

By the time he was sent to prison, More was ready to bid farewell to the "false flateryng world" and to accept his ordeal as "medicinable." He was interrogated in the Tower of London several times; Cromwell promised at least once that, if he conformed, he "might be abrode in the worlde agayne." More, however, answered that he had "fully determined . . . neyther to study nor medle with eny mater of thys worlde." He promised that henceforth his "hole study shulde be uppon the passyon of Chryst and [his] owne passage out of thys" life and into the next.[99] He had started a treatise on Christ's passion before he was committed to the Tower. He completed it there and composed a *Dialogue of Comfort* that reflects on history as tragedy and heaven as reward. He awarded the best lines to Antony, an aged Hungarian whose excitable young cousin Vincent seems never seriously to have threatened intelligence. Vincent had "nede of comfortable councell agaynst trybulacion." He was worried that the Turks' imminent conquest of central Europe would alter everything. Antony admitted the likelihood of that yet made his peace with the part that discomfort and defeat played in God's plan, suggesting that More, too, had come by then to terms with his predicament and peril and was ready to "let God worke, and leve off contention." But, as Richard Marius remarks, the Turks seem to have been standing-in for the reformers. So, when Antony notes that "christendome [is] very sore decayed," and that "the princes of cristendome" might have halted the Turks' "wonderful increase," had they only seen and reacted to the threat promptly, More likely had another "decay" and "increase" in mind. Marius makes a good case, but, on the whole, "serenity and composure" characterize More's last protagonist; perhaps the *Dialogue* is about consolation rather than contention.[100]

Antony's consolation is conventional. He transforms tribulation into a test, explaining that the world is a prison in which inmates are supposed to develop patience and perspective. The catch is that this prison is "so subtilly bildyed" that we forgot we are detainees. We are unfettered and seem so free, but

> by reason of this [perceived] favour, for a tyme, we wax . . . so wanton that we forget where we bee, wenying [supposing] that we were lords at large, where as we be in dede, yf we wold consider yt, evyn sely pore wrechis in prison, for of very trouth our very prison this earth is. And yet therof we cant us out, part by covenauntes that we make among us, and part by fraude, and part by violence to diverse partes diversly to our selfe, and chaunge the name therof fro the odyouse name of prison and call yt our own land and our lyvelod. Upon our prison we bild our prison: we garnysh yt with gold and make yt gloriouse.[101]

What did More's Antony mean when he mourned that we build our prison upon our prison? He was almost certainly deploring that Christians had grown accustomed to "the worldes wretchid welth." They deceived themselves ("and call yt our lyvelod") and distracted themselves with civic duty ("make yt gloriouse"). "In this prison, they bye and sell . . . they pipe and revell." More was quite explicit and emphatic about the disastrous effects of such "false perswasion." The faithful forget the advice offered in the apostle's letter to the Hebrews (13:14) and repeated in Augustine's *City*: the time given for "our litell while wandryng" on earth is better spent repenting than improving "our dwellyng citie here." "In this short sowying tyme of this wepyng world, must we water our sede with the showers of our teares." The harvest is in heaven.[102]

What of public officials? Could they not claim that their "litell while wandryng" on earth was well spent attending to others' welfare, that their neighbors' advantage was dear to them? Such statesmen—More was explicit—"know not well their own affeccion." They normally served themselves first, neighbors or constituents only after. They could be generous with gorgeous words and sentiments, but with little more. "They frame[d] them self a conscience," contriving to seem selfless.[103] Or perhaps, as More has Antony say earlier in the *Dialogue*, public officials simply underestimated their "dedly desier of ambiciouse glory," a desire that, at every turn, trumped conscience, irrespective of how well it was "framed." Ambition overwhelms administrators. "It is a thing right hard to touch pitch and never [de]file the fingers."[104]

More understood better than most that playing at politics was playing with fire. He gathered as much when still a safe distance from those who closely orbited the king's will, though near enough to see that the closer to the Crown a counselor gets, the likelier he is to be sucked in and—when the sovereign will turns—sent off.[105] But the *Dialogue* he wrote in prison remembers why so many were attracted to power: the more of it they possess, the more possessions they accumulate and the more others will defer to them. They then fool themselves into thinking they can "control other men and live uncommaunded." More's Antony takes the trouble to enlighten them, as "a great officer of the king's" had purportedly enlightened him, although his present discomfort also persuaded him that it was pointless to chase power. The officer's lesson, nonetheless, was a gem. He allowed that he once enjoyed being saluted with respect, having citizens "stand barehed" to signal their esteem for his position. But twenty men so standing, he went on, never warmed his head as well as a cap. "He toke never so mich ease with their beying barehed before hym as he caught one's grefe with a cough that came uppon hym, he said," after he stood capless before the king. However high he might climb, the officer knew that he must defer to those higher still. And there was danger when too many deferred to him, for he was then viewed from above with suspicion and envy. To placate those higher, he would have to grovel before them—and especially before the king, because "by the favour of great princes . . . as [their subordinates] rise upp high, so fall they down agayne as low."[106]

Notwithstanding the "grefe" that "came upon" public officials who deferred to higher-ups and the risk of falling from the heights to which they themselves ascended, their power was a powerful drug. It made them feel well, prosperous, divinely favored. And as long as their chaplains, not wanting to displease, assured them their feelings were well-founded, they would not listen to More's Antony or his "great officer" who warned counselors and courtiers, who "have the rule and aucthoritie of this world in their hand," to consider the prosperity they enjoy as "a fearfull signe of god's indignacion." Powerful citizens counted their positions and possessions as blessings. They did not want to know they were cursed.[107]

The *Dialogue* does not call on public officials to resign. Much as Augustine had in the fifth century, More recognized in the sixteenth that Christian magistrates were excellently positioned to protect their churches. At that, though, he failed dismally. But on one count he might have agreed with his admirers among historians (and even with a number of his enemies at the time) that he succeeded sensationally: he had not allowed personal ambition to interfere with what he perceived as his public duty. And he apparently learned—if not in office, in prison and disgrace—the moral and theological importance of an officeholder's discomfort. The office must not fit like a glove. As Augustine explained in his *City*, self-reproach and remorse must be part of the statesman's kit. Antony is emphatic: when duty requires a public official to "put to pain" malefactors, he must "in his hart be sory." Augustine directed officials in those circumstances to judge fairly, make the best of the mess, avoid the arrogance of power, and pray for deliverance. Antony may have recalled one of More's lectures on Augustine's *City* when he urged discomfort on the officials who, "in his own hart" he should admit—and act as though—the trappings of office only temporarily distinguish him from "every pore begger" he rules.[108]

So More's *Dialogue* is as inconsistent as Augustine's *City*. The two depict ambition as a distressingly perfect predator. They also agree that, in politics, its prey have no chance. Even the capless "great officer," who understands he is trapped in the chain of command, however "upp high" he may rise, knows as well that he will flatter those higher to avoid descending. Yet More's Antony also speaks soothingly, and the *Dialogue*, as the *City*, holds out a place in the Christian magistrate's "hart" where the "dedly desier of ambiciouse glory" may not reach. More and Augustine also held out hope for the good that may come when ambition is pitted against integrity, nothing good for government or for "the state," but something good for the soul.

Politics in "This Time of Teares"

While More was in prison, his daughter Margaret Roper wrote a revealing response to a letter she received from her stepsister Alice Alington. The bulk of

Roper's reply is a dialogue between father and daughter, reported or invented to answer Alington who earlier approached More's successor as chancellor, Thomas Audley, for help: surely, she implored, More might be rescued by his former friends. But Audley confided that he and they were mystified by her stepfather, "so obstinate in his owne conceite." Audley and the others swore the oath of succession at the king's bidding and could not fathom why he refused. Alington could not enlighten him and applied to Margaret Roper for information.[109] Roper, in turn, shared her stepsister's request with their father when, adding her own perplexity, they next talked in prison. Roper, in other words, pressed More, much as Alington or Audley might have, and the result is a dialogue, so cleverly crafted that historians speculate More wrote it—and Roper simply smuggled it from the Tower. Yet it seems unfair to reduce her role to that of go-between or stenographer on a hunch. She had an excellent reputation among Erasmici for intelligence and dedication to study. More prophesied, on another occasion, that his daughter's work was so erudite and sensible that it would be mistaken for that of an accomplished man of letters. Students of late medieval and early modern gendered identity may be tempted to take his prophecy as evidence of underappreciation—society's rather than her father's, of course—but they still see Margaret Roper as yet another figure in a frieze of conventionally submissive women of her time. But her letter to Alington ostensibly attests her proficiency as a provocateur, her memory for her father's finest phrases, and her ability to generate her own.[110]

What, for our purposes, is the most telling exchange in Roper's letter includes the parable of the jury More told to explain his contrariness. He mentioned that nearly all the jurors were friends of someone the defendant, a law officer, lately harassed. No wonder they were quick to think the worst. "They were skant come together," More said, when all but one agreed to convict. They pressed the holdout to "playe the gude companion," set aside his scruples, and vote with them. He replied by imagining what might happen should the jury reconvene at life's end. The other jurors, having voted their conscience, would be headed for heaven. "For doing against mine . . . at your request here, for good cumpany," he would be sent down to the devil. "If I shall then say to all you . . . maisters, I went once for good cumpany with you, which is the cause that I go now to hell . . . . Go now for good cumpany with me, wolde ye go?" The jurors' appeal for solidarity "nowe" looked weak indeed when one's place in the celestial city was at stake.[111]

The implication was that More's tenacity, here and now, was his ticket to heaven, yet his daughter found the flaw in his analogy. The jurors who voted for conviction were dismissively sketched in her father's story. They took no time to sift the evidence ("skant come together") and seemed improperly— and mistakenly—moved by local acquaintance. The holdout's reference to their "conscience[s]" was almost certainly offered facetiously. The jurors, that is, should hardly be compared with "good and so well learned" subjects who conformed and took the oath. Roper heard her father call them wise. He had done so again in the dialogue. "The credence that you may with reason geve their persons for their aforsayd qualities shoulde well move you to thinke the oth, of itself, as every man may well swere without peryll of soule [and] chaunge your owne conscience . . . to the conscience of so many other."[112]

More first disputed the "many" of his daughter's "so many." He maintains his opposition to the oath brings him in line with a flock far larger than any that could be assembled in England. Try as they might, the king, Cranmer, and Cromwell were not capable of fashioning any formidable challenge to the consensus of the faithful, living and dead, that confirmed the primacy of the pope, the importance of the sacraments, and the universality of the Roman Catholic church.[113] But More also addresses the question of the opposition's quality to add to the points he scored on its quantity. Notwithstanding his polite nod to their intelligence and virtue, those who conformed and took the oath, he tells Roper, are neither "so good" nor "so well learned." Their conformity proved politics prevailed over whatever virtues they possessed and made them opportunists. They swore the oath to protect their estates and improve their status. Roper has her father assess their capitulation and conformity ironically—and he likely did so in their conversation as well as in her correspondence. He notes that their views had changed, no doubt, "after great diligens to seke and finde out the trouthe," he adds. He "never heard my self the cause of their change," he admits, but assures his daughter that their "cause" must have been well weighed as well as curiously concealed. Some indecently concluded that the conformists "swere otherwise than they thinke or frame their conscience afreshe to thinke other wise than they thought," just to curry favor. Had they done so, their conformity corroborated what Pico claimed about the perversity of politics, in the letters and life More translated; what Hythloday described in *Utopia* as the contagious corruption at court; and what the *Dialogue* said about ambition. But Roper's facetious father refused to think ill of those counselors and courtiers who conformed. Their horror of disappointing Henry could be no greater than his; their fear of losing their wealth and friends, no greater than his. "If such thinges shoulde have tourned them," More went on, "the same thinges had been lykely to make me do the same, for in good faith, I knew fewe so faint hearted as my selfe."[114]

He was, of course, slyly self-effacing to underscore the cowardice of his conformist colleagues. Their inglorious reversal on the oath showed that they learned only too well the lesson featured in Hythloday's script and more succinctly put in More's history of Richard III's tyranny: principled politicians "do themselves no good."[115] The "faint hearted" opportunists were still in the king's service. They were prudent whereas More was principled and imprisoned. He had done himself "no good." He had charted his way through other crises rather well, however, so his court time is very difficult to characterize. Historians agree that he wrongly described himself as unheroic, as timid. Some insist that he was, to the contrary, a daring, radical individualist, and those who ardently admire his individualism never quite accept how thoroughly the church's "consensus of the faithful" shaped his conscience. They must cheer when More tells Norfolk, in Robert Bolt's stupendously successful *Man for All Seasons*, that, above all, the believing subject or "self" must assert its freedoms, as if the content of a conviction acquires dignity by having it subscribed voluntarily.[116] But other historians think More was a different sort of radical. They have him agitating for a significantly and comprehensively reformed polity. They miss what we chronicled as his reservations about far-reaching social schemes. They identify More with Hythloday's optimism in the *Utopia*. And they attribute the *Dialogue*'s skepticism to the former chancellor's discomfort and despair. Yet More's Antony in the *Dialogue* generally confirms what More's More in *Utopia* said about expectations that an equitable society would develop once resources were redistributed. The poor would not be appreciably better off, Antony predicts, and there would be no incentive to work. The *status quo* must do, More says, because "the rich man's substaunce is the well spring of the pore man's living."[117] And when he perceived that the anticlericals' disrespect for "lawes and orders amonge men" might result in the strongest and least scrupulous taking all from everyone else, More tried to assure that his world was not "deceived" and "chaunged." For he was sure that peace could not soon come again to a "worlde ones rufled and fallen in a wyldenes."[118]

Politics, at its best, was about peace, not about social or economic prog-ress. More believed that the Catholic church contributed fundamentally and decisively to preserving peace and that its clergy and courts had appropriately been awarded a degree of juridical autonomy. English kings had long under-stood that clerical immunities and liberties paid dividends, that by upholding standards for more discipline as well as for religious devotion, the church's authorities were tremendous political assests. But the evangelical anticlericals charged bishops with abusing the jurisdictions and freedoms they were given. The churches' courts, critics said, parodied justice and were especially soft on clerical crime. More replied that he found clerical officials so "well mynded to [the clergy's] amendement and correcyon" that, during his long career in law enforcement, he met many a delinquent priest who was "rather content to re-mayne in the king's prysons a month then in the bishops' a weke."[119]

Clerical justices, of course, were only human. More acknowledged that their critics had some legitimate complaints: a head count would come up with some who "love[d] authoryte" or leisure or "lawde and prayse" more than they loved truth. He further granted that the critics had a valid point to make about the best of all possible worlds: given the importance of each jus-tice's job, "none sholde be noughte." More nonetheless advised that it was utterly unrealistic to equate "sholde be" with "could be," to demand perfect justice "whyle this worlde standeth."[120] The anticlericals obviously had an ex-cellent reason for raising the bar to an unsustainable altitude and for assuring that the "spyrytualty," specifically, the church's courts could not measure up. They did not want to be brought before and judged in the very tribunals they had recklessly condemned. So they flattered the government by appealing to its courts. But an acerbic More saw through their tactics: "yf it wyll be so harde to fynde any one suche" unimpeachable and impartial judge "in the spyrytualty," he said,

> I can scant beleve but that it wold be somewhat ado to finde many such in the temporaltye eyther and specyally not onely such but those also that the kyng myght be sure to be suche, bysydes that, there must be many chaunges and many newe devyses of lawes for the mater, bycause fewe temporall men be suffycyently lerned in those lawes of the chyrche, by which that mater hath bene accustumed to be ordered before. And happely yf any such men be so suffycyently

lerned, yet is it possyble that those men whiche are so lerned, are not
those that are so pure and clene frome every spyce of pryde, covetyse,
and worldely love. And therefore were the heretykes lykely thus to
make mery a good whyle, before there sholde be founden good judges
for them.

More's assumption here is conventional: heretics resisted rehabilitation and
wanted only "to make mery" and be rid of the church's courts, clergy, and sacraments. They wanted to defer justice rather than get it. More argued that
competent clerical justices were closer at hand than critics surmised, but the
difficulties to which his passage alludes suggest rather more than the indispensability of the church, its laws, and courts. The "eyther" in the second line
speaks volumes. Courts were courts, necessarily imperfect. Clearly, for More
and Augustine, the political and juridical functions of the "spyrytualty" were
precincts of the terrestrial city.[121]

Far less so, the devotional life of the church! The sacraments were por-
tals through which grace poured from the celestial city. "As many as are
present . . . and are in cleane lyfe receive it spiritually." And "sacramentall re-
ceiving" makes them "more firmly knyt and unyd quicke lively membres in
the spirituall societie of sayntes."[122] The anticlericals' most trenchant criticisms of the church only attested that mortals were always truant and the
church's business on earth always unfinished. The sacrament of penance had
much the same effect, but, more effectively than the criticism, it inspired
Christians to "rule" themselves "wiselie . . . in this time of teares, this vale of
mysery, this simple wretched worlde."[123]

Audley must have heard the exhortation dozens of times, the conventional injunction to rule oneself "wiselie" and well. But he had difficulty believing More was prepared to eschew politics for self-government. Audley
suspected ulterior motives. He told Alice Alington Aesop's fable of the few
seemingly shrewd citizens who wished to govern their many peers. The ambitious few learned there would soon fall "a greate rayne the which sholde
make theym all fooles that sholde so be fowled or wette therewith." Their
precaution and plan: to take shelter until the rain passed, to emerge then as
wise as before, and to rule the fools who had been drenched in the down-
pour. But, as Audley recalled, the multitude turned so foolish after the "greate
rayne" that it refused to recognize the prudence and wisdom of the few, dry

politicians. For their part, frustrated, they wanted to relinquish their special standing and wished that they, too, had been caught in the deluge. The implication was that More, in prison, was biding his time, taking shelter, until those clouds passed that kept Crown and council from coming to their senses. So contrariness was a political ploy. Audley's predecessor was hoping to regain authority. More knew the fable well; it was Wolsey's favorite. Not surprisingly, More objected to Audley's application, yet he also quarreled with the premise that those who "longe to be rulers" could ever have been wise. To want to rule fools was a foolish ambition. To become a fool to rule—in the fable's terms, to wish to be wet, after having had the intelligence to stay dry—only substantiated Augustine's observation that the lust for power, the *libido dominandi*, afflicted all politicians and most mortals in this weeping world, "in this time of teares." The accumulation and deployment of power by some to the disadvantage of others, "the business of Babylon," was a dreadful necessity. For our two protagonists, Augustine and More, to invest it with any dignity was to be incorrectly political.[124]

Endgame

Audley's Aesopean explanation of More's motives seems to miss the mark. True, More was trying—and writing—to make a difference even after his resignation as chancellor. Then, as before, however, his disappointments prompted a pessimism that, especially at the end of his life, resembled Augustine's. For he agreed that there was no place in the terrestrial city free of its "feigned loves" and "fierce hatreds," save imaginations, select conversations, and—so rare—communities disavowing the lust to dominate.

Political theorists obviously have found other, less comprehensive, ways to quiet the brass and cymbals, to replace self-congratulation with self-questioning. Tocqueville talked about the quasi-feudal characteristics of Americans' experiment with democracy, for example, to historicize a political culture that appeared to want "nothing more than to interpret itself by itself," "by its own self-confirming narrative." As Sheldon Wolin sums up, Tocqueville aimed at "unsettling [his] present."[125] After visiting with Augustine and Thomas More, we should be able to say the same about their objectives, although current wisdom holds the contrary, namely that, for the two, "sanctions of religion and faith . . . "underpinned"—rather than unsettled—what Slavoj Žižek now calls society's "symbolic efficiencies." In this application, they refer to the deceits and illusions that enable repulsive rulers to jerry-rig their dignity and give repressive rules an inviolability of sorts. In other words, religion helps governments keep up appearances and pretend their assumptions are unproblematic.[126] This cannot hold true of the Thomas More who conjured up Hythloday and who told of the wise peasant at a pageant declaring that the king was no more than an ordinary man in fancy dress on a big horse. Does it hold true of Augustine, the contrarian, who grew disenchanted with and critical of the ways politicians and their publicists manufactured and manipulated public opinion? Despite his dependence on the government to suppress secessionists, he consistently favored an alternative to "the busy, rooted life of states known to ancient men." He instructed Christians engaged in empire maintenance in order to protect their churches to fret over, rather than flaunt as a virtue, their complicity in political culture. He instructed them to lament and repent the deceit and deference that underpins and sustains prevailing political settlements. They ought, in Peter Brown's words, to be "otherworldly in the world." I suspect that Thomas More, in addition to all else he did, was, on the whole, following instructions.[127]

Conclusion

Good shepherds judiciously use the rod. Neither Augustine nor Thomas More thought that it was inappropriate or impious to urge government to assist their catholic and Catholic churches, respectively. Both Augustine and More knew that governments ordinarily resorted to coercive measures, to the rod, but sublime, salvific ends sometimes justified gritty means. Who could deny the central importance of preserving the integrity of the sacraments through which God's grace reached this wicked world?

Because they understood that the relationship between religion and the rod, *in hoc saeculo*, was terribly unfortunate as well as necessary, Augustine and More renounced the expectation that "genuine justice" could be achieved in time. *Incorrectly Political* reviews their renunciations and sets them in the contexts of their impressive, complicated careers, ideally, to make the careers and renunciations more comprehensible. But not the least of this book's accomplishments, I hope, is to answer George Kateb's summons, which was re-issued at its start, a call for a more profound political pessimism.

For Kateb, pessimism and skepticism are correctives or antidotes for "the passionate sense of possibility" in politics that always seems a source of recklessness. Passions fly the flag unselfcritically over what Thomas More termed the "feigned loves" and "fierce hatreds" that characterize efforts to preserve or change regimes. "Canonical writers" were insufficiently pessimistic, Kateb claims, but I think that the fault lies with interpreters who tend to paper over "canonical" discontent. "Traditionalistic" interpreters of Augustine and More, for example, admit that their subjects expected the worst yet also "believed in the positive impact of Christianity on social and political life." If "impact" in such calculations refers to damage control, the traditionalists are right. They are mistaken about Augustine and More, however, if "impact" refers to meaningful rehabilitations of political relations. If "impact" in their analyses denotes extensive, redemptive changes, the traditionalists and their subjects come across as insufficiently pessimistic.[1]

Profound and agile wits wanted always to change laws as well as lives. That seems to be the assumption bracing the best "traditionalistic" studies. Robert Dodaro's exquisite discussion of "the just society in the thought of Augustine" is a superb example. Dodaro starts with Augustine's "assault on the Stoic ideal." He distinguishes between the Stoics' efforts to control emotions and Augustine's emphasis, following the apostle Paul, on Christians' responsibilities to express repentance and compassion for fellow creatures in sighs, groans, tears, and cheers. Deeply felt remorse for sin and gratitude for God's pardon became the "experiential basis from which to generate sympathy for others." Augustine normally did not apply this insight to statesmanship, but Dodaro does. He imagines that the bishop's "experiential basis" serves as the foundation for a Christian commonwealth in which the policymakers' sense of sinfulness and humility beget strong, creditable impulses to reconcile others and in which those impulses are enshrined in customs or laws that encourage civic virtue.[2]

Remorse, humility, and rededication led to personal righteousness (*in unoquoque justitia*): for Augustine, this was rudimentary, although one could only build so much on such a foundation, because *justitia,* righteousness or justice "in this life," he said, "was forgiving sins, not perfecting virtues."[3] Michael Hanby now suspects that this stipulation reflected Augustine's dislike for the Donatists' and Pelagians' adaptations of "essentially pagan virtues," yet, whatever the reason, the bishop certainly stopped short of proposing in any programmatic way a new Christian commonwealth.[4] To remember this, however, is not to forget that he occasionally wished the chasm between biblical ethics and political virtues might close. When he heard that critics of Christianity had exaggerated the divide, declaring that the Christian faith was incompatible with good citizenship, he answered that citizens would be well served by all laws formulated to correspond with the precepts of that faith. He surmised, for example, that the empire might be more secure if offenders were pardoned rather than punished. He imagined that Cicero had implied as much when he praised Caesar for having forgotten injuries done to him.

Whether fact or flattery, Cicero's statement suggested to Augustine—if for only a moment—that Romans, even without Christianity, had realized that public administration could dependably and to good effect align personal righteousness with political practice.[5] For that moment, he seems poised between what might be and what never could be. And there were several such moments in which Augustine spooned sentiments about forgiveness into his generally pessimistic prognosis for politics. Do they, the moments and sentiments, constitute countervailing evidence? Does that evidence, in other words, possess equal and countervailing force to the narrative knit in this book from Augustine's ambitions lost, his responses to Rome's humiliation and to the Roman empire's setbacks, his skirmishes with the Pelagians, and his *City*'s remarks on terrestrial preoccupations, political practice, and celestial rewards?

Three kinds of evidence, taken together, may qualify. The first is the kind we have just encountered, namely, the wishful thinking that only occasionally conditioned Augustine's pessimism. The second kind relates to the bishop's participation in politics. He served as something of a local magistrate, filed appeals for convicts in capital cases, and asked for government assistance against schismatic and heretical Christians. More's participation, of course, was more pronounced. For thirty months, he was chancellor of the realm. Had he and Augustine not also said that Christian magistrates could only hope to make bad situations and corrupt systems a little less dreadful, their interventions could be construed to rise to the level of countervailing evidence. Yet the two did so say and convey a warning that to invest great expectations in political practice, civic virtue, or political objectives was to be incorrectly political.

A third kind of evidence, which at first seems strikingly different from the first, ordinarily settles on the scales when interpreters attempt to compose a counterweight to Augustine's pessimism. That third type appears to consist of comments that drift from sentimentality toward sober assessment. Augustine's reference to organized crime is an excellent example: *remota justitia*, justice removed, his *City* proposes, governments are larceny on a grand scale. I argued in the fourth chapter that "justice removed" ought to be taken as a reference to an ineradicable defect or deficit. Other interpreters assume that the phrase suggests the availability of remedies and celebrates upright regimes. Only after justice had been removed, did politics resemble piracy; politicians were normally and normatively virtuous.[6]

This optimistic exposition holds that Augustine not only expected Christians to be helpful politically but also advised them to be hopeful about politics. Readers must choose whether the optimism or pessimism of interpreters corresponds with Augustine's views, passage by prickly passage; ideally, *Incorrectly Political* has supplied contexts that make the more pessimistic Augustine and More the compellingly clear favorites. The narrative does not minimize their political concerns or political participation. But it traces the development of their perceptions—which were developed at times in tension with their ambitions—that political regimes were to be used and could not be appreciably improved. Return now to Augustine's controversial phrase. Granted, my reading may be something of a minority report, but if one accepts the alternative, namely, that the passage confirms prospects for a truly just government, one improvises against the grain of the bishop's predominantly pessimistic outlook. A. J. Carlyle, nearly a century ago, appears to have discovered just that. He had been tempted to pair Augustine with Cicero after pinching some optimism from *remota justitia*. It seemed to him to imply that the state could stop stealing and strive to attain and preserve justice, as Cicero had commended when he identified justice as the *raison d'être* of rule. Nonetheless, after rummaging through Augustine's other remarks on justice, Carlyle conceded—without relinquishing his reading of *remota justitia*—that the evidence overwhelmingly supported a very different interpretation of the bishop's political philosophy. It looked as if Augustine, as might any analyst of goodwill, substituted wishful thinking for careful reasoning when the latter had yielded regrettable results. Augustine's "deliberate and considered omission of the quality of justice in his final definition of the state" set him a world apart from Cicero.[7]

"Deliberate," "considered" "final": the careers of More and Augustine culminated with confirmations that "genuine justice" was unattainable in time. That is not to say they were idle or indifferent, but it is to deny that they were enthusiastically and optimistically *engagé*. To exaggerate their engagement is certainly terribly tempting. Thomas More is acknowledged today as the patron saint of politicians, after all; Augustine is heralded in some circles as a pioneer of progressive political reform. But this may simply tell us that admirers or religiously committed activists are searching for replies to the Enlightenment conceit that the rational deliberation necessary to govern wisely and well cannot mix with religious devotion. Possibly the traditionalists' confidence that both More and Augustine believed that Christianity could make monumental differences in political practices and objectives derives from a distortion of what the two did and said to assure that political practices enabled Christianity—its church, sacraments, ministry, and missions—to make profound differences in personal behaviors and expectations.

Je m'accuse. Fifteen years ago, I included a short chapter on Augustine in a book that I wrote about soteriology and political theology. I maintained that his "dark view" of political culture was related to the theological anthropology he reasserted often during his debates with the Pelagians. I included his stipulations that the empire had been—and that government could continue to be—serviceable or useful in Christianity's efforts to stamp out heresy and win over heretics, schismatics, and skeptics. Yet I wrote two paragraphs that crossed the line and contended that Augustine, "having formulated the darker view, also offered a personalist platform for the renewal of political culture."[8]

The *Erasmici* were among many traditionalists who found that side of the line congenial. They had waded through Augustine's *City*, apparently without developing serious reservations about the prospects for political renewal in the early sixteenth century. They composed instructions for princes and magistrates as if most politically powerful patrons should—and would quickly—take to heart their counsel when it came, because it came after their careful study of history and after conscientious examinations of the literature of classical antiquity, that widely trusted treasury of moral and political philosophy. A rather crude optimism abounded; would-be tyrants could be browbeaten into agreeing with prudent and erudite *Erasmici* whose exhortations clearly marked the route to renewal. And the scholars' political participation, in theory, assured that the route was traveled as well as marked. Thomas More pointed out the flaws in that theory (yet he was slow to act accordingly). He said that the thirst "for offices and honowres" in public administration was insatiable. Neither successes nor sermons on virtue quenched it. "An hepe of hevines" ultimately crushed the best-intentioned counselors whose anguish and struggles to be heard were to no avail. True, a case could be made that More urged the wise to advise. He seldom wrote openly about his disillusionment. His keen desire to protect England from the dangers he associated with reformed religion kept him in the government. His *Utopia*, however, shows him happier contemplating mock-up republics—a goad or gadfly complaining cleverly and advising obliquely—than careering about court. Years before he dreamed up his ideal commonwealth, he translated Pico, who had warned his own friends to keep their distance from corruption, from the "laboure for offices and honowres" that feeds on ambition, to ill-effect. Earlier still, More appears to have found that same brief against political ambition (and related caveats about political involvement) when he read Augustine's *City*.

But we cannot claim that More "channeled" a pessimistic Augustine in the sixteenth century. *Incorrectly Political* is not a conventional study of influence and intellectual debts. There is no telling what More knew about Augustine, no telling whether he was alert to the disaffection with political service reported in the late 390s and, arguably, experienced in the late 380s. More probably was not familiar, as you are now, with how the bishop handled the disappointments of 410, the perfectionism of the Pelagians, and the challenges of church and community service. We hear only that he read and lectured on Augustine's *City*, but characteristically, he seldom cited sources. Yet More and Augustine were similar on some counts. Each was disturbed by his own political ambitions and by those of others. Both recognized that governments could be useful, especially against religious dissidents—Protestants and Donatists, respectively—who demanded that established churches be dismantled. But More and Augustine also understood that their governments were necessarily of extremely limited use, and each composed an endlessly generative, enviably entertaining, subtly disorienting work to say so. The two, I believe, belong in the same book; they were, after all, "on the same page."

Abbreviations, Editions, and Translations

Sources and Series

BA
Bibliothéque augustiniennes: Oeuvres de Saint Augustine (SCh)

CCSL
Corpus Christianorum Series Latina

Coll. Avell.
(*Collectio Avellana*) *Epistulae imperatorum pontificum aliorum*, CSEL 35.1.

CSEL
Corpus Scriptorum Ecclesiasticorum Latinorum

CSP
Calendar of State Papers and Manuscripts relating to English Affairs, existing in the archives and collections of Venice, 1202–1675. London, 1864–1947.

CTh
Theodosiani libri XVI cum Constitutionibus Simondianis. Berlin, 1905.

GCC
Gesta Conlationis Carthaginiensis. CCSL 149a.

LP
Letters and Papers, Foreign and Domestic of the Reign of Henry VIII. London, 1862–1932.

Maier, *Dossier*
Le dossier du Donatisme, ed. Jean-Louis Maier. Berlin, 1987–89.

PCBE
Prosopographie chrétienne du Bas-Empire, vol. 1. Paris, 1982.

PL
Patrologiae cursus completus, series Latina
PLRE
The Prosopography of the Later Roman Empire. Cambridge, 1970–81.
SCh
Sources chrétiennes
Zenoph.
Gesta apud Zenophilim. CSEL 26.

Ambrose

Apol.
De apologia prophetae David. CSEL 32.2.
Aux.
Contra Auxentium. CSEL 82.3.
Ep. (Ambr.)
Epistularum liber decimus. CSEL 82.1–3.
Ep. extra coll.
Epistulae extra collectionum. CSEL 82.3.
Explan. ps.
Explanatio psalmorum. CSEL 64.
Expos. evang.
Exposition evangelii secundum Lucam. CCSL 14.
Expos. ps.
Expositio psalmi. CSEL 62.
Ob. Th.
De obitu Theodosii. CSEL 73.

Augustine

Bapt.
De unico baptismo. CSEL 53.
Beata
De beata vita. CCSL 29.

Brevic.
Breviculus connlationis cum Donatistis. CCSL 149a.

Cat. rud.
De catechizandis rudibus. CCSL 46.

Civ.
De civitate Dei. CCSL 47–48.

Conf.
Confessionum libri tredecim. CCSL 27.

Cons. Evang.
De consensu evangelistarum. CSEL 43.

Contra Faustum
Contra Faustum Manichaeum. CSEL 25.1.

Contra Fort.
Contra Fortunatum disputatio. CSEL 25.

Contra Jul.
Contra Julianum. PL 44.

Contra Jul. imperf.
Contra Julianum opus imperfectum. CSEL 85.1.

Contra Man.
Contra epistulam [Manichaei] quam vocant fundamenti. CSEL 25.1.

Contra mend.
Contra mendacium. PL 40.

Contra Pel.
Contra duas epistulas Pelagianorum. CSEL 60.

Cresc.
Contra Cresconium grammaticum. CSEL 52.1.

De gestis Pel.
De gestis Pelagii. CSEL 42.

De mend.
De mendacio. PL 40.

Div. quaest.
De diversis quaestionibus ad Simplicianum. CSEL 44.

Don. post col.
Post collationem ad Donatistas. PL 43.

Enarr. Ps.
  Enarrationes in Psalmos. CCSL 38–40.

Ep.
  Epistulae. CSEL 34.1–2, 44, 56–57.

Ep.*
  Lettres 1*–29*: texte latin établi par Johannes Divjak. BA 46.

Exc. urb.
  De excidio urbis Romae. CSEL 46.

Gaud.
  Contra Gaudentium Donatistarum episcopum. CSEL 53.

Gen. litt.
  De Genesi ad litteram. CSEL 28.

Gratia et pecc.
  De gratia Christi et de peccato originali. CSEL 42.

Johannis evang.
  In Johannis evangelium tractatus. CCSL 36.

Monach.
  De opera monachorum. CSEL 41.

Nat. gr.
  De natura et gratia. CSEL 40.

Nupt.
  De nuptiis et concupiscentia ad Valerium. CSEL 42.

Ord.
  De ordine. CCSL 29.

Parm.
  Contra epistulam Parmeniani. CSEL 51.

Pecc. Mer.
  De peccatorum meritis et remissione et de baptsimo parvulorum ad Marcellinum. CSEL 60.

Petil.
  Contra litteras Petiliani. CSEL 52.2.

Retr.
  Retractionum libri duo. CCSL 57.

Sermo
  Sermones. PL 38–39.

Sol.
  Soliloquiorum libri duo. CSEL 89.

Vingt-six sermons
Vingt-six sermons au peuple d'Afrique. Ed. François Dolbeau. Paris: Institut d'études augustiniennes, 1996.

Erasmus

AW
Enchiridion militis christiani, in Erasmus, *Ausgewählte Werke*. Munich, 1964.
CWE
Collected Works of Erasmus. Toronto, 1974–.
EOO
Opera Omnia Desiderii Erasmi Roterodami. Amsterdam, 1969–.
Ep. (Eras.)
Opus epistolarum Des. Erasmi Roterodami. Oxford, 1947.

Thomas More

Corresp.
The Correspondence of Sir Thomas More, ed. E. F. Rogers. Princeton, 1949.
CW
The Complete Works of St. Thomas More. New Haven, 1963–.
TMU
Utopia, ed. George M. Logan and Robert M. Adams. Cambridge, 2002.

Others

Ep. (Jer.)
Hieronymus epistularum, pars III. CSEL 56.1.
Optatus, *De schismata*
Optatus of Mileve, *De schismata Donatistarum.* SCh 412–413.
Orosius, *Hist.*
Paulus Orosius, *Historiarum adversum paganos, libri septem.* PL 31.
Paulinus, *Vita*
Vita sancti Ambrosii, mediolanensis episcopi. Washington, 1928.
Pelagius, *Ad Dem.*
Epistula ad sacram Christi virginem Demetriadem. PL 30.

Pelagius, *Epist. doct.*
Epistula de malis doctoribus et operibus fidei et de judicio futuro. PL, supplementum 1.

Pelagius, *De vita*
De vita Christiana. PL 40.

Possidius, *Vita*
Sancti Augustini vita scripta a Possidio episcope. Princeton, 1919.

Prudentius, *Peristephanon*
Aurelii Prudentii Clementis Carmina. CSEL 61.

Tyconius, *Apoc.*
The Turin Fragments of Tyconius' Commentary on Revelation. Cambridge, 1963.

Journals

HZ
Historische Zeitschrift

JECS
Journal of Early Christian Studies

JEH
Journal of Ecclesiastical History

RA
Recherches augustiniennes

REA
Revue des études augustiniennes

RHE
Revue d'histoire ecclésiastique

SCJ
Sixteenth Century Journal

VC
Vigiliae Christianae

For translations of Cicero, Plato, and Plutarch, I have relied on the Loeb Classical Library. Translations from other sources are mine unless the endnotes identify the following translators.

Atkins
> *Augustine: Political Writings*, trans. E. M. Atkins, ed. Robert J. Dodaro. Cambridge, 2001.

Bettenson
> Augustine, *Concerning the City of God against the Pagans*, trans. Henry Bettenson. London, 2003.

Chadwick
> Augustine, *Confessions*, trans. Henry Chadwick. Oxford, 1998.

Fantazzi
> Erasmus, *Handbook of the Christian Soldier*, trans. Charles Fantazzi. *CWE* 66.

Hill
> Augustine, *Sermons*, vol. 3.4, trans. Edmund Hill. Hyde Park, N.Y., 1990.

Rogers
> More, *Selected Letters*, trans. Elizabeth F. Rogers. New York, 1961.

Teske
> Augustine, *Marriage and Desire*, in *Answer to the Pelagians II*, trans. Roland J. Teske. Hyde Park, N.Y., 1998.

Notes

Introduction

1. George Kateb, "The Adequacy of the Western Canon," in *What Is Political Theory?* ed. Stephen K. White and J. Donald Moon (London: Sage, 2004), 30–53.

2. *Civ.* 12.21; Hannah Arendt, *The Origins of Totalitarianism* (New York: Meridian, 1958), 457–59, "for political systems," and 478–79, for Augustine. For Kateb's admiration, see his "Adequacy," 51–52.

3. See Jean Elshtain's discussion of "countervailing" comments, *Augustine and the Limits of Politics* (Notre Dame, Ind.: University of Notre Dame Press, 1995), 19–42. James Gustafson's perceptive prefatory remarks for the fiftieth anniversary edition of H. Richard Niebuhr's *Christ and Culture* (San Francisco: Harper, 2001), xxvi–xxviii, express impatience with colleagues who labor the "historical inaccuracy" of Niebuhr's "ideal-typical method." One can appreciate the appropriateness of Gustafson's complaint, though, without also conceding that Niebuhr was right to combine Augustine's "eschatological hopes" with his supposedly "conversionist ideas," with the idea that Christ was "the transformer of culture."

4. I use the lower case when referring to Augustine's catholic church. Universality was not then widely accepted in North Africa as the church's defining feature. Augustine was trying to remedy that at the Council of Carthage in 411, where Donatists argued that the term "catholic" suggested their church's purity. In the final three chapters of this book, "catholic" will acquire its capital "C" inasmuch as the universality of Thomas More's church was then considered a defining trait worth defending.

5. R. R. McCutcheon, "Heresy and Dialogue: The Humanist Approaches of Erasmus and More," *Viator* 24 (1993): 359.

6. Spörl, "Augustinus: Schöpfer einer Staatslehre?" *Historisches Jahrbuch* 74 (1955): 70.

7. Kaufman, *Redeeming Politics* (Princeton, N.J.: Princeton University Press, 1990), 130–37, 146–48.

Chapter One **Augustine, Ambrose, and Ambition**

1. *Vingt-six sermons,* 22–23.

2. Carol Harrison, *Augustine: Christian Truth and Fractured Humanity* (Oxford: Oxford University Press, 2000), 3–4; Reginald Gregoire, "Riflessioni sulla tipologia agiografica della *Vita Augustini* di Possidio," *Augustinianum* 25 (1985): 22–26; and, for the ahistoricity of Augustine's theological insights, Robert J. O'Connell, *Images of Conversion in St. Augustine's 'Confessions'* (New York: Fordham University Press, 1996), 297–307.

3. *Conf.* 3.6–7; *Contra Man.* 19–26; and Phillip Cary, *Augustine's Invention of the Inner Self: The Legacy of a Christian Platonist* (Oxford: Oxford University Press, 2000), 87–89.

4. *Conf.* 5.6.10.

5. *Conf.* 5.10.19.

6. Claude Lepelley, "*Spes saeculi:* Le milieu social d'Augustin et ses ambitions séculieres avant sa conversion," *Studia ephemeridis Augustinianum* 24–26 (1987): 101–5.

7. *Bonae spei puer appellabar: Conf.* 1.16.26. Also see *Conf.* 2.3.6; *Sermo* 356.13; and, for the family resources, Claude Lepelley, "Un aspect de la conversion d'Augustin: La rupture avec ses ambitions sociale et politiques," *Bulletin de littérature ecclésiastique* 88 (1987): 230–31.

8. *Conf.* 4.12.19.

9. Ramsey MacMullen, *Christianizing the Pagan Empire* (New Haven, Conn.: Yale University Press, 1984), 41.

10. See *Conf.* 7.19.25 and Aimé Solignac, "La christologie d'Augustin au temps de sa conversion," *BA* 13:693–98. Daniel H. Williams, *Ambrose of Milan and the End of the Nicene-Arian Conflicts* (Oxford: Oxford University Press, 1995), details Ambrose's part in the christological controversies. Mark Humphries, *Communities of the Blessed: Social Environment and Religious Change in Northern Italy, AD 200–400* (Oxford: Oxford University Press, 1999), 167–68, mentions that Milanese Christians perceived their bishop more as pastor than as theologian. I argue for their general indifference to christological disputes in my "Diehard Homoians and the Election of Ambrose," *JECS* 5 (1997): 427–32.

11. *Conf.* 5.13–14 and Pierre Courcelle, *Recherches sur les Confessions de Saint Augustin* (Paris: De Boccard, 1950), 85–87, for "un echange de politesses officielle."

12. *Ipse mirarer; Conf.* 6.2.2.

13. *Ep.* 36.14.

14. *Civ.* 15.7.

15. *Conf.* 6.3.4.

16. Paulinus, *Vita* 6–9.

17. Corbellini, "Sesto Petronio Probo e l'elezione episcopale di Ambrogio," *Rendiconti Classi di lettere e scienze morali e storichi, Istituto Lombardo* 109 (1975): 187.

18. Neil McLynn, *Ambrose of Milan: Church and Court in a Christian Capital* (Berkeley: University of California Press, 1994), 48–50, but see my reservations in "Die-

hard Homoians," 436–39, along with McLynn's "Diehards: A Response," *JECS* 5 (1997): 448–49.

19. For Palladius' rancor (*"pungentemente risentito"*), see Tavano, "Una pagina degli Scolia Ariani la sede e il clima del concilio," *Antichità Altoadriatiche* 21 (1981): 145; for Palladius' accusation, see "Fragments de Palladius," 120, in *Scolies Ariennes sur le concile d'Aquilée,* ed. Roger Gryson, SCh 267 (Paris: Cerf, 1980), 302–4.

20. *"Gesta,"* 54–64, in *Scolies Ariennes,* 370–76, and Williams, *Ambrose,* 175–78.

21. Rita Lizzi, "Ambrose's Contemporaries and the Christianization of Northern Italy," *Journal of Roman Studies* 80 (1990): 166–67.

22. McLynn, *Ambrose,* 261–63.

23. *Ep.* (Ambr.) 18.32.

24. *Ep.* (Ambr.) 17.12–13. Ambrose probably used his association with the usurper Maximus, to whose court at Trier he had been sent as ambassador shortly before the altar crisis broke. Maximus subscribed to the Nicene or consubstantialist christology. When Ambrose was back in Milan, railing against pagan superstitions and warning against rescinding Gratian's orders for Victory's removal, he might well have reminded Milan that the "orthodoxy" of the usurper in Trier was an attractive alternative to the paganism in Rome and the "unorthodoxy" in Milan. For Valentinian II's nemesis to the north, see Kirsten Gross-Albenhausen, *Imperator Christianissimus: Der christliche Kaiser bei Ambrosius und Joannes Chrysostomus* (Frankfurt: Marthe Clauss, 1999), 68–70.

25. *Expos. evang.* 4.31 and *Apol.* 10–11.

26. *Potestas decepit; humilitas non destituit; Expos. ps,* 14.9; Manlio Sargenti and R. B. Bruno Siola, *Normative imperiale e diritto Romano negli scritti di S. Ambrogio* (Milan: Giuffrè, 1991), 37–38, citing *Ep.* (Ambr.) 75.

27. *Conf.* 6.3.3. See Frank Kolb, "Der Bussakt von Mailand: Zum Verhältnis von Staat und Kirche in der Spätantike," in *Geschichte und Gegenwart: Festschrift für Karl Dietrich Erdmann,* ed. Hartmut Boockman, Kurt Jürgensen, and Gerhard Stoltenberg (Neumunster: Wachholz, 1980), 44, 58–59, and 64, for Ambrose as "ein Machtmensch par excellence."

28. Dassmann, *"Fuga Saeculi:* Aspekte frühchristlicher Kulturkritik bei Ambrosius und Augustinus," in *Wege der Theologie: An der Schwelle zum dritten Jahrtausend,* ed. Gunter Risse, Heino Sonnemans, and Burkhard Thess (Paderborn: Bonifatius, 1996), 941–42.

29. Robert Markus, *Saeculum: History and Society in the Theology of St. Augustine,* 2nd ed. (Cambridge: Cambridge University Press, 1988), 27.

30. *Cum authoritate praedicet; Explan. ps,* 43.95. For Ambrose's citations from the prophetic books of the Old Testament and their part in fashioning a "rôle d'episcopus gouverneur," see Lellia Cracco Ruggini, "Prêtre et functionnaire: L'essor d'un modèle épiscopal aux IVe–Ve siècles," *Antiquité tardive* 7 (1999): 180–83.

31. See Girogio Barone-Adesi, "L'Urbanizzazione episcopale nella legislazione tardoimperiale," in *L'Évêque dans la cité da IVe au Ve siècle: Image et autorité,* ed. Eric Rebillard and Claire Sotinel (Rome: Ecole française de Rome, 1998), 53–56.

32. For previous efforts to reserve the basilica for the subordinationists' worship, see McLynn, *Ambrose*, 179–96, and Williams, *Ambrose*, 210–17.

33. *Aux.* 37.

34. *Ep.* (Ambr.) 20.4.

35. Marcia L. Colish, "Why the Portiana? Reflections on the Milanese Basilica Crisis of 386," *JECS* 10 (2002): 361–72.

36. *Aux.* 33 and *Ep.* (Ambr.) 20.8 and 20.19.

37. *Ep.* (Ambr.) 20.22.

38. *Ep.* (Ambr.) 20.27–28.

39. *Intra ecclesiam non supra ecclesiam; Aux.* 36.

40. *Conf.* 9.7.15

41. Moorhead, *Ambrose: Church and Society in the Late Roman World* (London: Longman, 1999), 185–96. McLynn, *Ambrose*, 307–9, disagrees.

42. *Ad altare accessi non aliter accessurus nisi plene promisisset mihi; Ep. extra coll.* 1.28.

43. *Ep.* (Ambr.) 51; Paulinus, *Vita* 24.

44. Gross-Albenhausen, *Imperator Christianissimus*, 120–24; John Matthews, *Western Aristocracies and Imperial Court, A.D. 364–425*, 2nd ed. (Oxford: Oxford University Press, 1990), 238–47.

45. Hervé Inglebert, "Les causes de l'existence de empire romain selon les auteurs chrétiens des IIIe–Ve siècles," *Latomus* 54 (1995): 33–35, discusses Ambrose's materialist and providentialist explanations for government successes and failures.

46. *Ut fides tua in mea voce loqueretur; Ep. extra coll.* 2.4–5.

47. McLynn, *Ambrose*, 351–54.

48. *Beata* 1.4; *Conf.* 6.11.19.

49. *Civ.* 5.26.

50. *Conf.* 10.36.59.

51. *Conf.* 3.4. James J. O'Donnell, *Augustine: Confessions*, 3 vols. (Oxford: Oxford University Press, 1992), 2:162–67, reconstructs the *Hortensius*, the reading of which, says Goulven Madec, *Petites études augustiniennes* (Paris: Institut d'études augustiniennes, 1994), 92–93, was "le point de depart" for Augustine's conversion.

52. Madeleine Moreau, *Le dossier Marcellinus dans la correspondence de Saint Augustin* (Paris: Études augustiniennes, 1973), 131–32.

53. *Contra mend.* 23.

54. *De mend.* 31.

55. *Conf.* 6.6.9 (Chadwick translation, rendering *sub stimulis cupiditatis*, "goads of ambition").

56. "Metteva in ansia"; Francesco Della Corte, "Le pagine Milanesi della *Confessiones*," in *Fede e sapere nella conversione di Agostino*, ed. Aldo Ceresa-Gastaldo (Genoa: Università di Genoa, 1986), 17–18; Therese Fuhrer, "Zwischen Glauben und Gewissheit:

Auf der Suche nach Gott und dem *vitae modus,*" in *Die Confessiones des Augustinus von Hippo,* ed. Norbert Fischer and Cornelius Mayer (Freiburg: Herder, 1998), 256–57; and Courcelle, *Recherches,* 80–81, for confusion in Augustine's exposition.

57. *Conf.* 6.10.16.

58. *Conf.* 6.14.24.

59. *in eodem luto haesitans; Conf.* 6.11.18–19.

60. *Conf.* 8.2.2 and 8.5.11–12; Peter Brown, *Augustine of Hippo* (Berkeley: University of California Press, 1967), 79–81; and Anton Van Hoof, "Die Dialektik der Umkehr," in *Die Confessiones,* 365–66. Historians tend to identify that "servitude" with what they and literary critics call "the divided self." The apostle Paul in Romans 7 is commonly credited with its paradigmatic formulation in the history of the Christian traditions, but Augustine's formulations are memorable, notably *Conf.* 8.5.11: *sed tamen consuetudo adversus me pugnacior ex me facta erat, quoniam volens quo nollem perveneram.* "Custom" may not be the best translation of *consuetudo,* which, Augustine explains, originated from him and kept him from achieving what his better half desired. For *consuetudo* as "le poids invetere des habitudes du corps," see Serge Lancel, *Saint Augustin* (Paris: Fayard, 1999), 138.

61. *Conf.* 8.2.4–5; Courcelle, *Recherches,* 383–91.

62. Lepelley, "*Spes Saeculi,*" 112–13.

63. *Conf.* 8.5.12.

64. *Conf.* 8.6.15.

65. *Conf.* 8.7.17–18. Perseverance was one of Augustine's foremost concerns during the last twenty years of his life when he consistently identified it as a divine gift and as much a part of his doctrine of grace as the *initium fidei,* for which, see Lancel, *Augustin,* 602–3.

66. Cochrane, *Christianity and Classical Culture: A Study of Thought and Action from Augustus to Augustine* (Oxford: Oxford University Press, 1957), 338–39, 343–44.

67. Ambrose, *De fide* 2.16 (CSEL 78).

68. *Conf.* 9.2.2 and 9.15.13.

69. *Conf.* 1.13.21.

70. Lepelley, "Rupture," 243.

71. *Sol.* 1.4.9.

72. *Ord.* 2.19.51–2.20.52.

73. Dennis Trout, "Augustine at Cassiciacum: *Otium Honestum* and the Social Dimensions of Conversion," *VC* 42 (1988): 140–41; Brown, *Augustine,* 119–22; Suzanne Poque, "La prière de catechumene Augustin en September, 386," in *Congresso internazionale su S. Agostino nel XVI centenario della conversione* (Rome: Institutum Patristicum Augustinianum, 1986), 79–84; and Bernard Bruning, "*Otium* and *Negotium* within the One Church," *Augustiniana* 51 (2001): 113.

74. *Sol.* 1.13.22.

246 — NOTES TO PAGES 33–37

75. O'Donnell, "The Next Life of Augustine," in *The Limits of Ancient Christianity*, ed. William E. Klingshorn and Mark Vessey (Ann Arbor: University of Michigan Press, 1999), 223–27.

76. *Sol.* 1.15.29 and *Ep.* 10.2.

77. *Conf.* 8.6.15.

78. "*Un bastion du paganisme*"; Lancel, *Augustin,* 38–39. Brown, *Augustine,* 132–37, stresses the philosophical character of Augustine's retreat, while George Lawless, *Augustine of Hippo and His Monastic Rule* (Oxford: Oxford University Press, 1987), 44–58, stresses the monastic.

79. *Quod potuissem esse nolui; Sermo* 355.2.

80. E.g., *Vingt-six sermons,* 112–13, 266–67.

81. Possidius, *Vita* 3. The quotes are from Weiskotten's translation. Possidius added some detail to Augustine's recollection in sermon 355—notably the suppliant's involvement in government—and underscored Augustine's longing "to rescue that soul from the dangers of this life." For Possidius' reliability, see Eva Elm, "*Die Vita Augustini* des Possidius: Wandlungen in der Beurteilung eines hagiographischen Textes," *Augustinianum* 37 (1997): 229–40. Augustine mentioned starting a monastery in Hippo.

82. Possidius, *Vita* 4; Lancel, *Augustin,* 348–56, for a map of, and comments on, the diocese.

83. See Martine Dulaey, "A quelle date Augustin a-t-il pris ses distances vis-à-vis du millenarisme," *REA* 46 (2000): 33–36, 56–59.

84. Nello Cipriani, "Le opere di Sant'Ambrogio negli scritti di Sant'Agostino anteriori all'episcopato," *La scuola cattolica* 125 (1997): 788–89, 796–97.

85. *Ob. Th.* 4.

86. *Nemo se hostiis polluat; CTh* XVI.10.10.

87. *CTh* XVI.10.12.

88. For Praetextatus and Tatian, respectively, PLRE 1.722–24 and 828. For Flavianus as "the driving force" of the pagan restoration attempted by usurper Eugenius, see Jörg Ernesti, *Princeps Christianus und Kaiser aller Römer: Theodosius der Grosse im Lichte zeitgenössischer Quellen* (Paderborn: Schöningh, 1998), 69.

89. *Civ.* 5.26; Elena Cavalcanti, "*Virtus et Felicitas:* Gli elogi degli imperatori cristiani nel V libro de *De Civ. Dei* di Agostino e I panegirici latini per Constantino e Theodosio," in *Paideia Cristiana: Studi in onore di Mario Naldini,* ed. G. Aureliano Privitera (Rome: Gruppo editoriale internazionale, 1994), 499–500.

90. *Sermo* 138.10.

91. Ernesti, *Princeps Christianus,* 82–87, 476–77.

92. *Sermo* 22.4; *Cons. evang.* 1.32.50; *Enarr. Ps.* 32.2.9.

93. *Intueantur qui nondum crediderunt; Vingt-six sermons,* 262–65.

94. *Civ.* 9.13–15.

95. *Cat. rud.* 3.5.

96. *Enarr. Ps.* 148.10–12.

97. *Vingt-six sermons,* 578. The very mention of repeal here, as early as 405, speaks volumes. Also consult Hervé Inglebert, *Les romains chrétiens face a l'histoire de Rome: Histoire, christianisme, et romanitas en Occident dans l'Antiquité tardive* (Paris: Institut d'études augustiniennes, 1996), 499, which aptly summarizes for Augustine: "*Oui, l'empire est chrétien, mais les chrétiens vont au cirque.*"

98. Markus, *Saeculum,* 29–33, 51–52, and Markus, "*Tempora Christiana* Revisited," in *Augustine and His Critics,* ed. Robert Dodaro and George Lawless (London: Routledge, 2000), 202–6.

99. Madec, "*Tempora Christiana:* Expressions du triomphalisme chrétien ou recrimination païenne?" in *Scientia Augustiniana: Studien über Augustinus und den Augustinerorden,* ed. Petrus Meyer and Willigis Eckermann (Wurzburg: Augustinus-Verlag, 1975), 112–36. But compare Hubert Cancik, "Augustin als constantinischer Theologe," in *Der Fürst dieser Welt,* ed. Jacob Taubes (Munich, 1983), 142–48.

100. *Sermo* 361.4 and 8.

101. *Contra Faustum* 22.76.

102. Markus, "L'autorité épiscopale et la definition de la chrétienté," in *Vescovi e pastori in epoca teodosiana* (Rome: Institutum Patristicum Augustinianum, 1997), 37–43.

103. *Vix respirare possimus; Ep.* 48. For municipal solidarity, see Werner Eck, "Der Episkopat im spätantiken Africa: Organisatorische Entwicklung, soziale Herkunft, und öffentliche Funktionen," *HZ* 238 (1983): 276–78; and Claude Lepelley, *Les cités de l'Afrique romaine au bas-empire,* 2 vols. (Paris: Études augustiniennes, 1979), 1:383–85, 399–401. Also see Lepelley, "Le patronat épiscopale aux IVe et Ve siècles: continuités et ruptures avec le patronat classique," in *L'évêque dans la cité,* 28–29, for the comparison with Ambrose. Neil McLynn, "Augustine's Roman Empire," *Augustinian Studies* 30 (1999): 36–40, suggests the fog's effect and confirms that "the real power-holding elite remained beyond Augustine's reach." "He was groping through a fog in the hope of grasping and manipulating the dimly perceived, barely accessible levers of power."

104. *Ep.* 103.2.

105. *Ep.* 103.3. For the facts as reported to and by Augustine, see *Ep.* 91.8 and, for Possidius' suit, *PCBE,* 777–78.

106. *Ep.* 91.1–2.

107. *Ep.* 103.2. For Nectarius' courtesy (*libenter audivi; gratanter accepi*), see Hendrik Huisman, *Augustinus' Briefwisseling met Nectarius* (Amsterdam: Babeliowsky, 1951), 121–22.

108. *Ep.* 91.3.

109. *Ep.* 104.8–12; *Sermo* 251.7.

110. *Ep.* 91.1.

111. TeSelle, *Living in Two Cities: Augustinian Trajectories in Political Thought* (Scranton, Penn.: University of Scranton Press, 1998), 107–9 and 158–65, also suggests that such constructive results contribute, in some measure, to a reconstruction of "the social world of an errant humanity."

112. *Ep.* 104.9, Atkins translation, answering *Ep.* 103.3.

113. Brown, *Augustine*, 353–64.

114. *Ep.* 91.10. Huisman, *Briefwisseling*, 117, suspects that Augustine saw the crisis at Calama as a chance to use fear to convert the pagans to Christianity.

115. Dodaro, "Secular City," 243–46. My reply to Dodaro, which follows in the text here, is argued at greater length in Kaufman, "Patience and/or Politics: Augustine and the Crisis at Calama, 408–409," *VC* 57 (2003): 22–35.

116. *Ep.* 91.6 and 138.10.

117. *Ep.* 91.6 and 104.9. Also see Huisman, *Briefwisseling*, 139–40.

118. *Johannis evang.* 40.10. Also see *Enarr. Ps.* 37.9.12–37.10.14.

119. *Ep.* 90 and 103.4.

120. *Ep.* 91.10; later, *Ep.* 138.14 and *Gen. litt.* 9.9.

121. *Ep.* 91.7; *Civ.* 22.6.

122. Ernest Fortin, "Justice and the Foundation of the Political Community: Augustine and his Pagan Models," in *Augustine: De Civitate Dei*, ed. Christoph Horn (Berlin: Akademie Verlag, 1997), 53. Also see Harrison, *Augustine*, 133–35, and Dodaro, "Secular City," 243, quoting Cicero's commendation of the *via in caelum* (*De re publica* 6.16.6).

Chapter Two **Limitations**

1. *Conf.* 6.6.9.

2. Torture was commonly used to extort truth from accusers and witnesses, but also from the accused. For Augustine's opposition, see *Civ.* 19.6 and *Ep.* 91; for legislation relevant to episcopal courts, Maria Rose Cimma, *L'Episcopalis Audientia nella costituzioni imperiali da Costantino a Giustiniano* (Turin: Giappichelli, 1989), and John Lamoreaux, "Episcopal Courts in Late Antiquity," *JECS* 3 (1995): 143–67; and, for a different take on Constantine's court reform, H. A. Drake, *Constantine and the Bishops: The Politics of Intolerance* (Baltimore: Johns Hopkins University Press, 2000), 323–29.

3. See Clara Gebbia, "Sant'Agostino e l'Episcopalis Audientia," in *L'Africa Romana*, ed. Attilio Mastino (Sassari: Dipartimento di storia, Università degli studi di Sassari, 1988), 2:693–94, and A. H. M Jones, *The Later Roman Empire* (Norman: Oklahoma University Press 1964), 1:517.

4. *Enarr. Ps.* 118.24.3, citing 1 Corinthians 6; *Sermo* 137.14; *Ep.* 33.5 and 48.1; and *Monach.* 29.37.

5. *Enarr. Ps.* 25.2.13; cf., Possidius, *Vita* 19.

6. *Ep.** 24.

7. Claude Lepelley, "Liberté, colonat, et esclavage d'àpres la lettre 24*: La juridiction episcopale de *liberali causa*," in *Les lettres de saint Augustin découvertes par Joannes Divjak*, ed. Lepelley (Paris: Études augustiniennes, 1983), 340–42; Kauko Raikas,

"*Audientia Episcopalis:* Problematik zwischen Staat und Kirche bei Augustin," *Augustinianum* 37 (1997): 476–77; and Joachim Szidat, "Zum Sklavenhandel in der Spätantike," *Historia* 34 (1985): 366–71. For the registration of freed slaves, see *Sermo* 356.4 and, for Augustine's impatience with slave traffickers, *Ep.** 10.

8. Raikas, "Problematik," 477–78, and Raikas, "The State Juridical Dimension of the Office of a Bishop and Letter 153 of St. Augustine to *Vicarius Africae* Macedonius," *Vescovi pastori in epoca teodosiana: Studia Ephemeridis Augustinianum* 58 (Rome: Institutum Patristicum Augustinianum, 1997), 691–92. Compare Kaufman, "Augustine, Macedonius, and the Courts," *Augustinian Studies* 34 (2003): 67–82.

9. Anne Ducloux, "L'Église l'asile, et l'aide aux condamnes d'àpres la constitution du Juillet 398," *Revue historique de droit français et étranger* 69 (1991): 145–49.

10. *Ep.* 152. For Macedonius, see *PCBE,* 659–61; for his skepticism, Madelaine Moreau, "Le magistrate et l'évêque: Pour une lecture de la correspondance Macedonius-Augustinus," *Recherches et travaux, Universitae Stendahl, Grenoble* 54 (1998): 112–15.

11. *Ep.* 153.3–4 and 138.12–14.

12. *Ep.* 153.20–21.

13. *Ep.* 236.1 and 250.2; Lamoreaux, "Courts," 155–56, for mediation.

14. *Per ipsos dies possemus fortasse causam ejus amica disceptatione finire; Ep.* 115.

15. Jean Doignon, "Oracles propheties, 'on-dit' sur la chute de Rome (395–410)," *REA* 36 (1990): 127–34.

16. Markus, *Saeculum,* 54–61, succinctly contrasts the apocalyptic and the triumphalist (Eusebeian) views, locating Augustine at neither extreme; Peter Brown, *Religion and Society in the Age of Saint Augustine* (London: Faber and Faber, 1972), 326–31, considers the church's collaboration and the possibilities for episcopal "predominance" in Africa from the 390s.

17. Patrick J. Geary, *The Myth of Nations: The Medieval Origins of Europe* (Princeton, N.J.: Princeton University Press, 2002), 56–58; Peter J. Heather, *Goths and Romans* (Oxford: Clarendon, 1991), 323–28; Richard Fletcher, *The Barbarian Conversion: From Paganism to Christianity* (Berkeley: University of California Press, 1997), 66–77; and J. H. W. G. Liebeschuetz, *Barbarians and Bishops: Army, Church, and State in the Age of Arcadius and Chrysostom* (Oxford: Clarendon, 1990), 59–61.

18. *Ep.* 96.1.

19. *Ep.* 111.3–8 and Karin Sugano, *Das Rombild des Hieronymus* (Frankfurt: Lang, 1983), 97–101.

20. Heather, *Goths,* 215–17.

21. Alexander Demandt, *Der Fall Roms: Die Auflösung des römischen Reiches im Urteil der Nachwelt* (Munich: Beck, 1984), 594–95.

22. Chaunu, *Histoire et décadence* (Paris: Libraire académique Perrin, 1981), 165–68, 188–91, 259.

23. *Enarr. Ps.* 99.9.12 and, for Ambrose's precautions, *Conf.* 6.2.2.

24. *Ep.* 29.10.

25. *Sermo* 62.6.9 and Robert Markus, *The End of Ancient Christianity* (Cambridge: Cambridge University Press, 1990), 113–21, for the trend and tribalizing.

26. *Sermo* 105.12; Gaetano Lettieri, *Il senso della storia in Agostino d'Ippona: Il "saeculum" e la gloria nel "De civitate Dei"* (Rome: Borla, 1988), 248–53; and Jean-Claude Frédouille, "Les sermons d'Augustin sur la chute de Rome," *Augustin prédicateur (395–411)*, ed. Goulven Madec (Paris: Institut d'Études Augustiniennes, 1998), 339–48.

27. *Sermo* 105.10; *Civ.* 1.3; Doignon, "Oracles," 140–41.

28. *Sermo* 81.9, citing Matthew 18:7 and 24:35.

29. *Sermo* 81.1–2. For a late-fourth-century celebration of Rome's "sacred graves" and "buried saints," see Prudentius, *Peristephanon*, 2.465–68, 2.529–84, and 12.1–66. Franz Weissengruber, "Zu Augustins Definition des Staates," *Römische historische Mitteilungen* 22 (1980): 31–35, contrasts the poet Prudentius with Augustine, whose route to righteousness passed, *durch Überwindung der Bindung des Diesseits*, through the conquest of what bound Christians to this world.

30. *Sermo* 105.11.

31. *Contra Pel.* 3.5.14.

32. *Sermones* 81.7 and 105.4–7 as well as *Ep.* 120.5.

33. *Exc. urb.* 1.

34. *Cat. rud.* 19.31.

35. *Exc. urb.* 3–4. Also see Harrison, *Augustine*, 216–17.

36. See *Exc. urb.* 8–9; *Sermo* 273.7–9; *Civ.* 12.9, 19.10–11, and 19.27. Also consult Frédouille, "Sermons sur la chute," 446–48.

37. *Sermo* 80.8; *Civ.* 19.4; Basil Studer, "Augustine and the Pauline Theme of Hope," in *Paul and the Legacies of Paul*, ed. William Babcock (Dallas: Southern Methodist University Press, 1990), 212–14; and Norbert Fischer, "Augustins Weg der Gottessuche," *Trierer theologische Zeitschrift* 2 (1991): 96–98.

38. *Ferre te vult; Sermo* 296.8.

39. *Sermo* 296.11, citing Matthew 6:20, and Otto Zwierlein, "Der Fall Roms im Spiegel der Kirchenväter," *Zeitschrift für Papyrologie und Epigraphik* 32 (1978): 69–70.

40. Orosius, *Hist.* 2.3.5; 4.6.34–35; and 7.8.4.

41. *Ep.* 138.4, usefully discussed in Herbert A. Deane, *The Political and Social Ideas of St. Augustine* (New York: Columbia University Press, 1963), 90–93.

42. See Quentin P. Taylor, "St. Augustine and Political Thought: A Revisionist View," *Augustiniana* 48 (1998): 292–95, for "deep pessimism"; for patriotism and providentialism, respectively, see François Paschoud, *"Roma Aeterna: Études sur la patriotisme romain dans l'Occident Latin a l'époque des grandes invasions* (Rome: Institut Suisse, 1967), 234–36, and Madec, *"Tempora Christiana,"* 132–33.

43. Pelagius, *Ad Dem.* 8; *De gestis Pel.* 35.61.

44. Pelagius, *Epist. doct.* 24.1. For Rufinus in Rome, Elizabeth Clark, *The Origenist Controversy: The Cultural Construction of an Early Christian Debate* (Princeton, N.J.: Princeton University Press, 1992), 202–3.

45. Augustine's thoughts on human freedom and fortitude evolved. Pelagians' expectations that he might find their positions compatible with his previously expressed views are quite comprehensible. And those very expectations probably hastened the development of his more pessimistic anthropology. We shall be discussing what evolved, but for the earliest stages of the evolution, see below, note 57, and Harrison, *Augustine*, chapter 3.

46. For Augustine's courtesy, *Pecc. mer.* 3.1.1; *Contra Pel.* 2.3.5; *Nat. gr.* 20.22, 69.73; and Yves-Marie Duval, "La correspondance entre Augustin et Pélage," *REA* 45 (1999): 378–79. See Charles Matthewes, "The Career of the Pelagian Controversy," *Augustinian Studies* 33 (2002): 203–6, for the Pelagians as spiritual trainers, and, for their objections to Manichaean determinism, Mathijs Lamberigts, "Le mal et le peche, Pélage: La rehabilitation d'un heretique," *RHE* 97 (2000): 102–3. Otto Wermelinger, "Neuere Forschungskontroversen um Augustinus und Pelagius," in *Internationales Symposion über den Stand der Augustinus-Forschung*, ed. Cornelius Mayer and Karl Heinz Chelius (Wurzburg: Augustinus-Verlag, 1989), 217, suspects that Augustine's reaction to the Pelagians' *enthusiastisch-optimistischen Vollkommenheitsstreben*, their lively, hopeful struggle to be pious (perhaps impeccably so) was, in part, an answer to nostalgia for the *Belle Époque* of Roman domination. Also see Brown, *Religion and Society*, 192–93, for Pelagius' distinction between genuine and nominal Christians, and 217, for Augustine's reluctance to scold "the new heretics."

47. *De gestis Pel.* 6.18 and, for Pelagius' denial (*ego vero numquam sic tenui*), 13.29–14.30. Also see *Gratia et pecc.* 2.3.3, 2.8.9, 2.12.13, and 2.16.17; *Pecc. mer.* 2.18.28; and *Retr.* 2.33.60.

48. *Ep.* 176.2–5 and Otto Wermelinger, *Rom und Pelagius: Die theologische Position der römischen Bischöfe im pelagianischen Streit in den Jahren 411–431* (Stuttgart: Hiersemann, 1975), 104–5.

49. *Ep.* 183.2.

50. *Coll. Avell.* 45.6–8, for Zosimus; Wermelinger, *Rom und Pelagius*, 199–202, for Honorius' rescript.

51. Jane Merdinger, *Rome and Africa in the Time of Augustine* (New Haven, Conn.: Yale University Press, 1997), 128–29. For the council's position on "true forgiveness," *CCSL* 149, 69–73; for Caelestius' position, *Gratia et pecc.* 2.6.6 and Wermelinger, *Rom und Pelagius*, 172–73.

52. *Tractoriae Zosimi* 2, PL 20, col. 694, and Brown, *Augustine*, 361–62, for the swinging and rioting.

53. *Contra Jul. imperf.* 1.123–25.

54. *Ep.* 177.2.

55. For Augustine's effectiveness, see Eric Rebillard, "Sociologie de la déviance et orthodoxie: Le cas de la controverse pélagienne sur la grâce," in *Orthodoxie, Christianisme, Histoire*, ed. Susanna Elm, Antonella Romano, and Rebillard (Rome: École français de Rome, 2000), 231–39.

56. Pelagius, *Ad Dem.* 2.1; Sebastian Thier, *Kirche bei Pelagius* (Berlin: de Gruyter, 1999), 320.

57. *Jubet per legem, dat per gratiam; Ep.* 157.9; *Conf.* 10.29.40. On this count, the *Confessions* represents a departure from Augustine's early anti-Manichaean intimations that sinners may make significant, albeit not sufficient, progress without special assistance. See Clark, *Origenist Controversy,* 228–32.

58. *Ep.* 140.5, 29, and 34. Also see Robert F. Evans, *One and Holy: The Church in Latin Patristic Thought* (London: S.P.C.K., 1972), 80.

59. *Ep.* 140.22, citing Romans 10:3. Cf. Pelagius, *De vita* 9.1.

60. *Contra Jul.* 4.3.21–22 and *Civ.* 5.12–15. Also consult Herve Inglebert, "Les causes de l'existence de empire romaine selon les auteurs chrétiens des IIIe–IVe siècles," *Latomus* 54 (1995): 46–48.

61. *Nullo modo germanae veraeque virtutes; Contra Jul.* 4.3.19.

62. *Contra Pel.* 3.5.15.

63. *Pecc. mer.* 2.15.22.

64. *Sermo* 131.2 (Hill translation).

65. *Pecc. mer.* 1.9.9–1.10.11.

66. *Nupt.* 2.34.58 (Teske translation) and Harrison, *Augustine,* 109–10.

67. *Contra Jul.* 5.4.16.

68. *Contra Jul.* 5.3.9 and 5.3.12 (*tradi desideriis suis*); *Contra Jul. imperf.* 2.63.

69. *Contra Jul.* 5.3.10 and 5.3.13; for the mistranslation, *Contra Jul. imperf.* 2.174.

70. Pelagius, *De vita* 13.5.

71. *Ratione utens, incipit peccato originali addere et propria; Pecc. mer.* 1.10.12.

72. *Contra Jul.* 4.3.25.

73. *Nat. gr.* 9.10 and 40.47.

74. *De gestis Pel.* 11.23 and 33.57. Also see W. Liebeschuetz, "Did the Pelagian Movement Have Social Aims?" *Historia* 12 (1963): 236–39.

75. John Milbank, *Theology and Social Theory: Beyond Secular Reason* (Oxford: Blackwell, 1990), 401, discussing current limitations put on civil religion, remembers that Augustine introduced what was then "the novel thought that reason itself can be perversely subordinate to a willful desire for a less than truly desirable object."

Chapter Three   **Using Government**

1. Donatist Christians referred to their churches as "catholic." To them, the term signified purity rather than universality. Augustine's arguments helped tilt the term toward the latter meaning. I use "catholic" to refer to the North African Christian opponents of the Donatists—Augustine and his allies, who knew them as the *pars Donati.* Here, I prefer the lowercase "c" in "catholic" to distinguish fourth- and fifth-century

catholic Christianity in Africa from the Catholicism that developed independently of this regional conflict, the Catholicism Thomas More defended in the early sixteenth century, and defends in our final three chapters here.

2. See Brown, *Augustine*, 141–45, and Lepelley, *Aspects de l'Afrique romaine: Les cités, la vie rurale, le Christianisme* (Bari: Edipuglia, 2001), 99–100.

3. Augustine's frustrations make that point, as do W. H. C. Frend's many splendid descriptions of the Donatists' interests and advances; for example, consult his "Donatus, '*paene totam* Africam *decepit*': How?" *JEH* 48 (1997): 611–20.

4. *Contra Fort.* 6–12.

5. *Cresc.* 3.5.5. Donatists, for their part, argued that the early fourth-century catholics cut themselves off or seceded from biblical, puritanical African Christians. To them, Augustine and his allies were apologists for that secession.

6. *Petil.* 3.25.29; *Bapt.*, 16.29.

7. *Zenoph.* 188.

8. See *Cresc.* 3.27.30–31; *Petil.* 3.57.69; Optatus, *De schismata* 1.14–15; *PCBE*, 179; and Bernhard Kriegbaum, *Kirche der Traditoren oder Kirche der Märtyrer: Die Vorgeschichte des Donatismus* (Innsbruck: Tyrolia, 1986), 85–87.

9. Compare W. H. C. Frend, *The Donatist Church: A Movement of Protest in Roman North Africa*, 2nd ed. (Oxford: Oxford University Press, 1985), 60–62, with Emin Tengström, *Donatisten und Katholiken: Soziale, wirtschaftliche, und politische Aspekte einer nordafrikanischen Kirchenspaltung* (Göteborg: Acta Universitatis Gothoburgensis, Studia Graeca et Latina, 1964), 190–92.

10. Optatus, *De schismata* 1.18–24.

11. Lepelley, *Aspects*, 348–49; Kriegbaum, *Kirche*, 32–43, 151–57.

12. See *Don. post col.* 33.56; Jean-Paul Brisson, *Autonomisme et Christianisme dans l'Afrique romaine de Septime Sévère à l'invasion vandale* (Paris: Boccard, 1958), 249–58; and Pierre Maraval, *Le Christianisme de Constantine à la conquête arabe* (Paris: Presses universitaires de France, 1997), 302–3.

13. Maier, *Dossier* 2, 122–23.

14. *Brevic.* 3.13.25 and *Ep.* 185.19–20.

15. Maier, *Dossier* 1, 271–72.

16. [*T*]*erreri me imperator voluit; GCC* 3.25.

17. See Maureen A. Tilley, *The Bible in Christian North Africa: The Donatist World* (Minneapolis: Fortress, 1997), 141–45; Tilley's edition of *Donatist Martyr Stories: The Church in Conflict in Roman North Africa* (Liverpool: Liverpool University Press, 1996); and Frend, *Donatist Church*, 293–94.

18. *Ep.* 87.4, citing Numbers 16.

19. *Petil.* 2.99.228 and *Ep.* 66.1. For Celer, see *Ep.* 57.2; for Pammachius, *Ep.* 58.1.

20. *Petil.* 2.83.184; *Ep.* 66.2; and Lepelley, *Aspects*, 236–38.

21. *Ep.* 66.1; *CTh* XV.5.21; and Optatus, *De schismata* 7.6–7.

22. *CTh* 16.5.37–39; *Cresc.* 2.3.4, for Donatists' objections to being included among heretical Christians; and, for Crispin's difficulties, *Ep.* 88.7; *Cresc.* 3.47.51; and Possidius, *Vita* 12.

23. *Cresc.* 3.43.47 and Maier, *Dossier* 2, 148–49, for the Donatist preface to the *Liber genealogous.*

24. *Cresc.* 1.31.36; *Bapt.* 4.10.16; *Petil.* 2.37.87; and *Ep.* 108.3. Also see the development of this argument in the *Adversus Fulgentium donatistam,* in Maier, *Dossier* 2, 264–65, and Albert C. De Veer, "La définition de l'hérésie et du schisme par Cresconius et par Augustin," BA 31, 761–62.

25. *Petil.* 2.32.73.

26. *Ep.* 97.2.

27. *Ep.* 100.2; *Cresc.* 3.48.53.

28. *Bapt.* 10.15; *Ep.* 93.17 and 185.13, 25, and 32.

29. *Parm.* 3.5.27.

30. *Cresc.* 2.18.21. Also see *Johannis evang.* 76.5 and *Petil.* 1.1.2.

31. *Cresc.* 2.37.47 and 3.66.75.

32. *Cresc.* 2.22.27 and *Parm.* 1.5.10, for accusations.

33. *Ep.* 52 (Parsons translation).

34. *Cresc.* 3.66.75–67.76.

35. *Cresc.* 4.66.83 and *GCC* 1.16, recapitulating *Ep.* 128, 4. Also see Albert C. De Veer, "L'exploitation du schisme maximianiste par Saint Augustin dans la lutte contre le Donatisme," *RA* 3 (1965): 219–37.

36. *Gaud.* 1.28.32 and Optatus, *De schismata* 3.4.

37. Compare Frend, *Donatist Church,* 171–77, 329–31, with Tengström, *Donatisten,* 60–73.

38. *Petil.* 2.83.184 (my italics).

39. *Ep.* 185.12; *Parm.* 2.3.6; and Optatus, *De schismata* 3.4.

40. See *Petil.* 1.24.26 and other sources discussed in Kaufman, "Augustine, Evil, and Donatism: Sin and Sanctity before the Pelagian Controversy," *Theological Studies* 51 (1990): 118–21.

41. *Ep.* 108, 14–18, and 185, 26–28; and *Cresc.* 3.43.47. Unlike Donatist moderates, to whom and about whom Augustine often wrote, Bishop Rogatus of Cartenna and a dozen or so other Donatist prelates so disliked the circumcellions that they seceded from the church, in the late 360s or early 370s; *Ep.* 93.11.

42. *Ep.* 76.3.

43. *Parm.* 2.9.19; *Cresc.* 3.60.66; and Maier, *Dossier* 2, 77–78.

44. *Parm.* 3.3.18 and, for Africa ablaze, Frend, *Donatist Church,* 222.

45. *Petil.* 2.88.195; *Parm.* 1.11.17 (*ad se non pertinere*) and 2.15.34; Hans-Joachim Diesner, "Gildos Herrschaft und die Niederlage bei Theuste," *Klio* 40 (1962): 179–81; Tengström, *Donatisten,* 84–87.

46. *Cresc.* 3.13.16, 4.25.32, and 4.50.60; *Petil.* 2.35.82 and 2.106.242.

47. *Parm.* 2.4.8; *GCC* 3.228–33.

48. *Ep.* 87.7; *Sermo* 47.17.

49. *Parm.* 1.5.10.

50. Pietro Romanelli, *Storia delle province Romane dell'Africa* (Rome: Bretschneider, 1959), 625–29. Not long after the uprising—and probably to capitalize on its failure—Aurelius and Augustine drafted plans for regional councils to deliberate with the secessionists. Nothing came of the plans, and Augustine blamed the Donatists' intransigence. Consult Émilien Lamirande, "Aux origenes du dialogue interconfessionnel: Saint Augustin et les donatistes, vingt ans de tentative infructueuses (391–411)," *Studia Canonica* 32 (1998): 203–28, micromedia document, section 2.1.2.

51. *GCC* 2.66 and 3.20. I borrow the term, "school for sinners" from Gerald Bonner's "Augustine and Pelagianism," *Augustinian Studies* 23 (1992): 34.

52. *Petil.* 2.93.202; Frend, *Donatist Church,* 254–55.

53. *GCC* 1.55.

54. *Ep.* 35.3; Brisson, *Autonomisme,* 374–77.

55. Optatus, *De schismata* 3.3.

56. *Il n'est pas moins étonnant;* Émilien Lamirande, "La conférence de Carthage (411) et les réactions de Saint Augustin: Un procès singulier, fatal aux donatises," *Studia Canonica* 32 (1998): 415–40, micromedia document, section 1.1.

57. *CTh* XVI.5.52, for the edict. For government's shift to a more proactive policy, consult Ernst Ludwig Grasmück, *Coercitio: Staat und Kirche im Donatistenstreit* (Bonn: Röhrscheid, 1964), 210–13, and, for a synopsis of the conference, Brown, *Augustine,* 331–34, and Lamirande, "Conférence," section 3.1.

58. *Parm.* 1.11.19 and *infra,* note 40.

59. *Ep.* 93.5, 11, and 49.

60. Compare *Ep.* 93.1. Pierre Cazier, "La *compelle intrare* d'Augustine, mise en perspective," in Cazier and Jean-Marie Delmaire, ed., *Violence et Religion* (Lille: Université Lille, 1998), 29–31, emphasizes the letter's caution.

61. *Ep.* 105.3 (Atkins translation).

62. *Fraternae caritatis inimici; Bapt.* 3.19.26.

63. *CTh* I.27.2, XVI.2.41, and XVI.5.52. For that "rod" and discipline, see *Ep.* 173.3, citing Proverbs 23:14, and 173.10, citing Psalms 72:11.

64. *Bapt.* 2.6.9; *Parm.* 2.6.11; and Bonner, *Augustine,* 302, for "dour fanaticism."

65. Frend, *Donatist Church,* 240–41; Possidius, *Vita* 9; and Brisson, *Autonomisme,* 187–88, 236–39.

66. *Quid ad haec respondetur; Parm.* 3.3.18.

67. *Ep.* 204.1; *Gaud.* 1.12.13–15.16.

68. *Gaud.* 1.20.22 and 1.31.39; *Ep.* 204.6–7.

69. Brown, *Augustine,* 335.

70. *Gaud.* 1.24.27. Also see *Parm.* 2.9.19.

71. *Gaud.* 1.20.23 and 1.35.45; *Ep.* 204.2.

72. Lancel, *Augustin*, 381. For African appeals *ad transmarina*, see, e.g., Maier, *Dossier* 2, 82–84; for Africa's "strong emphasis" on "disciplinary autonomy," Werner Marschall, *Karthago und Rom: die Stellung der nordafrikanischen Kirche zum apostolischen Stuhl in Rom: Päpste und papsttum*, vol. 1 (Stuttgart, Hiersemann, 1974), 222.

73. E.g., *Ep.* 185.19–20, citing Romans 13:2–4.

74. *Ep.* 87.7–8.

75. *Enarr. Ps.* 36.2.18 and 20 (*reus reum non facit*). Alfred Schindler, "L'histoire du Donatisme considérée du point de vue de sa proper théologie," *Studia Patristica* 17.3 (1982): 1308–9, asserts that Augustine and, before him, Optatus of Mileve missed the critical distinction between the kinds of government interference Donatists welcomed after Constantine and Caecilian and the intervention that catholics called for. But our evidence is insufficient to prove that Donatists petitioned only for the return of property, as Schindler says, whereas catholics pressed for the return and forcible "turn" of persons.

76. *Cresc.* 3.51.56; *CTh* I.27.2; and Lancel, *Augustin*, 366–67.

77. *Ep.* 105.7 and 185.8; *Enarr. Ps.* 21.2.3–6.

78. *Sermo* 99.9.

79. E.g., *Johannis evang.* 6.25–26

80. Tyconius, *Apoc.* 28–29. TeSelle, *Cities*, 36–39.

81. *Eine kollektive Heiligkeit war für ihn undenkbar;* Alfred Schindler, "Die Theologie der Donatisten und Augustins Reaktion," in *Internationales Symposion über den Stand der Augustinus-Forschung*, ed. Cornelius Mayer and Karl Heinz Chelius (Würzburg: Augustinus-Verlag, 1989), 144–45. Also see Evans, *One and Holy*, 107–8, and, for Augustine's Solomon, *Enarr. Ps.* 39.10.

Chapter Four **Used But Not Improved**

1. For Isaac's "woe"s and woes, see Tilley, *Martyr Stories*, 66–69.

2. Markus, *End*, 139–55.

3. Harrison, *Augustine*, 141–42.

4. *Rodulfi Glabri historiarum libri quinque*, ed. John France (Oxford: Clarendon, 1989), 3.6.19 and 4.5.14.

5. Kaufman, "Augustine, Martyrs, and Misery," *Church History* 63 (1994): 1–14.

6. *Sermo* 81.9.

7. *Civ.* 1.1.

8. See *Civ.* 17.6 and Isabelle Bochet, "L'écriture et le mâitre intérieur selon Augustin," *Revue des sciences religieuses* 72 (1998), 29–37.

9. See *Civ.* 1.2–5 and Gerard O'Daly, *Augustine's "City of God": A Reader's Guide* (Oxford: Oxford University Press, 1999): 80–94.

10. *Cor contritum et humiliatum dolore paenitendi; Civ.* 10.5, referring to Psalm 51:17.

11. *Civ.* 10.19.

12. *Civ.* 10.21. For unburied remains, *Civ.* 1.12–13.

13. *Civ.* 19.17 (Bettenson translation).

14. *Si religionem . . . non impedit; Civ.* 19.17.

15. *Civ.* 15.26.

16. *Civ.* 17.3–4.

17. *In Christo nusquam exsulem, in carne ubique peregrinum; Sermo* 302.2; *Civ.* 16.24.

18. *Enarr. Ps.* 124.7–8.

19. *Enarr. Ps.* 65.16. But, as we shall discover, Augustine countenanced Christians assuming political responsibility, though he specified provisions or conditions that made a world of difference without directing Christian officeholders to devise a different world order.

20. *Enarr. Ps.* 61.8; Lancel, *Augustin,* 379–81.

21. E.g., *Sermo* 96.7–8, extrapolating from 1 John 2:15, "love not the world."

22. *Civ.* 5.18. Johannes Van Oort, *Jerusalem and Babylon: A Study into Augustine's "City of God" and the Sources of His Doctrine of the Two Cities* (Leiden: Brill, 1990), 159–63, paraphrases: Christians in history were "in peregrination," always persecuted and patient. One suspects Augustine might have commended a more moderate response had he assumed, as do some prominent twentieth-century readers, that "divergence is not necessarily opposition," for which, see Johannes Straub, *Regeneratio Imperii* (Darmstadt: Wissenschaftliche Buchgesellschaft, 1972), 274, endorsing Werner Elert's observation to that effect.

23. *Quis ullo sermone digerit* [*miseriam communem*]? *Civ.* 22.22.

24. *Civ.* 5.5–8 and TeSelle, *Cities,* 61.

25. TeSelle, *Cities,* 56–62, 87–96, 160–65.

26. Dolbeau, *Vingt-six sermons,* 519; Lancel, *Augustin,* 562–66. John von Heyking, *Augustine and Politics as Longing in the World* (Columbia: University of Missouri Press, 2001), 33–43, 157–61, though, suggests that expressions of opposition or antagonism are evidence of Augustine's "rhetoric of excess." The *City* "sought to awaken and perfect the love of glory among political actors," "balancing Christian enthusiasm for eternal life" with devotion to civic duty, von Heyking allows, rather than denying, as Augustine did to Nectarius, that the two ought to be measured with the same scales.

27. See *Civ.* 19.12–16 and Stanislaw Budzik, *Doctor Pacis: Theologie des Friedens dei Augustinus* (Innsbruck: Tyrolia, 1988), 69–78, 268–71.

28. *Ep.* 138.10, for the concession.

29. *Ep.* 90.1, 91.1, and 104.10. For a discussion of public service and *philopatris,* see J. E. Lendon, *Empire of Honour: The Art of Government in the Roman World* (Oxford: Oxford University Press, 1997), 73–89.

30. Cicero, *De officiis* 1.34.125.

31. *Ep.* 151.14.

32. *Ep.* 136.2.

33. *Ep.* 95.3–5.

34. *Ep.* 138.11–14.

35. *Enarr. Ps.* 51.6.

36. Gaetano Lettieri, *Il senso della storia in Agostino d'Ippona: il "saeculum" e la gloria nel "De civitate Dei"* (Rome: Borla, 1988), 197–99.

37. Oliver O'Donovan, "Augustine's *City of God* XIX and Western Political Thought," *Dionysius* 11 (1987): 105–6.

38. *Enarr. Ps.* 90.1.8 and 90.2.2.

39. *Quam deserere nefas ducit; Civ.* 19.6.

40. *Civ.* 19.17. Miikka Ruokanen, *Theology of Social Life in Augustine's "De Civitas Dei"* (Göttingen: Vandenhoeck und Ruprecht, 1993), 27–28, submits that the *City's* nineteenth book represents Augustine's "theological thinking at its most mature and most genuine stage," emphasizing "the rather gloomy reality of human social life" and the Christians' higher calling, braced by "faith in and hope for the true justice, order, and peace of the transcendental-eschatological *civitas Dei.*"

41. *Ep.* 154.2.

42. 1 John 2:15; *Ep.* 155.7–8; *Sermo* 65.3.

43. *Ep.* 155.10–12.

44. Jakob Speigl, "Zur universalen Theologie Augustins: Die Religionsthematik in *De civitate Dei,*" *Augustiniana* 50 (2000): 58–60, speaks of the seepage.

45. *Civ.* 5.26.

46. *Ep.* 185.19–23.

47. *Johannis evang.* 11.14.

48. *Civ.* 18.54; *Petil.* 2.92.210; Robert Markus, *Conversion and Disenchantment in Augustine's Spiritual Career* (Villanova: Villanova University Press, 1989), 39–41 ("barrier"); Harrison, *Augustine,* 216–18 ("stemming the tide of man's sins with the sandbags of authority"); Markus, *Saeculum,* 148–49.

49. *Civ.* 2.18.

50. *Civ.* 1.pref.

51. *Civ.* 5.18–20 and *Ep.* 140.36.

52. *Civ.* 1.30; Markus, *Saeculum,* 57–58.

53. *Civ.* 2.17.

54. See *Civ.* 2.19–21; Cicero, *De re publica* 5.1; Robert Dodaro, "Eloquent Lies, Just Wars, and the Politics of Persuasion: Reading Augustine's *City of God* in a Postmodern World," *Augustinian Studies* 25 (1994): 84–86; and Catherine Conybeare, "*Terrarum Orbi Documentum:* Augustine, Camillus, and Learning from History," in *History, Apocalypse, and the Secular Imagination: New Essays on Augustine's "City of God",* ed. Mark Vessey, Karla Pollmann, and Allan D. Fitzgerald (Bowling Green, Ohio: Philosophy Documentation Center, 1999), 49–53.

55. *Civ.* 14.28 and, for emphasis on *natura vitiata,* see Pierre-Marie Hombert, *Nouvelles recherches de chronologie Augustinienne* (Paris: Institut d'études augustiniennes, 2000), 231, n. 5.

56. *Civ.* 5.21–22, 17.10, and 18.25–26.

57. Lendon, *Empire,* 236.

58. *Civ.* 4.4.

59. Lancel, *Augustin,* 560–61; Brown, *Augustine,* 306.

60. E.g., *Cons. evang.* 1.26.40, citing Jeremiah 16:19–21.

61. See Straub, *Regeneratio Imperii,* 292–95, for remarks on *renovatio* that first circulated in 1954. They distinguished Augustine's enthusiasm ("normative Augustinianism"), which acknowledged the impermanence of empires (*Hinfälligkeit; Vergänglichkeit*), from the narrative celebrations for a Christian society associated with Eusebius of Caesarea. Ruokanen, *Social Life,* 9–14, introduces scholars earlier in the twentieth century who saw little difference between the two.

62. Franz Georg Maier, *Augustin und das Antike Rom* (Stuttgart: Kohlhammer, 1955), 158–63, and, more famously, Wilhelm Kamlah, *Christentum und Geschichtlichkeit: Untersuchungen zur Entstehung des Christentums und zu Augustins "Bürgerschaft Gottes"* (Stuttgart: Kohlhammer, 1951), 137–40.

63. *Ep.* 33.5, 115, and 209.4–6.

64. *In . . . ecclesiis habitat gentium latitudo; Civ.* 16.2.

65. *Probi . . . in interiore homine tam grande mysterium atque honorant intus in corde; Civ.* 16.2.

66. Kamlah, *Christentum,* 145–48, wrote of "the church now" as a community (as a *Gemeinde-Jetzt*) to distinguish it from the *ecclesia sanctorum.* But Joseph Ratzinger expressed reservations about Kamlah's emphasis on interiority and supplied an explanation of Augustine's eschatological-transcendental *ecclesia* and *civitas Dei* more accommodating to the community of the sacraments; Ratzinger, "Herkunft und Sinn der *Civitas*-Lehre Augustins: Begegnung und Auseinandersetzung mit Wilhelm Kamlah," *Augustinus Magister* (Paris: Études augustiniennes, 1954), 474–79.

67. Van Oort, *Jerusalem,* 126–27; Maier, *Augustin,* 180–81; Kamlah, *Christentum,* 158–64; and, for "no positive relation," F. Edward Cranz, "*De Civitate Dei* 15.2, and Augustine's Idea of the Christian Society," reprinted from *Speculum* (1950), in *Augustine: A Collection of Critical Essays,* ed. Robert Markus (Garden City, N.Y.: Anchor, 1972), 410–12.

68. *Civ.* 18.2 and 18.22.

69. Henri Xavier Arquillière, *L'Augustinisme politique: Essai sur la formation theories politiques du moyen âge,* 2nd ed. (Paris: J. Vrin, 1956); Walter Ullmann, *The Growth of Papal Government in the Middle Ages: A Study of the Ideological Relations of Clerical to Lay Power,* 2nd ed. (London: Methuen, 1962); Kaufman, *Redeeming Politics* (Princeton: Princeton University Press, 1990), 77–104.

70. Kamlah, *Christentum,* 318–19, and Johannes Spörl, "Augustinus: Schöpfer einer Staatslehre?" *HZ* 74 (1955): 62, 66–68, 74–76.

71. For which, consult Basil Studer, "Zum Aufbau von Augustinus *De Civitate Dei,*" *Collectanea Augustiniana,* ed. Bernard Bruning, Mathijs Lamberigts, and J. Van Houten (Leuven: Peeters, 1990), 2:947–50.

72. *Civ.* 18.1 (Bettenson translation).

73. Van Oort, *Jerusalem,* 273–74; Lettieri, *Senso della storia,* 126–27 (*indissolubili*); and *Civ.* 2.20, for luxury, debauchery, and, *publici inamici.*

74. Lettieri, *Senso della storia,* 256–57.

75. *Civ.* 15.17 (Cain) and 15.26 (Noah).

76. Markus, *Saeculum,* 29–32, for euphoria; 177–78, for "living space."

77. Markus, *Saeculum,* 96–102, quoting Williams at 102.

78. Von Heyking, *Augustine,* 1–12, 81–89, 216–21, "foreshadow" at 87; Elshtain, *Augustine,* 34–42; and Brown, "Introducing Robert Markus," *Augustinian Studies* 32 (2001): 181–87, "opacity" at 184. But also see Brown's "Political Society," in *Augustine: A Collection of Critical Studies,* 321–22, where *saeculum* seems less opaque and more "sinister . . . a penal existence marked by misery and suffering . . . by a disquieting inanity."

79. *Civ.* 14.19.

80. O'Daly, *Augustine's City,* 23.

81. *Civ.* 18.51.

82. *Civ.* 18.49.

83. But Williams, "Politics and the Soul," *Milltown Studies* 19/20 (1987): 63–67, admitting it as one of the *City's* "paradoxes," suggests that a detached or "indifferent" politician was the deliverance Augustine was counting on. John Milbank's protest that, in the *City,* "it is quite precisely the political order . . . that we are saved from," though, corresponds more closely with the claims argued here. See Milbank's "An Essay against Secular Order," *Journal of Religious Ethics* 15 (1987): 209.

84. Höffe, "Postivismus plus Moralismus: zu Augustinus' eschatologischer Staatstheorie," in *Augustinus: "De Civitate Dei",* ed. Christoph Horn (Berlin: Beck, 1997): 279.

85. *[I]d esse jus, quod ei, qui plus potest, utile est; Civ.* 19.21.

86. *Civ.* 19.21; Ruokanen, *Theology,* 69–76; and Höffe, "Positivismus," 266–69.

87. *Civ.* 14.28 and 15.3.

88. *Civ.* 5.19.

89. *Civ.* 13.5 and 21.16.

90. Again, *Civ.* 19.6.

91. *Enarr. Ps.* 93.3, quoting Philippians 2:15.

92. *Sermo* 56.14.

93. *Civ.* 11.3 and 19.14; *Ep.* 153.3–4; and O'Daly, *Augustine's City,* 204–5.

94. James Dougherty, *The Fivesquare City: The City in the Religious Imagination* (Notre Dame, Ind.: University of Notre Dame Press, 1980), 38–40, for example, is generally correct but a bit too categorical about Augustine's "not"s with reference to "Christians [who] 'use' the civil peace and 'comply' with state authority. They do not build the

city," Dougherty insists, "they do not reform its laws, they do not meddle in the public affairs of their host country."

95. Spörl, "Augustinus," 70 (*Weltverneiner*); also see Ruokanen, *Theology*, 110–11.

96. *Civ.* 19.4.

97. *Paci supernae patriae suspirantes; Civ.* 15.6.

98. Plato, *Republic* 6.496c.

99. *Necesse est miseria consequatur et quae inerat augeatur; Civ.* 15.4.

100. R. W. Dyson, *The Pilgrim City: Social and Political Ideas in the Writings of St. Augustine* (London: Boydell, 2001), 46–47.

101. *Ep.* 220.3.

102. *Civ.* 17.8 (spread); *Civ.* 22.6 (safety); and *Ep.* 199.46 (expansion and contraction).

103. *Civ.* 18.45, but also 4.3 and 4.5.

104. See Lettieri, *Senso della storia*, 306–7, and Ernest L. Fortin, "The Why, Not the What," *Review of Politics* 59 (1997): 366–67.

105. Dodaro, "Lies," 89.

106. *Sermo* 361.20; *Div. quaest.* 66.2.

107. Markus, *Saeculum*, pp. 117–21.

108. E.g., *Enarr. Ps.* 61.23. Augustine discusses ambition and conversion in the context of political practice, explaining how God ensured officials did not convert "to earn the good fortune of Constantine," *Civ.* 5.25.

109. *Civ.* 20.9; on wars, *Civ.* 4.15.

110. *Enarr. Ps.* 61.8, citing Matthew 23:2–3 and 7:23; for "perfectly harmonious," *Civ.* 19.13.

111. Milbank, *Theology and Social Theory*, 391–92.

112. *Civ.* 1.35.

113. *Civ.* 18.48.

114. See *Sermo* 355.2; Martijn Schrama, *"Praeposito Tamquam Patri Oboediatur:* Augustinus über Frieden und Gehorsam," in *Collectanea Augustiniana*, 2.877–78 (*Gemeinschaft von Gesinnungsfreunden*); and Lawless, *Augustine*, 60–61.

115. *Delebo eum de tabula clericorum; Sermo* 356.14; for unfallen angels, *Civ.* 10.7.

116. *Hic nusquam; Enarr. Ps.* 99.11. Kevin L. Hughes, "Local Politics: The Political Place of the Household in Augustine's *City of God*," in *Augustine and Politics*, ed. John Doody, Kevin L. Hughes, and Kim Paffenroth (New York: Lexington, 2005), 154–55, citing *Civ.* 19.14–19.16, makes the case that the family is someplace in which charity can be learned to the extent that "the household becomes a safe house, a refuge from a culture whose ethos is established by the passion for glory, the *libido dominandi*."

117. *Johannis evang.* 77.3.

118. *Sermo* 80.8.

119. *Civ.* 1.21.

120. *Civ.* 8.19.

121. *Ep.* 140.37.

Chapter Five   Thomas More, At Work in the World

1. CW 4:102–5 (laws); CW 4:122–23 (disputes).
2. CW 4:70–71.
3. *Ep.* (Eras.) 4:17.
4. *Ep.* (Eras.) 10:136–37.
5. Stapleton, *The Life and Illustrious Martyrdom of Sir Thomas More* (New York: Fordham University Press, 1966), 13. But neither Stapleton nor Erasmus offers an entirely trustworthy account. More would likely have been surprised to have found himself—at a tender age—a budding statesman, scholar, and saint. Yet one should be wary as well of replacing his premature maturity, self-assurance, and determination with a torturous ambivalence which has him trying to reconcile allegedly intense personal or political ambitions with a selfless devotion to Christianity. We will have more to say about More's ambition and ambivalence in this and subsequent chapters.
6. "This child . . . will prove a marvelous man"; Roper, *More,* 198. For Morton's pontificate and part in Henry VII's administration, see Christopher Harper-Bill, "Archbishop John Morton and the Province of Canterbury, 1486–1500," *JEH* 29 (1978): 10–12, and S. B. Chrimes, *Henry VII,* 2nd ed. (New Haven, Conn.: Yale University Press, 1999), 241–42.
7. CW 2:89–92.
8. CW 4:60–61.
9. CW 4:58–59.
10. John Guy, *Thomas More* (London: Arnold, 2000), 23; Roper, *More,* 197.
11. *Hujusmodi nihil expectabam. . . . subirascebar Moro*"; *Ep.* (Eras.) 1:6.
12. *Principium negotiosis nugis; Ep.* (Eras.) 3:111.
13. Stapleton, *Life,* 8–9.
14. *Corresp.* 6–8 (Rogers transl.).
15. For Colet on conformity, see his *Oratio ad clerum in convocatione* (1510) in Samuel Knight's *Life of Dr. John Colet, Dean of St. Paul's,* 2nd ed. (Oxford: Clarendon Press, 1823), 238–50, and John B. Gleason, *John Colet* (Berkeley: University of California Press, 1989), 180–84.
16. See Nicholas Harpsfield, *The Life and Death of Sir Thomas Moore,* ed. E. C. Hitchcock (London: Early English Text Society, 1932), 17, and *Ep.* (Eras.) 4:17–18 (*meditans sacerdotium*). The point urged on Ulrich von Hutten in 1519 was that More, unlike Martin Luther, had not rushed into the priesthood, only to repent the rush and the choice. In 1521, Erasmus manufactured Colet's dislike of Luther's darling Augustine (*Ep.* [Eras.] 4:515). Alternatively, one could argue that "Erasmus' language [on More] is playful, almost ironical, and . . . proverbial" ("be a chaste husband rather than a lewd priest"); Guy, *More,* 32.
17. Richard Marius, *Thomas More: A Biography* (London: Dent, 1985), 36–38; Roper, *More,* 198.

18. See Fox, *Thomas More: History and Providence* (New Haven, Conn.: Yale University Press, 1982), 4 and Elton, "The Actor Saint," *New York Review of Books* 32 (January 31, 1985), 7–8.

19. Guy, *More*, 47–58, commenting on *Ep.* (Eras.) 4:20 and 4:294. Also see Russell Ames's still useful inventory of More's early work, *Citizen Thomas More and His Utopia* (Princeton, N.J.: Princeton University Press, 1949), 181–90.

20. Cf. Germain Marc'hadour, "*Fuitne Thomas Morus in* Aulam *Petractus?*" in *Acta Conventus Neo-Latini Sanctandreani*, ed. I. D. McFarlane (Binghamton: State University of New York Press, 1986), 444–46.

21. Elton, *Studies in Tudor and Stuart Politics and Government*, vol. 1 (Cambridge: Cambridge University Press, 1974), 1:132–33.

22. James McConica, "The Patrimony of Thomas More," in *History and Imagination*, ed. Hugh Lloyd-Jones, Valerie Pearl, and Blair Worden (London: Duckworth, 1981), 59–61.

23. *Ep.* (Eras.) 1:450–52; Peter Ackroyd, *Life of Thomas More* (New York: Random House, 1998), 130–32.

24. CW 3.2:102–104.

25. CW 3.2:106.

26. CW 3.2:204–205.

27. CW 3.2:228–31.

28. *Acts of Court of the Mercers' Company, 1453–1527*, ed. Laetitia Lyell and Frank D. Watney (Cambridge: Cambridge University Press, 1936), 320; Roper, *More*, 199–200; Marius, *More*, 50–51; Guy, *More*, 43–44. Ackroyd, *More*, 110, however, thinks Roper's story is implausible.

29. CW 3.2:104.

30. CW 3.2:230–33.

31. CW 1:116.

32. CW 1:111. For Pico's remark, CW 1:376.

33. Fox, *More*, 29–31.

34. Henri De Lubac, *Pic de la Mirandole: Études et discussions* (Paris: Aubier, 1974), 402–5.

35. CW 1:58–59 and 1:298–99.

36. Heinrich Reinhardt, *Freiheit zu Gott: Der Grundgedanke des Systematikers, Giovanni Pico della Mirandola* (Weinheim: VCH, 1989), 108–9. More's slimmed-down biography deletes Gianfrancesco's discussion of Pico's esoteric interests, for which, CW 1:308–10.

37. CW 1:74–75.

38. CW 1:53, 1:294, and 1:304–14.

39. CW 1:62, 1:68–69, and 1:328–29.

40. CW 1:66; Guy, *More*, 37–39.

41. *CWE* 66:61; *AW* 63. I cite Hajo Holborn's edition of Erasmus's *Enchiridion* (*AW*) when my translations differ from those of Charles Fantazzi (*CWE* 66). For the comparison with Aquinas, see Erasmus' preface to the 1518 edition (*CWE* 66:9–10); for the inquiry that led to the composition of the *Enchiridion*, Otto Schottenloher, "Erasmus, Johann Poppenruyter, und die Entstehung des *Enchiridion militis christiani*," *Archiv für Reformationsgeschichte* 45 (1954): 113–16.

42. *CWE* 66:94; *AW* 99–100.

43. *CWE* 66:22–23.

44. *Tu fratrem, in cibo aut potu cultuve judicas. At Paulus te judicat ex factis tuis; AW* 80; *CWE* 66:77. And, for the contrasts with monasticism (*im Unterschied zur monastischen Sonderform hat die christliche Frömmigkeit im allgemeinen ein durchaus welthaftes Gepräge*), consult Alfons Auer, *Die vollkommene Frömmigkeit des Christen nach dem "Enchiridion militis christiani" des Erasmus von Rotterdam* (Düsseldorf: Patmos-Verlag, 1954), 196–206.

45. *CWE* 66:60.

46. CW 1:103 and 1:372–73. Also see Germain Marc'hadour, "Sir Thomas More, chevalier chrétien," *Moreana* 38 (2001): 37–38.

47. CW 1:112.

48. CW 1:78–79.

49. CW 1:90–91 and 1:328.

50. CW 1:84; De Lubac, *Études*, 44.

51. CW 1:87–88; CW 1:350.

52. CW 1:352–53.

53. CW 1:86.

54. Stanford Lehmberg, "Sir Thomas More's Life of Pico Della Mirandola," *Studies in the Renaissance* 3 (1956): 64–67; Marius, *More*, 37–39.

55. G. D. Ramsay, "A Saint in the City: Thomas More at Mercers' Hall, London," *English Historical Review* 97 (1982): 276–88. For dating, see Heinz Holeczek, *Humanistische Bibelphilologie als Reformproblem bei Erasmus von Rotterdam, Thomas More, und William Tyndale* (Leiden: Brill, 1975), 38–39.

56. Lorenzo Polizzatto, *The Elect Nation: The Savonarolan Movement in Florence, 1494–1545* (Oxford: Oxford University Press, 1994), 90–91, 117–18, 161–64, and 306.

57. CW 15:470–73; Ackroyd, *More*, 161–63; and Ames, *Citizen More*, 186–87.

58. CW 4:38–39.

59. *Mercers' Company*, 329–33.

60. *Sic vivo et volo;* CW 4:56–57.

61. More and his companions at Bruges reminded the king's council in 1515, two months after their arrival, that they had "soo short warnyng" and had to leave England with "lityll and skarse [time] to prepayr our self"; *Corresp.* 21.

62. Logan, *The Meaning of More's Utopia* (Princeton: Princeton University Press, 1983), 3.

Chapter Six **Utopia?**

1. TMU 240–41; CW 4:243. I cite the former when I prefer its English translation. Citations with my initials in parentheses (pik) signal that translations in the text are my alternatives to both.

2. TMU 242–43. More first tried a Latin title, *Nusquama;* See James Romm, "More's Strategy of Naming in *Utopia,*" *SCJ* 22 (1991): 179–80.

3. CW 4:154–56, 166–68.

4. *EOO* 2.1:308.

5. *Perversis opinionibus a pueris imbuti;* CW 4:86.

6. CW 4:62–64.

7. CW 4:80–82; CW 12:213–16; and Dominic Baker-Smith, *More's Utopia* (New York: HarperCollins, 1991), 112–13.

8. Dermot Fenlon, "England and Europe: *Utopia* and its Aftermath," *Transactions of the Royal Historical Society,* 5th ser., 25 (1975): 124–25.

9. CW 4:92–94.

10. CW 1:78–79; CW 4:56–57.

11. *Quae suam novit scenam eique sese accommodans;* CW 4:98. Also see Cicero's *De re publica* 2.30.52; his *De officiis* 1.6.19 and 1.44.157; and Quentin Skinner, "Sir Thomas More's *Utopia* and the Language of Renaissance Humanism," in *The Languages of Political Theory in Early Modern Europe,* ed. Anthony Pagden (Cambridge: Cambridge University Press, 1987), 130–34. To place More's debts to Cicero in the context of More's "engagement of the classical theorists," see Logan, *Meaning,* 74–111.

12. Compare Cicero, *De officiis* 1.31.114 with CW 4:98–101.

13. CW 4:102–103; Ackroyd, *More,* 179; Logan, *Meaning,* 122–23.

14. Cicero, *De officiis* 3.22.86; Baker-Smith, *Utopia,* 125–27.

15. CW 4:102–3 (pik).

16. For More's suspicions about *Romanitas,* see Eric Nelson, "Greek Nonsense in More's *Utopia,*" *Historical Journal* 44 (2001): 902–8.

17. CW 4:70.

18. Logan, *Meaning,* 44–47; Fox, *More,* 62–63.

19. Greenblatt, *Renaissance Self-Fashioning: From More to Shakespeare* (Chicago: University of Chicago Press, 1980), 33–34.

20. TMU 63.

21. CW 4:52–54. "All hope of ideal politics appears to have receded into the far distance, more remote from the reader than the fantastic inventions of the poets"; Baker-Smith, *Utopia,* 94–95.

22. TMU 109–121.

23. Nagel, "Lies and the Limitable Inane," *Renaissance Quarterly* 26 (1973): 173–80.

24. CW 4:343.

25. TMU 73–75 (my emphasis).

26. TMU 70.

27. *Ep.* (Eras.) 1:486 and 1:568.

28. CW 4:112–13.

29. Compare CW 4:238–41 and CW 3.2:228–31.

30. *Optarim verius quam sperarim;* CW 4:246.

31. Logan, *Meaning,* 61.

32. *Regno nunquam deest tempestas; EOO* 4.1:182.

33. *EOO* 4.1:175.

34. *EOO* 4.1:177–78, 194, and 210; Plutarch, *Moralia* 58–59.

35. *EOO* 4.3:144–58.

36. CW 15:94–95, 108–9, and 120–21.

37. CW 15:537.

38. But Dorp renewed his protest soon thereafter; Henry De Vocht, *Monumenta Humanistica Lovaniensia* (Louvain: Uystpruyst, 1934), 80–82, 160–63. Also see Kaufman, "The Disputed Date of Erasmus' *Liber Apologeticus,*" *Medievalia et Humanistica* 10 (1981): 148–51.

39. CW 4:4–37; Logan, *Meaning,* 26–31.

40. CW 4:126–29, 144–45.

41. TMU 130–31.

42. See *AW* 55 and Martin Fleisher, *Radical Reform and Political Persuasion in the Life and Writings of Thomas More* (Geneva: Droz, 1973), 5–20.

43. CW 4:174–79; Baker-Smith, *Utopia,* 171–72; and Roland Galibois, *Religion et socialisme dans l'Utopie de Thomas More et dans les éscrits du premier Tillich* (Laval: Presses de l'Université Laval, 2002), 80–82 and 131–32.

44. J. H. Hexter, "*Utopia* and Its Historical Milieu," in CW 4:lv–lvi, lxvi–lxvii, and lxxix–lxxxii.

45. Quentin Skinner, "More's *Utopia,*" *Past and Present* 38 (1967): 158 and 168.

46. TMU 143.

47. Baker-Smith, *Utopia,* 161–62, 223.

48. Fox, *More,* 51.

49. CW 4:145 catches the irony somewhat better than TMU, pairing the deliberate provocation of younger Utopians with *per convivii libertatem* as "the relaxed atmosphere of the feast." Despite TMU's translation, "the freedom of mealtime talk," the young examinees' impromptu responses hardly made conversations "free."

50. *Ep.* (Eras.) 1:129–30 and 1:566–68.

51. CW 4:146–47.

52. CW 4:121–33.

53. Greenblatt, *Renaissance Self-Fashioning,* 39–42, suspects that More is rather unself-conscious here and that Utopian regulations express a subliminal "craving for order" (56), for which, also consult Marius, *More,* 162–64. I will suggest that More consciously, cleverly conveyed to his friends and first readers a lesson about both the improbability and the peril of radical political change. There is evidence that they got his message.

54. Erasmus, *Opus de conscribendi*, in *EOO* 1.2:222–38 and 432–41; *AW* 55, again; Kaufman, "More's *Monstra*; Humanist Spirituality and Ecclesial Reaction," *Church History* 56 (1987): 29–30; and, for "spur" and "stimulus," CW 4:192–93.

55. TMU 146.

56. CW 4:209.

57. *EOO* 4.1:214.

58. *EOO* 2.7:18.

59. *EOO* 4.1:218.

60. TMU 202.

61. Logan, *Meaning*, 257.

62. CW 4:103.

63. CW 4:68.

64. Plato, *Republic* 421d–422a, 464b–466c.

65. CW 4:104 (pik).

66. CW 4:239; François Chirpaz, *Raison et déraison de l'Utopie* (Paris: Harmattan 1999), 21.

67. *Ep.* (Eras.) 1:162 and *EOO* 2.1:84–86.

68. TMU 247.

69. CW 4:244.

70. Baker-Smith, *Utopia*, 208–12.

71. TMU 246–49; Bradshaw, "More on Utopia," *Historical Journal* 24 (1981): 25–27.

72. CW 4:109; TMU 106–7. Cf. Bradshaw, "More," 20–21, 26–27.

73. TMU 246–48.

74. Richard S. Sylvester, *"Si Hythlodaeo Credimus:* Vision and Revision in Thomas More's *Utopia*," *Soundings* 51 (1968): 288–89.

75. CW 4:248.

76. CW 15:280–83, 302–5. Erasmus earlier angered More's correspondent, probably John Batmanson, with related comments on monks' sense of superiority. His *Praise of Folly* illustrated how *omnia omnium*, in the cloisters, resulted in quite the reverse of humility and harmony (*EOO* 4.3:162). More mentioned the Carthusian's bitter, arrogant, scalding reply (*calore scripsisti*) to make much the same point (CW 15:202).

77. Plato, *Republic* 473a.

78. Plato, *Republic* 591c–592b.

79. Nelson, "Nonsense," 899.

80. Fenlon, "England," 129.

81. Ackroyd, *More*, 174.

82. CW 4:30–31 (marvels); TMU 256–57 (monsters); Kaufman, "More's *Monstra*," 25–26 (both).

83. TMU 25.

84. TMU 4–7, 272–73, and, for "deafening silence," Guy, *More*, 91–92.

85. *Doctissimus alioqui;* CW 15:218.

86. CW 4:8.

87. TMU 12–17, CW 4:10–13.

88. Marius, *More*, 187–88.

89. TMU 260–63.

90. Peter R. Allen, "*Utopia* and European Humanism: The Function of the Prefatory Letters and Verses," *Studies in the Renaissance* 10 (1963): 100–107.

91. CW 4:37 and Logan, *Meaning*, 74, for *Utopia*'s demonstration of "the absolute futility of . . . the humanist solution to the problem of counsel."

92. Dominic Baker-Smith imagines More thought the implementation of his ideal was difficult but not impossible. It is unclear, however, whether the ideal he hoped to have implemented was the "conjunction of political power and philosophical intelligence"—in which case John Guy is correct to suggest that More was on a Ciceronian mission to have politicians put Plato's ideals into practice—or, as I argue, a tension between the "critical frame of mind" and "the resistant contingency of actions." See Baker-Smith, "Uses of Plato by Erasmus and More," in *Platonism and the English Imagination*, ed. Anna Baldwin and Sarah Hutton (Cambridge: Cambridge University Press, 1994), 95–97 and Guy, *More*, 216–17.

93. CW 4:98.

94. CW 4:7 (Budé) and 4:194 (lawyers).

95. CW 4:103.

96. CW 4:98–99.

97. TMU 13–15.

98. Michael Oakeshott, *The Politics of Faith and the Politics of Skepticism* (New Haven, Conn.: Yale University Press, 1996), 99–102.

99. CW 5.1:289 and Ackroyd, *More*, 283–85, for "siren voices."

100. Hugh Trevor-Roper, "The Intellectual World of Sir Thomas More," *American Scholar* 48 (1979): 74–76.

101. CW 5.1:118.

Chapter Seven   **Crisis**

1. *Ep.* (Eras.) 3:547.

2. CW 4:55.

3. CW 15:139.

4. CW 15:144–47.

5. *Corresp.* 253.

6. See Barbara Harris, *Edward Stafford, Third Duke of Buckingham, 1478–1521* (Stanford: Stanford University Press, 1986), 165–68 and 188–92.

7. Fox, *More*, 102–6, collects passages from *Last Things* to illustrate its "unrelieved morbidity" and to suggest that More "had been extremely perturbed by" the death

of the much loved duke. For "outraged sense," Dermot Fenlon, "Thomas More and Tyr-anny," *JEH* 32 (1981): 462–63; for Elton's surmise, his *Studies in Tudor and Stuart Politics,* 1:137, 145–46.

8. Roper, *More,* 208.

9. Warham's remark (1525) is quoted in Peter Gwyn, *The King's Cardinal: The Rise and Fall of Thomas Wolsey* (London: Barrie and Jenkins, 1990), 578–79. For More's ad-miration, CW 3.2:270; for "magisterial bearing," Ackroyd, *More,* 180–82.

10. *Corresp.* 278; Gwyn, *Cardinal,* 373–75; and Roper, *More,* 205–8. Repossessing this "likelier prospect," though, is not quite the same as endorsing Richard Marius' depiction of More as "a functionary" following orders "faithfully and without question." It is true that the Speaker previously wrote against both war and immoderate taxation, but he also lost no love on the French and had his Utopians hire mercenaries. And, in 1523, Wol-sey was assuring all who had reservations that the Habsburgs would do most of the fighting. Cf. Marius, *More,* 206–11.

11. Tyndale extended his analysis back to England's wars with France in the early fifteenth century, *Expositions of Scripture and Practice of Prelates,* ed. Henry Walter (Cambridge: Cambridge University Press, 1849), 300–303.

12. CW 15:372–73.

13. CW 15:364–65, 386–87. See *Concilia Magnae Britanniae et Hiberniae,* ed. David Wilkins (London, 1737), 3:622–23, for the pope's proposals and *Letters and Papers Illus-trative of the Reigns of Richard III and Henry VII,* ed. James Gairdner (London, 1861), 1:94–95, for the appeal to which Innocent was responding. Complaints about the abuse of sanctuary immunities were common during the fifteenth century. *Objectiones et ar-gumenta contra et pro privilegiis sanctuarii Westmonasterii,* a treatise repeating and an-swering them, was copied at about the time of the crisis narrated by More. See Longleat MS. 38, notably 95v–99v, 130r–132r, 216, 231r–232r, and for dating and related informa-tion, Kaufman, "Henry VII and Sanctuary," *Church History* 53 (1984): 472–73.

14. CW 6.1:303 and Tyndale, *An Answere unto Sir Thomas More's Dialogue,* ed. Anne M. O'Donnell and Jared Wicks (Washington, D.C.: Catholic University of America Press, 2000), 152. When I refer simply to anticlericals in what follows, readers should supply "evangelical"; More, after all, confronted an ideologically charged protest calling for a considerable, comprehensive desacralization of the clergy. Ethan H. Shagan, *Popu-lar Politics and the English Reformation* (Cambridge: Cambridge University Press 2003), 131–61, usefully lays out the relationship (or "resonance") between local anticlerical sentiments, which More accepted as sometimes legitimate complaints, and evangelical anticlericalism in the late 1520s and early 1530s, which he took to be terribly subversive, calamitously heretical.

15. Roper, *More,* 234.

16. Guy, *More,* 114; Roper, *More,* 235.

17. Fisher's sermon is reprinted in *The English Works of John Fisher, Bishop of Ro-chester (1449–1535),* ed. Cecilia A. Hat (Oxford: Oxford University Press, 2002), 85–89.

The title page (76) indicates that Wolsey made the assignment. For ambassadors' reports of the ceremony, see CSP, Venetian (1520–1526), 122–24.

18. CW 5.2:734–35; CW 6.1:183–84; Roper, *More*, 235.

19. CW 5.1:318–19.

20. *Nebulonis insania;* CW 5.1:270.

21. CW 5.1:274.

22. CW 5.1:276–79.

23. CW 6.1:153.

24. CW 8.2:786–87.

25. *Mentiris . . . stolide et sacrilege;* CW 5.1:476.

26. CW 5.1:526–27.

27. CW 5.1:674; CW 8.2:639.

28. *Corresp.* 446–47.

29. CW 5.1:48; CW 8.1:250–51 ("so sodeynly").

30. CW 5.1:618–19.

31. Consult Douglas Trevor, "Thomas More's *Responsio ad Lutherum* and the fictions of humanist polemic," *SCJ* 32 (2001): 751–53.

32. CW 6.1:325–26.

33. CW 5.1:646–47; CW 8.1:485.

34. Hat, *Fisher,* 156–57 and 162–63; for the Steelyard, Ackroyd, *More,* 246–47.

35. CW 6.1:337–38; for Fisher on vernacular translation, see Richard Rex, *The Theology of John Fisher* (Cambridge: Cambridge University Press, 1991), 158–62.

36. Tyndale, *Expositions of Scripture and Practice of Prelates,* ed. Henry Walter (Cambridge: Cambridge University Press, 1849), 291.

37. CW 8.2:706–9; CW 6.1:292–93.

38. CW 7:402.

39. CW 7:46–49, 70–71. Also see CW 6.1:378–88.

40. CW 7:23.

41. CW 9:85–87.

42. Ackroyd, *More,* 311, and *Corresp.* 387.

43. CW 7:214–15.

44. CW 7:439–40, reprinting Foxe's account. For "devocyon," CW 7:130.

45. CW 7:187, citing 1 Corinthians 3:13–15.

46. CW 7:205–6.

47. CW 7:217–23.

48. CW 7:118.

49. CW 7:173–74.

50. CW 6.1:138.

51. CW 6.1:144.

52. The previous chapter expresses my reservations about Bradshaw's case for More's commitment to reform in *Utopia.* Hence, while I agree that arguments for con-

tinuity ought to be made, I cannot endorse everything said about "More's continuing commitment" in Bradshaw's "Controversial Sir Thomas More," *JEH* 36 (1985): 560–67.

53. CW 6.1:433; Bradshaw, "Controversial," 569.

54. Tyndale, *Answere*, 46–47.

55. CW 8.1:259 and CW 6.1:178.

56. CW 8.1:574.

57. CW 6.1:33–34, 198–203.

58. CW 8.2:906.

59. CW 6.1:204–5.

60. CW 5.1:178–80; CW 8.1:126–27.

61. CW 6.1:119. Miracles, for More, also demonstrated the spirit's "leadership" in the Catholic church, although reformers protested that many miraculous events were frauds, staged to dupe commoners into accepting the church's authority. More's rejoinder turned that protest on its tail: the exposure of frauds attested that God monitored the church and assured that faith was not abused. But the greatest miracle, More would likely have admitted, was the consent (or consensus) of so many Catholics over time and across regions. See CW 6.1:62, 85–88, and 243.

62. Bagchi, "Tyndale, More, and the Anatomy of Heresy," *Reformation* 2 (1997): 265 ("fundamentalism"); Ackroyd, *More*, 262; Craig D'Alton, "Charity or Fire? The Argument of Thomas More's *Dyaloge*," *SCJ* 23 (2002): 65–68 ("tight control"); and Brian Gogan, *The Common Corps of Christendom: Ecclesiological Themes in the Writings of Sir Thomas More* (Leiden: Brill, 1982), 134–35, 160–63, and 211–12.

63. CW 10:351.

64. CW 10:196–99, 371–72.

65. CW 9:158.

66. CW 6.1:368–69.

67. CW 7:167–68.

68. "Never no new bygonne": CW 8.2:606–7.

69. CW 9:190 (St. German); CW 10:124–29 ("sholde medle").

70. CW 9:161–62; CW 10:135–37.

71. CW 6.1:406.

72. CW 6.1:409.

73. CW 6.1:410.

74. See CW 9:118–20, for More's denials ("never any of them any strype or stroke gyven them, so mych as a fylyppe on the forhed"). Also see Marius, *More*, 394–406, who gauges that More made "a much stronger effort . . . to ferret out heresy" than did Cardinal Wolsey when he was the chancellor.

75. CW 8.1:16.

76. Roper, *More*, 210.

77. J. J. Scarisbrick, *Henry VIII* (Berkeley: University of California Press, 1970), 193.

78. *Corresp.* 495 and LP 4.3:5864, 2622, for the king's confidence.

79. Wolsey coupled his comments on what the church should not and could not have done with policies that featured what England could and would do to protect it from heresy. Hence, More's controversies, notably his *Dialogue Concerning Heresies* and *Supplication of Souls*, "were all of a piece with Wolsey's policies." See William Rockett, "Wolsey, More, and the Unity of Christendom," *SCJ* 35 (2004): 138–39.

80. LP 4.3:5791, 2588.

81. See Henry Ansgar Kelly, *The Matrimonial Trials of Henry VIII* (Stanford: Stanford University Press, 1976), 86–87, for Catherine's protests, and 96–99, for Fisher.

82. Scarisbrick, *Henry VIII*, 179–80.

83. Gwyn, *King's Cardinal*, 539–48.

84. LP 4.3:5733, 2540.

85. *Corresp.* 497.

86. LP 5:71, 85. For Chapuys' not-so-secret work against annulment, see Rex, *Fisher*, 179–81.

87. Roper, *More*, 225; Guy, *More*, 155–56; Kelly, *Trials*, 174–79.

88. See Stanford E. Lehmberg, *The Reformation Parliament, 1529–1536* (Cambridge: Cambridge University Press, 1970), 81–87, for early agitation in the Commons; for the slices of "the Cromwellian coup" served up here, see John Guy, *The Public Career of Sir Thomas More* (New Haven, Conn.: Yale University Press, 1980), 127–28, 164–65, 194–201; Rockett, "Unity of Christendom," 143–53; and CW 10:lviii–lxii.

89. Bradshaw, "Controversial More," 552–54.

90. CW 9:87.

91. CW 9:28–29.

92. CW 9:33–34, 44–49.

93. CW 9:109.

94. CW 10:223.

95. CW 10:58–59.

96. CW 8.1:253; CW 6.1:86–88; CW 7:196–97.

97. CW 8.1:36; Peter Marshall, "Forgery and Miracles in the Reign of Henry VIII," *Past and Present* 178 (2003): 43–50, 62–65.

98. Roper, *More*, 230–54; Guy, *More*, 186–96.

99. *Corresp.* 552; CW 12:29–30.

100. CW 12:8 ("decayid") and 38 ("leve off contention"); Marius, *More*, 472–77.

101. CW 12:272–73.

102. CW 12:41–42.

103. CW 12:226–27.

104. CW 12:160.

105. CW 3.2:204–5.

106. CW 12:219–22.

107. CW 12:44–49.

108. CW 12:162–63; *Civ.* 19.6.

109. *Corresp.* 512.

110. Compare Walter M. Gordon, "Tragic Perspective in Thomas More's Dialogue with Margaret in the Tower," *Cithara* 17 (1978): 3–12; Elaine Beilin, *Redeeming Eve* (Princeton, N.J.: Princeton University Press, 1984), 24–28; and CW 12:lx–lxv with Kaufman, "Absolute Margaret: Margaret More Roper and 'Well Learned' Men," *SCJ* 20 (1989): 443–56. For More's prophecy, see *Corresp.* 302; for Erasmus' admiration, *Ep.* (Eras.) 4:577.

111. *Corresp.* p. 523.

112. *Corresp.* 515, 520, 524, 529. It should not be left out of our account that Roper herself conformed. More affectionately referred to her as his temptress, as a second Eve, for urging him to comply, but nothing ought to be inferred from that to suggest that he doubted her virtue or learning.

113. *Corresp.* 525–26; Gogan, *Common Corps,* 243–46.

114. *Corresp.* 527.

115. CW 2:81.

116. "That's my self"; Bolt, *A Man for All Seasons* (New York: French, 1962), 70. The screenplay has More, who was brilliantly portrayed by Paul Scofield in the first film version, explain that he steadfastly defends the church's independence, "because *I* believe it," with the "I" emphatically pronounced.

117. CW 12:179–81. John Guy's study of More's chancellorship, *Public Career,* 80–93, is often said to have stressed More's commitments to radical reform. See, for example, Bradshaw, "Controversial," 561–64, but also note Guy's implication (84–85) that More's chief contributions as chancellor were to oversee administrative efficiencies and to maintain the momentum generated by his predecessor Wolsey. "Nor was there anything socially 'radical' about [More's] orders and decrees in Chancery and Star Chamber"; *More,* 141.

118. CW 6.1:405.

119. CW 9:49.

120. CW 9:70.

121. CW 9:152–53.

122. CW 13:177.

123. *Corresp.* 519.

124. *Corresp.* 512–13, 518–19.

125. See Sheldon Wolin's *Tocqueville Between Two Worlds: The Making of a Political and Theoretical Life* (Princeton, N.J.: Princeton University Press, 2001), 230–34, 565–66.

126. See Slavoj Žižek, *The Ticklish Subject: The Absent Centre of Political Ontology* (London: Verso, 1999), 322–34, for the efficiencies, and, for "underpinning," Edmund Bosworth, "Sects and Violence," *London Times Literary Supplement* 5281 (June 18, 2004), 12–13.

127. Brown, *Augustine,* 322–24.

Conclusion

1. Ruokanen, *Theology of Social Life*, 12–13, for "traditionalistic" interpretations.

2. Robert Dodaro, *Christ and the Just Society in the Thought of Augustine* (Cambridge: Cambridge University Press, 2004), 183–214.

3. *Potius remissione peccatorum constet quam perfectione virtutum; Civ.* 19.27.

4. Hanby, *Augustine and Modernity* (London: Routledge, 2003), 21.

5. *Ep.* 138.

6. *Civ.* 4.4.

7. Carlyle, *A History of Political Theory from the Roman Lawyers of the Second Century to the Political Writers of the Ninth*, 2nd ed. (London, 1927), 165–68.

8. Kaufman, *Redeeming Politics*, 146.

Index

PETER IVER KAUFMAN

is professor of history and religious studies at the University
of North Carolina, Chapel Hill.